ON ISLAND TIME

Wildlife, Windsleds, and a Wedding on Madeline Island

PATRICIA SPAULDING

Quill House Publishers
Minneapolis, Minnesota

On Island Time
Wildlife, Windsleds, and a Wedding on Madeline Island
Patricia Spaulding

Copyright © 2011 Patricia Spaulding. All rights reserved.

Learn more about the author, this book (including the lost chapter), and Madeline Island at www.patriciaspaulding.com.

The cover photo of the Madeline Island Ferry is by Ros Nelson, Watermark, Washburn, Wisconsin. The map on page 4 is from the Madeline Island Chamber of Commerce and is used with their permission.

ISBN – 13: 978-1-933794-44-0
ISBN – 10: 1-933794-44-5
Library of Congress Control Number: 2011930989

Quill House Publishers, PO Box 390759, Minneapolis, MN 55439
Manufactured in the United States of America

DEDICATION

To Doug,
my partner in this adventure and in life.

MADELINE ISLAND AND THE APOSTLE ISLANDS

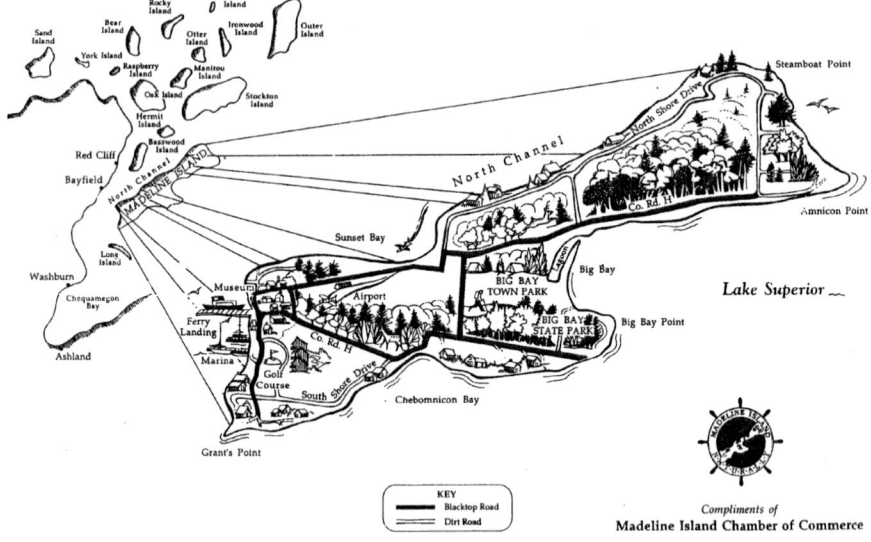

TABLE OF CONTENTS

Prologue 7
Buying the Lot 11
Raspberry Island Light 25
Heirlooms 37
Planning the House 46
Gene 52
Infatuation 57
Bell Street Tavern 66
Construction 74
Travel at Your Own Risk 83
More Construction 90
Windsled 92
Stranded 100
Still More Construction 103
Islanders 105
Indian Cemetery 119
Even More Construction 122
Tree Farmer 126
When Will Construction End? 133
A Smile South of Washburn 136
Moving Day 140
Sweet Airs 147
Fourth of July 152

Nature's Will 156
Bears 160
Golden Birch Time 165
Wildlife Superhighway 169
The Lake Is the Boss 175
Uninvited Guest 183
Island Controversies 186
Island Generosity 192
Fisherman 196
Night Walk 200
Leaving 202
September Wedding 207
Acknowledgments 213

PROLOGUE

I'm sitting directly behind the pilot, the only passenger in a narrow, single-engine plane. Normally I wouldn't think of setting foot in an airplane with only one engine and two seats, but on this occasion curiosity won out over cowardice. This flight is a birthday present from my husband, Doug.

The plane taxis onto the landing strip and then stops. We're at Madeline Island's tiny, single runway airport, located a mile and a half from La Pointe, the only town on the island. The propeller on the nose of the plane is rotating furiously and the growl of the engine is so loud that I can see the pilot's lips moving but I can't make out what she is saying.

She leans over the top of her seat so I can hear her better. "This is the first plane I learned to fly—it's a J-3 Piper Cub—and it's still my favorite. I've taken hundreds of passengers on this trip."

She's obviously detected my jitters and is trying to reassure me.

"Anything special you'd like to see on your flight?"

I nod. "Our house here on the island, but I'd like to save it till the end."

When we first visited Madeline in 1975, I never thought we'd own a home here someday, never realized how much I'd cherish this land, never dreamed I'd learn a new way of life on the island. Now I'm about to view the island I have grown to love from a fresh perspective.

The pilot adjusts several dials on the instrument panel, then turns back toward me. "There's another set of controls in front of you. Once we've been up for a while, you can try your hand at flying."

"Uh, I'll think about it," I say. Fat chance, say the butterflies in my stomach.

She revs the engine to an even higher speed, and the noise level ratchets up several more notches to an almost unbearable din. We taxi down the runway and just before the pavement ends we take off in a fluid ascent.

Now there's so much to see that I barely notice the butterflies doing cartwheels in my stomach. We're high above the glittering azure waters of Lake Superior, waters so clear that I can see the rock shelves and submerged boulders along the shoreline below.

We leave Madeline Island behind. Spread out in front of us are the Apostle Islands. The densely wooded islands look like intricately shaped pieces of a jigsaw puzzle strewn across a cerulean blue tablecloth. There are twenty-two of these puzzle pieces, all in varying shades of green.

Though I've never before seen them from the air, I can name every one of these islands.

Ever since my older son was born—and he's over thirty years old now—our family has vacationed in this area. Over the years we've traveled by boat to the shores of almost every one of these islands, all but Eagle and Gull, which are bird sanctuaries where visitors are not allowed, and North Twin, which can only be visited with a special permit due to its unique vegetation.

At home in Minneapolis we eat on place mats imprinted with a map of the Apostles, flat beige islands resting on a motionless powder-blue Lake Superior. The archipelago lies just off the tip of the Bayfield Peninsula at the northernmost point in Wisconsin. If the names of the islands were erased from the map, I could identify every one by its distinctive shape. Today, beneath the wings of the Piper Cub, the map comes to life.

Below us now, with two lighthouses on its shore, is Michigan Island. One of these lighthouses was a mistake; it was supposed to have been built on a different island and it wasn't tall enough on Michigan to be visible to ships looking for its guiding light. To correct the error, a second, taller, lighthouse was constructed. Off in the distance is Stockton Island. I can make out the long white arc of the beach at Julian Bay. Attached to the end of the beach is the verdant green triangle of Presque Isle (French for "almost an island").

No matter what their shape, all of the islands are thickly forested and many have a sandspit at the southern end. The features that distinguish one from another on the ground are mostly invisible from the air. As we fly over Basswood, I cannot catch even a glimpse of the remnants of a quarry we have visited. And from the air there is nary a hint of the yawning mouths of the sea caves that punctuate the shorelines of Devils and Sand.

Though early maps of the Ojibway and French voyageurs showed between twelve and twenty-eight islands, today we know there are twenty-two.

Just as their numbers have changed over the years, so have their names. The Ojibway named the islands for their natural features, the French missionaries named them for the twelve apostles, and in the 1700s Henry Schoolcraft renamed them the Federation Islands, giving each island the name of a state. Rocky Island has been variously known as Maple Sugar Island, Rice's Island, and Mississippi.

By 1986 all but one of the islands became part of the Apostle Islands National Lakeshore. The island that wasn't included is the one I know best.

"We're going to turn back to Madeline now," the pilot says. "We'll fly low so you can see all your favorite places, and then we'll end with your house."

From the air Madeline looks different than the rest of the Apostles. Unlike the unbroken greenness of the other islands, it has roads, houses, a town.

Hundreds of years ago, however, Madeline would have looked like all the rest. That was before the arrival of the Ojibway, before the voyageurs, before all the others who made this place their home.

Two years before Columbus landed on the shores of America, the Ojibway migrated from the Gulf of St. Lawrence to Madeline. Several hundred years later the French arrived in the area. Their missionaries came to save souls, their entrepreneurs to buy furs. La Pointe was the site of a fort and fur trading post as early as 1693. The songs of the French voyageurs filled the air as they paddled their thirty-six-foot long birchbark canoes laden with furs, transporting their valuable cargo to Canada. When the fur trade declined, others came to Madeline in search of fortunes in fish and timber. Still others came to farm the thin soil. Around the end of the nineteenth century when the railroad reached Bayfield, the tourist business boomed. Visitors stayed at the Madeline House and were towed by barge from Bayfield to Madeline Island for Fourth of July celebrations. In 1898 Colonel Fredrick Woods of Lincoln, Nebraska, constructed the first in a string of summer homes along what is still known today as Nebraska Row.

The plane approaches the northern tip of the island, the area where huge waves thunder toward shore when a nor'easter is blowing in. Off in the distance I can see Big Bay, the gentle curve of its barrier beach with the lagoon behind, where I've taken countless hikes along boardwalk paths. We pass over the campground at Big Bay State Park and continue down the south shore of the island where homes sit along low banks with sandy beaches. We swoop down toward the small village of La Pointe. I spot the marina at the edge of town, then Main Street with Grandpa Tony's restaurant, Tom's Burned Down Café, the post office, and a single gas pump. The ferry is just pulling into the dock, ready to release another load of tourists.

I've been so absorbed in the familiar sights that the sound of the pilot's voice startles me. "We're on our way to your house now."

We head up the northern side of Madeline with its high banks and pebbly shores. The land is thickly forested and wild looking except for the occasional dock at the waterline. I catch brief glimpses of stairways marching up the sides of the banks and the glint of the sun on windows of homes mostly hidden from view.

Then, there it is just ahead. Our house. The house our island contractor distilled from our dreams.

My heart skips a beat as I catch sight of the dark brown logs and fieldstone chimney. They are barely visible through the stands of white birch clustered around the house. I can just barely make out the weathered cedar log swing out in front. I smile as I think of the many times Doug and I have retreated there for quiet conversation or to take in the view. The plane follows the path of our driveway as it undulates in gentle curves toward North Shore Road. Then, too soon, we head back toward the airport. Several deer are grazing near the runway; they scatter as the plane touches down on the tarmac. As I climb down the steps I realize that I have been so fascinated by the trip that my fear of small planes has been forgotten and my butterflies have been freed.

That night, when the house is quiet, I rummage through the hall closet for a sweater, pull it around my shoulders, and wander out onto the front deck. I lean on the railing and gaze out at the dark waters of the lake, remembering the day, thinking about this island.

Like those who came here before me, I too came as a foreigner; I too traveled a long distance before I was ready to call Madeline my second home. My journey was measured not in miles but in experiences. I had to learn how to live on an island. I needed tutors. I found them in the natural world and among the year-round residents of the island. From them I learned what I needed to know. And I am learning from them still.

BUYING THE LOT

It's almost nightfall. I'm standing on the deck of the Island Queen, watching as the street lights of Bayfield wink on in unison. After two hundred miles cooped up in an air-conditioned car, the dense warmth of the lake air feels luxurious. It enfolds me in its balmy embrace.

The ferryboat's engines begin to rumble. The floor vibrates gently, tickling the bottoms of my feet. The last car—one of twenty that had been waiting in line—drives on board. A young man in a blue work shirt unwinds the tawny rope from a stout wooden post on the dock. The captain switches on the bright light atop the pilothouse; suddenly it's noontime on the deck. The engines work hard, chugging noisily, and the water churns beneath the boat as the ferry slowly pulls away from the dock.

I feel my excitement rising. Maybe the last-minute trip to the grocery store for marshmallows, the frantic search for Steve's swimsuit, and the arguments over which board games we should bring along were worth it after all. As usual, our family of four had barely found enough time in the rat race of our city lives in Minneapolis to get ready for our annual week-long summer vacation to Madeline Island. Doug and I both worked late last night, and Bob and Steve, our teenage sons, went out with friends that they won't be able to see "for one whole week."

At thirteen and sixteen, I'm somewhat amazed that they're willing to tear themselves away from their friends and spend time with their "bo-ring" parents. But after years of vacationing here, Madeline Island has become a special place for all of us, and this year our trip holds added allure because we're going to look at property on the island. Maybe we'll find a piece of land where someday we'll build a cabin of our own, a place we can visit for more than just one week a year.

Once the ferry clears the piers of the Bayfield dock, the deck lights are extinguished, the engines throttle down, and a hush settles over the boat. The sky is spangled with thousands of stars—so many more than we can see at home in Minneapolis. As I listen to the steady drone of the engines moving us leisurely through the water, I feel my breathing ease and my body unwind. The cares of my city existence begin to slip away. I'm heading to a place where I don't have to multi-task. I don't have to juggle my work schedule, my kids' activities, and the needs of my aging father. For one week I can simply enjoy being with my family in this place of incredible natural beauty.

The ride lasts only twenty minutes, but by the time the boat gently thumps against the dock at Madeline—once, then twice—I feel lighter, more buoyant. As always, the ferry has performed its magic. Some strange alchemy was at work while I was on board. It has transmuted my harried, hurried state of mind into blissful peace and contentment.

*****

A few days later I found myself in the company of a realtor, my husband and our two sons, tramping around vacant lots on Madeline Island.

Dave Stuart, the realtor, a beefy man in his sixties with thinning brown hair, had just shown us several pieces of property; each had a driveway to the potential house site. We climbed back in our cars and caravanned to the final lot. We stood on the gravel road in front of a parcel of land dense with trees and tall undergrowth. It looked impenetrable.

"There's no driveway on this lot. We're going to have to hike through the underbrush if you want to see the house site," Dave said. "Are you up for it?"

"Sure. Great," Doug answered, nodding vigorously.

The word "Yes" was barely out of my mouth before Doug and Dave plunged into the chest-high undergrowth, leaving Bob, Steve, and me to follow. It was a sultry August afternoon, a day better suited to lolling on the beach than hiking through mosquito-infested woods. But hike we did— if you could call stumbling through tall grasses, tripping over the rotting trunks of fallen trees and slogging through mud puddles, hiking.

After fifteen minutes we began to feel a slight breeze, a signal that we were nearing the lake. We stepped into an open area in the woods where there was a bit of breathing room between the trees. In front of us we caught glimpses of the sun glinting off the brilliant blue waters of Lake Superior.

Dave Stuart stood in the middle of the clearing. "Right here," he said, sweeping his arm in a grand arc. "This would make an ideal house site. And," pausing dramatically, his arm outstretched in the direction of the lake, "*there's* your view."

My eyes widened. I couldn't move. I didn't want to move. Even though I was covered with dozens of mosquito bites, jagged red scratches etched my legs where the brambles had caught them, and my new white tennis shoes were now a sodden gray, I barely noticed any of it. I was mesmerized.

This *was* a perfect site for a house. Encircling the clearing were multiple stands of forty-foot birch trees, their papery white bark glowing in the afternoon sunlight. Hemlocks, maples, and aspen dotted the periphery of the open glen.

And then there was the view. Doug walked across the front of the lot, peering between the branches of the trees, trying to get a glimpse of the lake. He discovered a downed tree that had fallen parallel to the front edge of the lot. It made an ideal platform from which to view the lake lying sixty feet below at the base of a steep bank.

Standing on this perch, Doug called to the rest of us. "You've got to see this. Come join me."

Doug reached down and pulled me up next to him. Bob and Steve clambered up beside us.

At the first sight of the view I abruptly drew in my breath. Scattered across the incredibly blue waters of Lake Superior were a handful of islands, each wrapped in a soft blanket of jade green. Over to the left was Basswood where we had hiked to the remains of the old quarry. On the right was Hermit, named for the solitary exile who lived out his last years there; beyond was Oak, the tallest of the islands; and then Raspberry, the site of our first island picnic. Every summer for the last sixteen years we had vacationed here. We had taken our small, eighteen-foot powerboat out on these waters to visit the islands.

Squinting, Doug said, "I think I can just make out the lighthouse on the banks of Raspberry."

I looked in the direction he was pointing. I could see it too. The red-roofed lighthouse on Raspberry Island has been shining its beacon since 1863. Sitting high atop red clay banks, its initial lighting was in July, the same month as the Union victory at Gettysburg.

It seemed appropriate that our house would have a view of Raspberry Island and its lighthouse, the destination of our first family boat trip in the Apostle Islands back when our children were preschoolers.

"I remember that lighthouse," said Bob. Then, turning to his brother, "You probably don't, though. You were just a baby."

"I was not. I was two years old." Steve gave Bob a shove. "And I *do* remember going there."

"Amazing view, isn't it?" Dave said, temporarily derailing the sibling rivalry.

As we climbed down from the tree he continued, "Let me show you the property irons along the front—so you'll know the boundaries of the lot. This piece of land is a bit unusual—it has three irons across the frontage. I know where the two outside irons are, but I haven't been able to find the one in between." Dave walked to the north and located the first iron; we gathered around a rusty metal pipe with a fuchsia plastic ribbon tied around the top. Then he strode off in search of the second one, leaving us to trail after him.

When we caught up with him, he was crouched down in the tall grass, hunting for the second iron.

"Who's the owner of this lot?" Doug asked.

"An old guy in his eighties." Dave said. Still searching for the iron, he barely looked up. "Name is Robinson. Elmer Robinson. He lives over on the mainland, in Washburn."

A minute later Dave stood up and held down the tall grass with his foot so we could see what he was pointing at. "Here's your other iron." After we had all obligingly gathered around to look at the second iron, Dave removed his foot from the grass and leaned back against the trunk of a nearby birch. "Back in the 1950s, Robinson and a partner bought up three miles of property along the north shore of Madeline. And they purchased Manitou Island as part of the deal."

"They bought the whole island? The one that's now part of the Apostle Islands National Lakeshore?" I asked.

"Yup. Hard to believe, isn't it. But a lot of the islands were privately owned at that time. Except Madeline, of course. This island has had people living on it for hundreds of years."

"Can I take a look at the plat map?" Doug pointed at the map Dave had tucked under his arm. "Maybe I can find the third iron."

A civil engineer, Doug was familiar with such maps. He pored over this one for several minutes and then walked along the front of the lot to the spot where he thought the third iron should be located. We all helped him search, but none of us could find another property iron.

Dave turned to face Doug. "You know, if you're interested in this lot, you better make up your mind pretty quick. I showed it to another guy yesterday. He sounded like he really wanted it."

Back at our car, at Dave's urging, we promised to call him the next day to tell him what we thought of the lots.

But what *did* I think? Did I really want a house on an island? It was a four-hour drive to Bayfield. And then we'd have to wait for the ferry. It seemed so inconvenient. And what kind of people live on an island anyway? I had read that Madeline's population shrinks from 2000 in the summer to 200 the rest of the year. Who were these year-round islanders? Did I want to live among them?

Yet I could not deny that I loved this particular island. After all, I'd known Madeline almost as long as I'd known my older son. My relationship with the island began just a few months after Bobby was born.

* * * * *

When we first visited the area it wasn't Madeline Island we came to see. It was Bayfield. A tidy little town of clapboard Victorian homes, it sits daintily at the edge of Lake Superior. From its harbor, sailboats, fishing boats, and power boats launch to explore the Apostle Islands and the surrounding waters.

It was October of 1975 when Doug, six-month-old Bobby, and I traveled to Bayfield for the fall Apple Festival. Our friends Mary and John Gustafson had rented a condo several miles from Bayfield and invited us to join them for the weekend. For several years they had regaled us with the details of their previous visits to the area, and now we were eager to experience it for ourselves.

It was our first trip away from home since our son was born. A first-time parent, I was nervous about traveling with a new baby and all his paraphernalia. I reminded myself that Mary loved children, and Bobby would have four adults instead of the usual two attending to his needs.

On the first morning of our visit we parked our car on the outskirts of town and, with great anticipation, began our hike into Bayfield. As we rounded the corner at the top of the hill above town we saw that the main street was filled with a brightly colored mass of moving bodies. We stopped for a moment to take in the scene before we plunged into the sea of people.

Rittenhouse Avenue was lined with booths of vendors from the orchards in the hills high above Bayfield. Apples in every conceivable form were sold at these stands: apple pies, apple turnovers, caramel apples, apple jams and jellies, apple cider, and even apple-stuffed bratwurst. On Manypenny Avenue we found a children's carnival and a variety of booths selling arts and crafts—many with apple and northwoods motifs.

The crowds moved to the beat of a variety of musical groups. On one corner a band from Ecuador played their Andean flutes. On another street a local group played bluegrass music. And marching down the middle of Rittenhouse Avenue was a Canadian bagpipe band in kilts and full Scottish regalia. Through it all, Bobby slept contentedly in his baby carrier on Doug's back.

Bayfield charmed us with its historic main street and distinguished old Victorian houses. But as it turned out, the highlight of our weekend was not this attractive little town. It was two-and-a-half miles away across the waters of Lake Superior, and the only way to reach it was by ferryboat. Madeline Island was the most unforgettable part of our trip.

Mary and John had camped on Madeline several years before. They didn't tell us what to expect, but it was clear they were excited to show us the island.

We parked our car on the deck of the ferry, and all of us climbed the stairs to the outdoor passenger area. The October sun warmed us as we sat on the shiny red wooden benches, watching the crowded streets of Bayfield fade into the distance. In front of us was a large emerald island embellished with flashes of crimson and gold. From a distance there were no signs of civilization. Trees covered the land and marched down to the water's edge. As the ferry drew nearer to the island, we caught a glimpse of an occasional rooftop peeking through the trees. The twenty-minute ferry trip carried us to another world.

We drove down the dock and into the tiny town of La Pointe. It was little more than a main street with a handful of restaurants, two gift shops, and a real estate office. In contrast to the crowds and bustle of Bayfield, we saw very few people on the streets of La Pointe. We didn't stop in town. Our destination was Big Bay Park. The blacktop road gave way to gravel and the town streets to pine forests. Beneath the tall trees the carpet of bracken ferns had turned golden. Deer grazed at the edge of the woods. The stillness was palpable.

In the parking lot at Big Bay we unloaded the picnic basket, and Mary and John led the way down the path toward their favorite spot on the beach. We paused for a moment at the top of the long flight of stairs to the water. To the left stretched the two mile, white sand beach on the shores of Lake Superior; to the right a stream widened into a lagoon studded with tiny islands. As we descended the stairs, we heard the trill of a loon from somewhere along the shore. A cool autumn breeze blew the watery fragrance of the lake toward us as we spread a blanket on the beach for our picnic lunch. After lunch we hiked the trail between the beach and the lagoon.

What I remember most about our first visit to the island were the fall colors. Miraculously the photographs we took that day reveal the intensity of the brilliant crimson, fuchsia, and amber maple trees set against an impossibly blue, crystalline sky. John was so captivated by the colors that he lay down on his back in the leaves with his camera pointed skyward to capture the stained glass hues of the leafy canopy backlighted by the abundant sunlight.

As we left we stopped again at the top of the stairs overlooking the beach. I drank in the colors, the aroma of crisp fall leaves on damp earth, the stillness broken only by the gently lapping waves. I felt soft wings in my heart break free and soar. I knew this visit would not be our last.

And so began our love affair with Madeline Island.

* * * * *

It was more my husband's dream than mine. At least at first.

Ever since that initial visit to Madeline Island, Doug had dreamed of buying property there. When we were only a few miles out of Bayfield on our way home, Doug said, "Some day I'd like to own a piece of 'the rock.'" One visit and already he had picked up the nickname the locals used for the island. He turned toward me. "What about you?"

I hesitated. He was so full of enthusiasm; I hated to douse his excitement with cold water. But as usual I was less adventurous than Doug. "I'd like to own a lake cabin, but I've always imagined buying something closer to Minneapolis, an hour or two away."

"But to be on an island in Lake Superior, wouldn't that be worth the four hour drive?"

"Well . . . maybe. Actually I'd like a small lake. You know, one with warm water where you could go swimming and take leisurely rides in a pontoon boat."

"Oh, geez, Pat, a pon*toon* boat?" he said, shaking his head in disbelief. "I was thinking a powerboat. It'd have to have a deep hull, though, so it would be stable out there on the Big Lake."

"But the water temperature in Superior is only fifty-five degrees in the summer. I've read that if you're in the lake more than fifteen minutes, hypothermia can set in, and then you're done for."

Doug sighed.

Our dreams didn't match, but we were young and in no position to buy anything anyway so we tabled our discussions. What we did agree on, however, was that this was the perfect place for a summer vacation. Every August we returned to the area and stayed for at least a week.

* * * * *

At first it was the three of us taking these trips; then in 1978, with Steve's birth, we became four.

During our vacations, Doug always managed to find time to stop by all the realty offices in the area to pick up their brochures. He poured over the descriptions of vacant land for sale. Sometimes if we spotted a for sale sign along one of the roads on Madeline, we would drive down the driveway and inspect the lot. Doug would assess the trees on the lot. (Were there hardwoods? Did they look healthy? Was there a mixture of species?) He would point out the ideal site for a house, and he would even figure out where the holding tank and propane tank should be placed.

At first I went along to humor him. Let him have his fantasies, I told myself. They're harmless. We can't possibly afford to turn them into reality.

Or so I thought. But dreams are interesting. If we want something badly enough, sometimes we find a way to make it come to pass.

* * * * *

Though it happened slowly and imperceptibly, I realized one summer that I had been converted. After many years of vacationing in the area, I too began to imagine owning a cabin on the shores of Lake Superior. So what if it was four hours away and the water was freezing cold even in the middle of summer? I had succumbed to the pleasures of the area—the pure air and crystal clear waters of Lake Superior, the red clay cliffs and sea caves along the shore, the Apostle Islands waiting to be explored, and the sense of peace and tranquility that filled my whole being whenever we spent time in this magical place.

But if my dreams were going to match Doug's, my conversion was still not quite complete. Though Doug had his heart set on Madeline, I had misgivings about living on the island. I had come to love the town of Bayfield, and I knew we wouldn't spend as much time there if it required an expensive ferry ride.

The ferry. That was another thing. Ever since I can remember I have had difficulty getting anywhere on time. I had visions of frantic trips through northern Wisconsin, exceeding the speed limit to make sure we didn't miss the last ferry of the day. And I knew who would be held responsible for the rush.

I don't know exactly how I got converted to the idea of living on the island. But something shifted subtly when we looked at the lots on Madeline. I began to realize that living on an island accessible only by ferry offered a lifestyle different from that on the mainland—a lifestyle that was even more removed from our fast-paced, big-city existence in Minneapolis.

Back when Steve was in kindergarten, Doug and I went to the first parent-teacher conference with some trepidation. How was our second son, who had been an animated, energetic preschooler, adjusting to the demands of kindergarten? His teacher, Mrs. Ryan, told us that Steve was getting along fine except that he was having trouble "sitting flat."

Steve was not the only one. Our whole family has always had trouble sitting flat.

Only a few months before we met with the realtor on Madeline, I had changed jobs; I went into private practice as a psychologist and spent my days seeing one client after another. Every hour on the hour I would usher one person out of my office, another person in. I barely had time to eat lunch. In order to attract as many clients as possible, I scheduled evening appointment times several nights a week. In addition, I faced the challenge of building a new business. When I wasn't seeing clients, I was networking with therapists and other professionals.

I was also trying to learn how to leave my work at the office and not worry over people who were dealing with difficult life situations. However, I found it hard not to think about the young woman who confessed that she rarely got through the day without contemplating suicide or the couple who insisted they wanted to save their marriage even though they reported a new version of their on-going conflicts every time I saw them. I knew if I was going to survive in this profession, I was going to have to turn off the troubles of the day as I switched off the lamp on my desk.

Doug's days were just as hectic. As a consulting engineer his hours were packed full of site visits, phone calls and client meetings.

With a thirteen and sixteen-year-old at home, our weekends and evenings were full too. I loved watching my sons participate in baseball games, cross-country meets, quiz bowl competitions, and jazz band concerts, but I longed for a few moments to catch my breath.

Then there was Dad. Ever since my mother died eleven years earlier, my father had been a welcome guest at our dinner table twice a week. Because I knew how much he looked forward to spending time with all of us, I didn't have the heart to cut back on those invitations. At eighty-one, Dad had a surplus of time and not enough activities to fill all the vacant minutes. Though he had many friends and was a member of a number of clubs and organizations, I knew that he still had too much time on his hands. I wondered if he was lonely.

In contrast, I felt as if my days were bursting at the seams. I knew I was lucky to have a life brimming over with work and people I loved; yet I wished I could slow my pace so I had time to appreciate this abundance. It seemed so unfair that life worked this way. While I longed for more free time and fewer things to fill it with, my father wanted the opposite.

Our house in Minneapolis often felt like Grand Central Station, a place where the four of us crossed paths and offered each other hurried hellos as we dashed off in different directions.

I longed for a home that would *be* a destination rather than a central hub from which passengers were dispatched to a multitude of other locations. I wanted a place to gather. I wanted to spend hours together rather than a few minutes in the car on the way somewhere else. I yearned for a place without schedules, where each day could unfold according to its own rhythm.

J. B. Jackson, a pioneer in the field of landscape studies, says that urban environments make us increasingly concerned with time and movement rather than place and permanence. Our lives in Minneapolis were flooded with time and movement. The island seemed an ideal spot to discover a sense of place and permanence.

If I was looking for a place where our family could gather to enjoy time together without a lot of distractions, then clearly the island was the place to be. If I wanted a place where I could immerse myself in the wonders of the natural world and return refreshed to my life in the city, then Madeline Island was a superb choice.

* * * * *

Back when I still considered Doug's fantasies harmless, we had driven down a driveway with a for sale sign and had found a house at the end of the road. We became so intrigued that we called the realtor and scheduled an appointment to see the place. All four of us looked over every square inch of the house, walked the entire length of the 500-foot driveway, and hiked down the long trail to the water's edge where we discovered a small sand beach. We even videotaped our tour. We called the house the "propane place" because there was no electrical service to that part of the island and an elaborate system of small propane tanks had been installed to provide light, heat, and fuel for the appliances. Our whole family mentally moved into the house, placing our books on the shelves, rain slickers on the hooks in the back hall and the makings for s'mores in the kitchen cupboards. Every day for the rest of our vacation and for weeks afterward we discussed the possibility of buying the propane place. Finally we concluded that the lack of electricity was too big a drawback. Reluctantly we all mentally moved out.

The "propane place" was a catalyst. It further fueled our desire to own a piece of "the rock." And the next summer, the summer of 1991, was when we found a realtor and began to look at property in earnest.

* * * * *

The doors of our Jeep had barely banged shut after saying goodbye to Dave Stuart when Doug said, "I really liked that last lot we looked at."

"Me too," Bob and Steve chorused from the back seat.

Doug continued, "I think we should make an offer on it. Tomorrow."

"Tomorrow! What on earth is the rush?" I wanted to know.

Bob and Steve were quiet, knowing enough not to enter into the fray.

"Well, didn't you like it?" Doug asked.

"Sure. I just want some time to think it over, that's all."

"What is there to think about? We've been looking at lots for years. And you heard Dave say that someone else was interested in it."

I grimaced. "That's the oldest ploy in the book! When my mother was a realtor she used to get mad when agents would try to pressure their clients into making an offer by saying that some fictitious 'other person' was interested in the house they liked."

"Maybe so, but that lot is perfect and I don't want to lose out on it. In fact, I think we should offer $500 more than the asking price just in case there are competing offers."

I wanted to yell, "Are you nuts!" but I realized Doug must really be smitten with this piece of property. My husband is not known for lavish spending. Over the years, despite the fact that his closet was full of fraying, ten-year-old button-downs, he would insist he didn't need any new shirts. Or, as we were putting away the groceries, he would want to know why I had bought the high-priced, name-brand granola when the store brand was just as good and only half as expensive. He is not stingy by any means, but he is careful about money.

So now, if Doug was willing to pay *more* than the advertised price, I knew he must be head-over-heels, crazy-in-love with this lot.

It *was* an exceptional lot. But I was nervous. I had only lived in two houses in my entire life, the one in which I grew up and the one Doug and I bought after two years of marriage. Neither Doug's family nor mine had ever owned a lake cabin. It seemed extravagant to even *think* of owning two homes. What would we be getting ourselves into?

But, I reasoned, our attraction to this island was not some giddy, giggling, recent infatuation. We knew the place wasn't perfect. But then, no place is. Our affection for this island had a lengthy history; it was more like the tenderness shared by long-married spouses who know their partner's bulges and bald spots, but find them endearing rather than a reason to search out a shiny new relationship.

I, too, was ready to say yes.

* * * * *

Two days after looking at the lot with the realtor, it was ours. The offer, sweetened with an extra $500, had been accepted. Undoubtedly the owner had been amazed to learn that someone was willing to pay him more than the asking price for his property. As far as we knew, a competing offer never materialized.

We got the news just as we were about to leave for a boat trip to picnic on the sandspit at Michigan Island. We changed our plans and instead boated from the La Pointe marina to the shore of our lot. The beach consisted of a narrow, five-foot-wide strip of rock-studded land at the base of sixty-foot banks. We picked our way gingerly along the shore, stepping over large boulders and several downed trees whose bark had been bleached silvery white by the combined forces of sun and wind. The four of us perched on one of these trees, sitting side by side to eat our sandwiches.

After lunch, contented, I watched as Doug, Bob, and Steve skipped rocks, trying to outdo each other. How many times had I observed such contests from the shores of these islands? Early on it was Doug patiently teaching our sons to search out slender, flat stones, showing them how to hold the rocks parallel to the water, how to flick their wrists just so, and how to count the bounces as their rocks skimmed across the surface of the water. Now teenagers, the pupils delighted in besting their teacher, showing their old man what feats young bucks could perform.

As I watched, I idly sifted through the sand at my feet, searching for interesting stones. This too was an oft repeated pastime. I lifted a piece of sandstone from the clutter of pebbles surrounding me. A sedimentary rock, it was formed from layers of compacted sands from island beaches. I turned it this way and that, admiring its perfect oval shape, its shadings of reddish gold. I brushed my fingertips across its rough surface; it felt like fine grit sandpaper, the kind used for the final polishing of furniture. I turned it on its side. Stacked upon each other were layer after layer of different shades of sandstone. Like the circles inside the trunk of an old tree, there were almost too many strata to count. The surface of the stone was pale rust, beneath that a strip of pinkish salmon, then a band of creamy white, and on and on.

If I knew how to read these layers, each one would tell a story. Each one contained a record of experience, a bit of history. After sixteen summers here, our memories too were layered atop each other, year by year—from the time Bobby rode in the baby carrier on Doug's back, to the summers when two blonde preschoolers used buckets and shovels to build rudimentary sandcastles on the beach at Big Bay Park, till this year when two long-legged teenagers outpaced their parents as we hiked for miles along forested island trails.

For several minutes I absently stroked the surface of the sandstone, lost in remembering.

Doug broke my reverie. "Hey, Pat, time to get going?"

I stood up, stone in hand, hesitated a moment, then carefully slipped it in my pocket.

* * * * *

On the last day of our vacation, we stopped by Dave Stuart's office to finish some paperwork.

Just before we left, he handed us a piece of paper. "When you get ready to build, you'll probably get lots of advice about who to hire. I've put together a list of contractors and builders who do good work. You might hear about some people who aren't on this piece of paper, but if they're not listed here, they're not here for a good reason."

We knew we couldn't afford to build anything on the lot for a long time, so we filed Dave's list away for the future. We had no idea when that day would come. Nor did we know that once we had opened the door to island life, there would be no turning back. As it has done to so many people, Madeline Island had cast its spell over us. The island would no longer be a once-a-year vacation destination; it would become an essential part of our lives.

As we drove home we talked about our property, trying to remember every detail. We were so happy to be one step closer to our dream—our dream of having a place of respite from our busy city lives, our dream of a gathering place where we could enjoy the company of family and friends.

Every year after that when we vacationed in the area, the four of us visited our land. We hiked through the thick underbrush until we reached the house site, often bringing a picnic lunch as a reward for surviving the difficult trek. Frequently on these visits, Doug would walk along the front of the lot, searching for the third property iron. It bothered him that he couldn't find it.

We also explored the property by boat again and again, checking out the shoreline and stopping to walk the beach. All of these visits to the lot on North Shore Road added to our store of dreams, dreams about a house high on a bank overlooking Lake Superior with a view of Raspberry Island lighthouse.

RASPBERRY ISLAND LIGHT

We had longed to see Raspberry Island lighthouse ever since our first visit to Madeline Island, but it took us five years to get there. We finally made the trip in 1980.

That year, just after the Fourth of July, my mother fell ill with a life-threatening illness that was difficult to diagnose. She contracted Goodpasture's syndrome, a disease so rare that the collection of specialists treating her consulted articles from medical journals they carried on their clipboards. They told us that Goodpasture's is an autoimmune disease characterized by rapid destruction of the kidneys and lungs. Her condition was grave, they said; the prognosis uncertain.

I couldn't let myself think about losing her. How would I go on without her? My mother who always took time to listen—to my childhood tears over skinned knees and bicycle wrecks, my teen-age heartaches after break-ups with boyfriends, and my new-mother fears for my young children. My mother who provided a role model for me as she coupled caring for her family with a full-time job and performed this balancing act during the late 1950s when neither my father nor most of society approved of such a combination. She and I had always been very close. Even during my teenage years, I never went through the usual phase of mother rejection.

She was hospitalized after the onset of her symptoms in early July, and I watched helplessly as, one after another, her vital organs faltered and began to fail. I spent hours every day at the hospital, leaving Bobby and Steve with a babysitter. I knew the summer was hard on them. In August, when my mother miraculously improved enough to leave the hospital and return home, Doug and I decided we could take a much needed family vacation. I knew Mom's health was still very precarious, and I called every day while we were gone to see how she was getting along. For me this trip was a respite from a world of illness and hospital rooms and intensive care units. For my children it meant time with parents instead of babysitters.

We rented one of the condos near Bayfield where we had stayed with our friends, the Gustafsons. The condos were on the water with a marina out front and a private dock for each unit. One of our favorite pastimes was walking the docks of the marina to check out the sailboats and chuckle at the inventive names chosen by their owners: *Luna Sea, The Incredible Hull, Tooth Fairy, Weak Moment, Hydrotherapy.*

Often during the trip I woke in the middle of the night as worries about Mom hurtled through my head. Would she get better? Would she have to return to the hospital? Was this a disease she could ever recover from? And always the question I kept trying not to ask forced itself into my consciousness: Was she going to die? The questions with no answers went on and on for what seemed like hours. I tried to calm myself. And then, when the dervishes in my brain slowed their whirling, I began to hear the music of the sailboats as their rigging tinkled against the masts in the soft nighttime breezes. It lulled me back to sleep.

Our daytime strolls along the docks of the marina were not sufficient for very long. Soon we had the urge to be out on the lake. We discovered the excursion boats that offered narrated cruises around the islands. We took the Grand Tour and after that the Sunset Cruise. Then, not satisfied to merely gaze at the islands from the boat, we decided to take a cruise that stopped at one of the islands and gave us time to explore.

The destination of our excursion was Raspberry Island, and it was the highlight of our week-long vacation. The island is located along the old shipping channel, and on its shores is the third lighthouse built among the Apostles.

As the tour boat pulled up to the dock at Raspberry Island, our two energetic sons bounced up and down with excitement. We walked down the gang-plank, and I looked up at the long flight of concrete stairs stretching to the top of the bank and then down at my two-year-old and five-year-old sons. We are going to have to make a game out of this, I thought, or Doug and I will end up hoisting our sons as well as ourselves up these stairs.

"Ok, guys," I said, "Let's count the steps!"

Steve ran out of numbers pretty quickly, but he got into the spirit of the game and marched up the steps as fast as his chubby two-year-old legs would take him.

"Seventy-four, seventy-five, seventy-six! We made it!" Bobby crowed as we crested the bank.

There in front of us sat the red-roofed lighthouse. It looked more like a grand old country home than a light-keeping station. Perched atop the two-story, white clapboard house was the tower that had once held the old kerosene-powered light.

A National Park Service ranger standing at the front door of the lighthouse waved to us. "Would you like a tour?"

We all nodded enthusiastically.

He showed us around the double dwelling where two keepers and their families used to live until the light was automated in 1947. From his description it was clear that the life of a keeper was demanding. The brass fittings and glass prisms of the light had to be polished. Coal had to be hauled for the steam boilers which powered the fog horn. Most importantly, the light had to be tended; many times a night the keeper climbed the stairs of the tower to trim the wicks of the lamp and make sure its beam was shining.

He pointed at a flight of steep, narrow stairs. "Come on up and take a look."

When we reached the top of the tower none of us said a word. Even Steve, who usually chattered nonstop, was silent as he looked around with wide-eyed fascination. On the green velvet lawn of the lighthouse was a miniature scene. A few Lilliputian tourists sat at tiny picnic tables while others played with a diminutive croquet set. But there was nothing small about the broad blue expanse of Lake Superior in front of us. Nearby several emerald islands popped their heads out of the water.

"Look. Down there." Bobby pointed. "Is that the boat we came on?"

"Yup." Doug nodded. "That's it."

Steve looked solemn. "It's so little."

The tour boat looked very small indeed as it bobbed up and down below us in the vast expanse of blue that seemed to go on forever.

The ranger pointed to a utilitarian-looking plastic beacon in the side yard. "See that post over there? The one with the small light on top and the solar panel on the side? That's the light that signals to ships today." He told us that the new plastic beacon is a far cry from the old lamp that used to be located in the tower. Before automation, every night at dusk the keeper would climb the stairs to light the lamp. It was outfitted with a fifth order Fresnel lens, handcrafted in France. We had seen the original light on display at the Apostle Islands Visitor's Center in Bayfield. It is a masterpiece of glasswork with a series of ornate bull's eye shaped prisms. Thinking about that elegant light, I could imagine that on a sun-drenched day like today, the rotating lamp would have caught the sunlight and sent it dancing across our faces.

After the tour we hiked a half-mile through the woods to the beach. And yes, this time our sons did need to be carried part way. But they wanted to get down in a hurry when they caught sight of the gentle curve of golden sand. There they built the first of many sandcastles and splashed through the water at the shoreline. As I sat on the beach near them, I watched with delight as Bobby and Steve joyfully slid down a small bank into the water. I leaned back against the warm sand with the cool water of Lake Superior gently lapping at my feet, and I drank in the clean smell of the lake and the nearby pines. As I relaxed, I felt the tension of those long days at the hospital drain from my body. I relished this moment of tranquility in the midst of a summer that had been anything but peaceful. The world of sickness and hospitals was real, but so was this world with Bobby and Steve splashing in the sparkling water. Life contained both these contradictory worlds. And the darkness of one made the lightness of the other more precious. The beauty of the natural world and the pleasures of sharing this time with my family supplied the balm I needed so much that August.

Finally it was time to head back to the other side of the island. I stood up and brushed the sand off my legs. "Come on, guys; grab your towels. Time for dinner."

We joined the rest of the tour group and found seats at one of the picnic tables on the grounds of the lighthouse. We were sitting high on a bluff, sixty feet above the water, facing west and looking out over Lake Superior on a warm, clear evening. We opened the steaming packets on our paper plates to find lake trout that had been cooked in foil over an open fire. Even our normally picky-eater sons scarfed down their food.

As we finished dessert we watched the crimson sun begin its descent into the lake. Both boys were silent, worn out after playing at the beach.

In this quiet moment once again my thoughts turned to Mom. I wished she had been there with us. She would have been the one to make a game of climbing the stairs to the lighthouse. She would have been full of questions for the tour guide and would have been down in the sand helping Bobby and Steve build their first sand castles and splashing with them in the water. And she would have savored this peaceful scene at sunset.

My thoughts were interrupted by the two older women conversing at the table next to ours.

"Look over there, about thirty-some miles away, that's the North Shore of Minnesota. And there to the west, the sun is going to go down right over Sand Island," said the woman in the bright red T-shirt.

"Should be a splendid sight," responded her friend as she used her napkin to sweep the crumbs off the table.

Suddenly Steve, our younger son, burst into tears. "Mommy, don't let the sun go down," he wailed. "Daddy, please don't let it go down."

The two older women chuckled, and the woman in the red T-shirt reached over and patted Steve's arm, but he was inconsolable. Steve has always been able to voice his feelings and did so even at the age of two.

I lifted him onto my lap and held him close. As I rocked him back and forth and tried to comfort him, I caught a glimpse of the lighthouse glowing golden in the sunset. Like that sturdy tower, I knew I needed to stay strong even as the winds of that summer buffeted my shores.

Nothing I said or did quieted Steve's sobs. I couldn't understand why he was so upset. Days later I realized that at two years old he probably didn't understand that the sun was going to come up again, that it was not going to set forever.

It was only many years afterward that I understood there might have been another reason for his sadness. Steve's dismay that night at sunset was most likely tied to the palpable fear and sadness I was feeling as I watched helplessly over my mother's decline that summer. At some wordless level I think he felt my fear and grief, and it became a two year old's lament at the sun's descent and impending death.

My mother died less than a month after our trip to Raspberry Island. She was only sixty-nine years old and had always been full of energy. I was devastated to lose her.

When I think of that summer I remember how helpless I felt. Helpless in the face of my mother's journey toward death. Helpless to calm my son's fears at seeing the sun disappear. Indeed I was helpless. I could no more prevent my mother from dying than I could keep the sun from setting. The cycle of nature removed the sun from the sky that August evening and my mother from the world that September.

* * * * *

Our first visit to Raspberry Island has become an oft-told family story. The reminiscing usually begins when we gather on the front deck of our island home. As I look at the small scrap of land in the distance, I remember the surge of excitement that accompanied our first foray onto the island. But like the warp and woof of tightly woven cloth, those happy memories are inextricably intertwined with grief and sadness. I blink back tears as I think of that summer—Steve sobbing as he watched the setting sun, and then so soon afterward, the death of my much beloved mother.

That visit was the first of many times in this region of natural beauty that I was to confront both faces of nature—the bright, benign face, which supplied a sense of peace and calm to my life unavailable to me in the city, and the other face, dark and unfeeling, under whose gaze the cycle of life moved inexorably forward no matter who or what was in its path. Nature, which generously provides us with the beauties of sparkling waves and a glowing sunset, can just as easily snuff out the lives of those we love.

As I stand on the deck, listening to Doug recount the familiar story, I catch a glimpse of Raspberry Island lighthouse. It steadies me—just as it did that summer long ago when my world felt so tenuous and insecure. I pick up the binoculars for a better view. There it is, the red-roofed building with the tower in the center, standing solidly at the edge of a windswept cliff as it always has, its bright light ready to guide sailors to safety amid tumultuous storms.

*****

By the time we bought the lot on the island we had amassed many such stories drawn from our adventures during vacations to the Madeline Island area. I remembered the sandstone rock I picked up on our beach the day we learned the lot was ours. Like that rock, our memories are layered one atop the other. With each vacation and each adventure, our relationship to the area deepened.

We stayed at the same condos near Bayfield for about a dozen years until we heard about a house we could rent. Hal and Marsha Powell's log cabin sat on the shore of Lake Superior near Bayfield. It had a flight of stairs down to the lake with a sandy beach in its own sea cave. Such sea caves, found in a few places along the shores of the mainland and several of the Apostle Islands, are formed when centuries of wave action carve hollows in the sandstone cliffs that border much of the south shore of Lake Superior. One of my favorite things about staying at the Powell's cabin was the sound of the waves echoing in the sea cave. When the waves were gentle they gurgled like a contented, just-fed baby, but when the waves came crashing in, the cave amplified the sound into a deep, thunderous roar.

The logs of the Powell's cabin were over a hundred years old. It had originally been built on farmland in the middle of Wisconsin. Marsha answered a newspaper ad, and they purchased the house, took it apart log by log, and reconstructed it on the shores of Lake Superior.

We rented the cabin sight unseen. As we drove down the long winding driveway under the tall maples with balsam and ferns crowding the edges of the road, we didn't know what to expect. When we first caught sight of the dark brown log cabin with robin's egg blue shutters and a fieldstone chimney, we knew a week would never be long enough. We were right. By week's end we had gone swimming in the sea cave, built a campfire in the fire pit which Hal Powell had outfitted with a circle of logs planed into benches, napped in the hammock overlooking Lake Superior, discovered a walking path to a nearby waterfall, and sat on the front porch at dusk as we watched twilight descend over the lake. Every summer for the next eight years we came back for a week in August.

A few weeks before our second visit to the Powell's log cabin, we bought a small powerboat. It was a used, sixteen-foot Smokercraft with a deep V hull, which we hoped would be seaworthy on Lake Superior. We knew it was a small boat for the big lake, but we thought that if we were careful and avoided using it in rough weather, it would probably be safe. Now we were not limited to islands visited by the excursion boats; we could visit any of the Apostle Islands we wanted.

Each day of our vacation, Doug got up in the morning and spread out the map of the Apostle Islands on the kitchen table. "Which island shall we visit today?" he asked as we all gathered around. This question always sparked an animated discussion.

"Let's go to York. I love the beach there," I said.

Eleven-year-old Bob had other ideas. "I want to hike the quarry trail on Stockton."

His younger brother shook his head. "No way!" Steve said. "Remember last time, how we saw bears on the beach at Stockton. I want to go to one of the islands that doesn't have any bears—like Devils."

There were so many islands to choose from. Did we want to visit an island with a lighthouse? There are six islands with lighthouses and one island, Michigan, has two. Did we want to visit an island with an abandoned brownstone quarry? (Basswood and Stockton.) Or one with the remnants of an old commercial fishing camp? (Manitou.) Or maybe the island where President Calvin Coolidge picnicked on flat rocks at the water's edge? (Devils.) Or an island with a two-mile-long crescent-shaped beach with the remnants of a shipwreck twenty feet from shore? (Stockton.)

Before we made our decision, because we were also learning to be good boaters, one of us would check the weather forecast on the local NOAA (National Oceanic and Atmospheric Administration) weather station and someone else would check the wind direction and estimate the wind speed. We learned to temper our choices with this information and to decide which destinations made the most sense, given the conditions. We started with the closest islands first and with added courage and calm waters we ventured farther and farther away from the mainland. Despite our precautions, we were still novice boaters on Lake Superior, probably the most challenging of the Great Lakes. We had a lot to learn during those first boat trips.

On a picture perfect day with blue sky, puffy white clouds and gentle breezes, we decided to boat all the way around Madeline Island. As we motored along the north side of the island the waters were calm and we got close enough to have a house tour of the cabins along the shore.

Just after we rounded the tip of the island, conditions changed drastically. Suddenly our little boat was tossed around like a child's toy in four- to five-foot waves that were taller than our boat. The Smokercraft sat low in the water and had no top to shield us. Bob and Steve and I cowered in the bottom of the boat and covered our heads with beach towels. Doug stood at the front, working hard to hold onto the steering wheel as he piloted the boat through the rough water. All the while he hummed "Victory at Sea." I think he was trying to convince us that everything would be ok, but I could see his grip tightening on the wheel and worry lines furrowing his brow.

Over and over again our small boat rode up the side of a giant swell, careened wildly over the top of the wave, and then plunged down into the deep hole on the other side. I held tightly to the gunnels and tried to focus on Bob and Steve rather than the waves crashing over us. Suddenly the motor sputtered and stopped. I ripped the towel off my head and looked around frantically.

"What's wrong?" I yelled to Doug.

"We're out of gas. I have to switch to the other tank."

Somehow, with the boat heaving and rolling uncontrollably, he managed to switch the outboard motor to the auxiliary gas tank. As he pulled the cord on the motor, I held my breath. It caught, hesitated, and then died. Doug pumped the gas line to prime the engine. He pulled the cord once more. This time it caught and held, then gathered strength. Finally we were moving forward again, and I could let out my breath. But not completely. Over and over again high waves came crashing against the side of our too-small boat.

After what seemed like hours we rounded the southern tip of the island. Suddenly we found ourselves again in calm waters. I collapsed against the side of the boat. I tried to stretch out my fingers. I had been clinging so hard to the edge of the boat that my hands felt like claws.

Bob crawled out from under his beach towel. "I don't want to go out in this boat ever again," he said.

"Me either," Steve added. "Not if it's like today."

"What . . . What happened out there?" I said to Doug when I had recovered enough to speak.

"I'm not sure." Doug said. "There wasn't a storm. I don't know where those waves came from."

What we hadn't known was that conditions could be so different from one side of an island to the other and that islands can offer protection from wind and waves.

We had just completed our first of many boating lessons on Lake Superior. We learned that weather conditions within the Apostle Islands can vary widely. We learned that a boat trip can suddenly turn frightening even on a sunny day without a dark cloud in the sky. We learned that conditions on the lake can change in a matter of minutes. We learned that if you pay attention to wind direction and speed, you can hide behind an island during a storm. Most of all we learned respect for the Big Lake.

* * * * *

Chastened and wiser after our Madeline boating trip, we continued to explore the Apostles. Each time we discussed which island to visit, Doug would mention Outer. Outer—the farthest island from the mainland, located at the periphery of the Apostles, beyond which are the open waters of the Big Lake with nowhere to hide in the event of a sudden storm. We had visited almost every other island except for Outer, and Doug longed to achieve what he considered the ultimate destination. The rest of the family, however, was not as excited about this goal as he was. For Bob and Steve and me, memories of being pummeled by waves as we huddled under wet beach towels were still too vivid.

Finally, incredibly, there came a day when the waters of Lake Superior were like glass. We had experienced this only a few times before. Once in a while on a very hot, humid day in August the lake is nearly still and remains that way for the whole day. On just such a day, when Doug suggested we go to Outer Island, we all agreed.

It was twenty-five miles to Outer—one way. There was barely a ripple on the lake's surface as we skimmed across the water. An hour later we landed our boat on the long sandspit at the southern tip of the island. We ate our picnic lunch and explored the inland bog behind the beach. But this was not enough for Doug.

"Let's go up and take a look at the lighthouse. It's supposed to be a beauty and the view would be—"

"But it's at the other end of the island. Six miles away," I said.

Doug shrugged. "We made it this far. What's another few miles?"

"And getting into that dock is no piece of cake." I grabbed the navigation guidebook. "The book says—"

"Pat, you're such a worrier. We'll be fine."

The boys had been quiet till now.

"Yeah, Mom. Stop worrying," Bob said.

Steve picked up the picnic basket. "Let's go."

It was no use. I was outvoted. By testosterone.

After we pushed off from shore, I picked up the guidebook again and read its suggestions about how to land at the dock. "It says here that we should point our boat toward the stairs that climb up the side of the cliff. And approach the shore in a straight line. And we need to have someone look out for large rocks."

Within fifteen minutes the lighthouse came into view. Bob, Steve, and I all watched for boulders while Doug steered the boat, and we managed to arrive safely at the dock. The volunteer lighthouse keeper met us at the top of the long flight of stairs and offered to give us a tour.

He told us that nearly the whole island had been logged. In the 1920s, the Schroeder lumber company clear cut the timber on the southern half of the island and constructed a narrow gauge railroad that hauled the logs to a dock at the southwest side of the sandspit where we had picnicked. The Lullabye Lumber Company built a logging camp on the northeast shore of the island in the 1940s. They did a more selective harvest of hardwood on the island's northern half.

It was hard to believe that this island, now completely covered with dense forest, had once been logged and partially clear cut.

"There's a trail," said the lighthouse keeper, pointing to a narrow path which abruptly disappeared into the woods. "Part of it's pretty overgrown and full of mosquitoes this time of year. Anyway, it goes out to Lullabye, and you can see what's left of the bunkhouses, the paymaster's shack, and a sauna. There's a fancy five-seat outhouse and even a couple of rusty trucks from the camp."

He also told us he'd heard about an old steam engine hidden somewhere on the island in tall grass. "Officially it doesn't exist. The story goes that when the loggers had finished their work and were packing up their equipment, a couple of the workers took the engine for a joy ride. It broke down. Rather than admit what they'd done, they listed it on the manifest and said it was shipped off the island."

I could tell by the look on his face that Doug was adding the Lullabye Trail to his list of future must-sees. If it hadn't been for the mention of mosquitoes, I was sure we would have been heading down that trail within the hour.

Instead we decided to climb the lacy iron fretwork stairs to the top of the whitewashed Italianate lighthouse. When we reached the lookout deck, I had to admit that the view was worth the trip to Outer Island. In one direction we looked down into the tops of the giant trees of an old growth forest that the loggers had spared. In the other direction it was easy to imagine I was standing on the Atlantic or Pacific coast. The vast open waters of Lake Superior went on forever. I glanced over at Doug. He had the satisfied smile of a Boy Scout who had just received the final merit badge for the rank of Eagle Scout.

* * * * *

Sixteen years had passed from the time we first visited the area until we bought a piece of land on Madeline Island. Sixteen summer vacations plus several during the winter months. With each visit our relationship to the area deepened. We treasured our opportunities for adventure as we boated around and tramped across the Apostle Islands; we relished the slower pace of life that renewed our spirits and gave us much-needed time to appreciate each other; and we learned respect for nature, especially the Big Lake.

These experiences became part of the fabric of our family history, part of what created the tightly-woven bond we had with the area, part of what had made us all joyfully say yes to the property with a view of Raspberry Island lighthouse.

HEIRLOOMS

My father died suddenly, of a thoracic aneurysm, on a lovely day in May. It was 1995; Doug and I had picked up Bob at the end of his sophomore year of college at Valparaiso University and then had driven to see Doug's parents. We were in Chicago when we got the call. Dad had been taken to the hospital in Minneapolis, and his condition was grave.

The highways in Wisconsin were a blur as thoughts raced through my head: Was he in pain? Was he going to die? Could anything be done? Would we get there in time to see him? Questions that would have to wait for answers—answers I might not be able to bear.

Like pages in a photo album, images floated into my consciousness: Dad sitting in the chair between my bed and my sister Penny's, reading *The Wizard of Oz*; Penny and I begging for "just one more chapter" and Dad readily agreeing. Dad, Mom, Penny, and I on one of Dad's camera trips, walking through a golden fall forest until he found the perfect shot for the photo he would take to the next meeting of the Minneapolis Camera Club. Dad sitting at his "ham" (amateur) radio table talking to people all over the world. Two small blonde heads snuggled on either side of him on the couch as he read *The Wizard of Oz* to Bob and Steve and they begged for "just one more chapter."

We didn't get there in time.

As I left the hospital, I wanted to still the soft morning breeze, silence the birds singing their exuberant spring songs, and dull the world's cloak of brilliant green. I wanted a somber world, one that mirrored my sorrow.

After the funeral Doug and I, Penny, her husband, Keith, and our five children gathered for supper around the dining room table in Dad's house. We set the table with Mom's best china and silver. That same table where Penny and I had blown out candles on numerous birthday cakes and eaten countless Sunday pot roast dinners. We cried, we laughed, we shared family stories, we supported each other in our shared grief.

* * * * *

It had been four years since we bought the lot on Madeline Island. In the intervening time we had continued to visit the lot frequently during our annual week-long vacations to the area. Building a house on the lot was still nothing more than a dream for the future. And after my father's death that dream was relegated to a distant corner of my mind. Another house took precedence. All my energy was focused on cleaning out the home in which I grew up. It was the most difficult task my sister and I faced following my father's death. My parents had built the two-bedroom brick bungalow in Golden Valley in 1940, two years after they married, and they had lived there the rest of their lives. It was the only childhood home Penny and I had ever known.

How is it that a house becomes more than just a container for the stuff of our daily lives? Together lumber and insulation and glass and stone provide shelter from the elements. And within that shelter a succession of daily events occur in the lives of the humans living there. But how does a mere dwelling place imprint itself into our hearts? How does it become a home? I had never bothered to raise such questions before. I simply took home for granted. But now, as Penny and I sorted through the accumulation of family possessions in our childhood home, I couldn't pick up one of my mother's china tea cups or look through my father's record collection without those questions pushing themselves into my consciousness.

All the rooms in the small house were bursting at the seams. Dad hadn't cleared out much of anything since my mother died fifteen years before. In addition, the house had a huge attic, which had become a convenient excuse to save anything and everything that might have value someday to someone.

It took a long time to work our way through the crowded attic. We tossed things out of the window at the south end of the attic into a Dumpster parked in the driveway. But there always seemed to be a suitcase packed with baby clothes or a cardboard box crammed full of high school yearbooks that triggered old memories and begged for further inspection.

Not only our family's things, but also the odds and ends of my grandfather's and my Aunt Florence's estates were in the attic. It also contained the remains of a dead squirrel.

* * * * *

When faced with a house full of the remnants of a family's life, how is it we decide what to keep and what to give away? We find we can easily part with some things, while others become heirlooms worth preserving.

Some of the decisions were easy when we cleaned out my family home. Though Doug and I didn't know when, we knew that someday we would build a house on Madeline Island. So I saved practical items—kitchen utensils, pots and pans, dishes, sheets and blankets—things we could use in our future island home, but they were certainly not heirlooms.

When Penny and I decided what to save from our family home, the monetary value seemed to make little difference. The worth of things we saved was not measured in dollar signs but rather by the memories attached to them. I kept the blue glass pitcher that reminded me of hot summer days when I came in from an afternoon of playing in the back yard and Mom poured tall glasses of lemonade from that pitcher for me and my friends. Penny could not part with the white milkglass cake plate with the fluted edge on which Mom served all of our homemade birthday cakes.

When I found the dark red immigrant trunk from my mother's side of the family shoved back under the eaves in the attic, I knew I had to keep it. "Your ancestors brought everything they owned to the New World in this trunk," my mother had told me. I sat on the floor looking at this rudimentary box with the crude dovetailed joints. Half of the original hand-made metal hinges that attached the cover to the box were missing, but amazingly the thin rope handles remained intact. I looked at the neatly painted, faded white letters on the side of the trunk. There was the name of the owner, Christian Roschen, and his address in the New World. He knew he was bound for Lake City, Minnesota, Nord America, but what did he imagine it would be like? What hopes and dreams were captured in those faded letters? I wondered how old he was when he left Germany and where he found the courage to board a ship that would carry him across the ocean to a land he had never seen. The cursive writing on the trunk was graceful, and the capital letters had added flourishes and curlicues. Was that Christian's flowing penmanship? Or could it have been his mother's? What did it take for a mother to watch her son depart for a new life in a world she could barely imagine?

I saved the trunk knowing that one day it would have a special place in a house that hadn't yet been built on an island surrounded by Lake Superior. I saved it because it is a vestige of my family's past. To me it is a family treasure because it reminds me of my roots. It was important to my mother, and because of her it became important to me, and I hope it will have significance for my children. Such things are my heirlooms. My parents are gone and someday I too will be gone, but, through objects like the trunk, pieces of my family history will be passed down to future generations.

* * * * *

One of the most interesting heirlooms we found was a photograph in an old book. As I gazed at the formal portrait of a large family gathered in two tidy rows, one of the children caught my eye. She was the youngest, the one with big eyes bordered by straight blonde bangs. Eight years old, sober and unsmiling, she stands in the front row of the family portrait. Beside her is her brother, Fritz, and in the second row her two sisters, another brother, her father, and stepmother. There was no hint of deception in this photo, yet it was based on a falsehood.

I discovered the photograph of my mother and her family in a dusty volume that chronicled the history of Wabasha County, Minnesota. Published in 1920, it contained photos and descriptions of families from the area. The section about the Charles Brusehaver family, probably written by Charles himself, boasts of their eight-room, gas-lighted house, their "fine circular barn," their "high grade Guernseys," and lists the birthdates of each of the children, adding that they "all . . . are now residing at home." For all the world, my mother's family looked like a unified whole. And the accompanying description made it sound so. But reality was more complicated.

Three years before the photo was taken, Ann, the children's mother, died in childbirth. At first Charles struggled to keep the family together; then in despair he retreated to the haze of alcohol. Since no one could take them all, the children were parceled out to relatives. The boys were sent to their uncle's farm where they could help earn their keep, and the two older girls stayed in town with their maternal grandmother. Gladys, my mother, went to live with a childless aunt and uncle. Sometimes envied by her sisters because she took piano lessons and had her own room, she recalled feeling lonely, separated from her siblings in a quiet house.

Despite the fact that the children were scattered among three households, for the sake of Wabasha County history, they were gathered for a family photo. Not long after the photographer snapped the photo, they returned to their separate homes.

Charles Brusehaver's despair lifted when he married Mattie, his housekeeper. When they had a child, he formed a new family, grew distant from his other five children, and remained estranged from them for the rest of his life. The house with eight rooms and gas lights that once had been home to my mother and her siblings was now inhabited by his newly formed family.

But thanks to their maternal grandmother, these displaced children did not lose their sense of family. Grandma Caroline was determined that the siblings remain close. She gathered the children in her home for each of their birthdays and for every holiday. Caroline taught them the importance of family. Strong bonds developed between the siblings. And they nurtured those connections for the rest of their lives. As children they may have lost their parents and their family home, but they never lost their love for one another or their desire to be together. When the Brusehaver siblings married and had families of their own, the size of their family gatherings increased.

When I was growing up there was never any choice about how we would spend Memorial Day. We always went to Hastings, Minnesota, for the annual Brusehaver picnic. It was truly an old-fashioned family gathering. Each household brought hampers of food, picnic tables were placed end to end, covered with a hodgepodge of tablecloths, and a feast was laid out on those groaning boards. There were roasting pans filled with fried chicken, pot roast and ham; heaping bowls of coleslaw, mashed potatoes and strawberry jello studded with sliced bananas and marshmallows; platters of deviled eggs dusted with paprika; as well as chocolate cake, ice box cookies, and pies—pecan, apple, blueberry, and lemon meringue—for dessert. After everyone had eaten, the tables were cleared and the older generation played cards, usually Euchre or Cribbage, if someone remembered to bring a board. Meanwhile, the next generation picked up bat and ball for a genial game of softball, a tradition I disliked because I was much younger than most of my cousins and was never much help to my team.

My mother and her siblings also gathered every Christmas season for a family dinner. Early on it was rotated between homes. A winter variation of the Memorial Day spread was assembled once again, only this time it was eaten indoors. I loved those gatherings, delighting in the hide-and-seek games we played in the old farmhouses of my relatives. In later years the group outgrew the houses, and the gathering was moved to the private room of Wiederholt's Restaurant in Miesville.

Besides those annual events, my mother and her siblings got together in smaller groups throughout the year—for birthdays, holidays, or for no reason at all except to enjoy each other's company. Because of those childhood years of living separately, they never lost their love of spending time together.

My fathers' family was much smaller. He was raised essentially as an only child, his older sister having died from consumption when she was sixteen and he was eight. Dad's family moved often during his childhood. They lived in many different houses in Minneapolis; most of them were rented and were located within a few blocks of each other. But from early on, no matter where they lived, family gatherings were an important part of his life too.

If holiday get-togethers were the norm in my mother's large family, it was Sunday dinner that brought my father's family together. After my paternal grandmother died, five years before I was born, those gatherings were always at our house with my mother in the kitchen. Sometimes my great-aunt, Florence, was at our table, but always Pop, my father's father, was there. I have often wondered if Pop and my Dad were close, but my father's loyalty to his father was never in doubt. In my grandfather's declining years when he no longer drove, my father visited him every single day and brought him to dinner at our house every Sunday evening.

Though they grew up very differently—my mother with four siblings in a small town, my father in a family of three in the city—both of my parents learned to value family. And family get-togethers held a special place in their lives. They passed these values on to my sister and me.

* * * * *

It took almost nine months, but finally Penny and I had sorted through everything, and our family home was empty and clean. Nine months of combing through the remains of our family's life. Nine months of grieving, of saying good-bye to the only home the four of us had ever shared. Nine months. The same amount of time it takes to grow a baby. But instead of growing, at the end of nine months the house seemed diminished.

We had removed all the things to which memories were attached. In keeping with the current expectations for getting a house ready to put on the market, we neutralized the décor. Off came the kitchen wallpaper with the stylized harvest gold daisies; in its place we slathered on several coats of creamy white paint. Up came the avocado green shag carpeting in the living room, exposing the original oak flooring. Down came the over-sized, ornate brass chandelier in the dining room, the one with golden swans supporting each of its six arms. It always had seemed a bit too large for our ten-by-twelve dining room, but my mother thought it was perfect. In its place we suspended a simple light fixture that did not call attention to itself. Compared to the six gilded swans, it was hardly noticeable.

When we were through, everything was bland and beige, with nary a hint of the family who used to live in the house.

Despite the fact that we had done everything possible to eradicate all vestiges of our family from the house, I still found it surprisingly hard to walk through the rooms for the last time. Vivid memories pushed their way past every spotless new surface. After closing one of the freshly painted kitchen cupboard doors, I let my fingers drop to run across the dials of the stove. I paused at the oven dial, its numbers faint from wear, and suddenly the air was fragrant with the yeasty sweet scent of Mom's freshly baked caramel rolls, reminding me again that I wished I had asked her to write down the recipe.

As I stood in the middle of the bedroom I shared with my sister Penny for twenty years, I could picture the two of us in our twin beds falling asleep as the strains of Tchaikovsky's *Swan Lake* wafted in from the living room where my father sat reading the editorial page of the *Minneapolis Star* in his overstuffed brown chair.

Lingering in the doorway, I remembered the Saturday mornings when I was a teenager trying to sleep till noon and Penny was still an exuberant grade-schooler. Our morning routines were incompatible. There she was, using the handle of her toy carpet sweeper to prop up the blanket on her bed and make a tent. She sat inside her sanctuary, noisily feasting on saltines and feeding the crumbs to Floppy and Floppy Junior, her long-eared, stuffed dogs. Meanwhile I burrowed deeper and deeper under the covers, trying to escape the sounds of crackling waxed paper and loud munching from the next bed.

That simple two-bedroom bungalow was the center of my universe for the first eighteen years of my life, and it was the geographic center of my family until now, when it was time to sell it to some other family. Even after my sister and I married and had our own homes and families, we returned to the brick house with the dark brown shutters in Golden Valley to celebrate birthdays and holidays around the oval dining room table that was quite literally located in the center of our family home.

After my father's death, the walls of our childhood home continued to draw us together as Penny and I sifted and sorted through the contents of the house. Sifting, sorting, and remembering. Remembering the countless everyday moments of shared family life—the jostle of two adults and two children sharing one small bathroom as we got ready for the day ahead, the family dinners around the kitchen table that were an every night occurrence. Family time under its roof had provided the brackets around the rest of my life.

I paused in the entry hall. How could we sell this house? I knew it was nothing more than simply a structure. But when that structure is the repository for countless stored memories of family togetherness, it becomes a home. It seemed wrong to turn it over to strangers.

Over and over again during the many months we cleaned out the house, I had the same thought. I knew it made no sense, but I was afraid that if I couldn't physically return to these walls, somehow the memories of those precious years together would grow dimmer and dimmer and might eventually be extinguished.

I lifted my hand to the knob of the heavy oak front door and turned back for one last look. And as I glanced around the empty living room, a new thought emerged, one that tempered my sadness. I thought of what I would take away with me, of what I carry with me always—the sure knowledge of what it means to be loved and nurtured by family.

* * * * *

Less than a year later, Doug's dad died. A year after that his mom had a heart attack and agreed to move to an apartment in an assisted living complex in Minneapolis where she would be closer to us. Once again Doug and I found ourselves clearing out a childhood home, this time the two-story, two-bedroom house where Doug grew up in Mt. Prospect, Illinois. Once again our dreams of a house on Madeline Island were deferred by the pressing task at hand.

Not long after she moved to Minneapolis, Doug's mom died. In a little over three years, Doug and I had lost our three remaining parents. Buffeted by one loss after another, there was no time to grieve the first death before we were faced with a second and then a third. Those three years became a blur.

In addition to the heirlooms we saved from our family homes, Doug and I received another kind of legacy from our parents. It was a bequest that allowed us to build our house on the island long before we thought it would be possible. Each of our families had lived frugally and, to our surprise, both left sizable estates. We wished our parents could have been with us for many more years, but that was not to be. It seemed appropriate that our inheritance allowed us to build a home that would become a family gathering place.

We would pay tribute to this legacy in a variety of ways. My maiden name, Parlin, is a derivation of Mac Farlane, making me a descendant of a large clan that lived on the shores of Loch Lomond in Scotland. We named our house *Birkenloch* to honor my father's Scottish heritage. In Gaelic *birk* means birch and *loch* is lake, the two most beautiful natural features of our home site. Inside the house we placed a number of family treasures from each of our families. From my mother's side there is the dark red immigrant trunk with the rope handles and the destination, "Nord America," hand lettered on the side. The set of Indian Tree china that belonged to Doug's mother is stacked carefully in the cupboard and used regularly for family dinners.

We hoped that our house on the island would become a visible expression of the link between our parents, our children, and ourselves, and someday our children's children. The three years during which we said goodbye to our parents and our family homes was one of the most painful passages of our lives, but we slowly emerged and began to look forward to the future when we could begin the process of creating Birkenloch, a tangible symbol of the importance of family in our lives.

As the previous three years had so poignantly taught me, our real dream for this house lay not in the structure that would be erected on this lot. Only when our house was filled with the love and laughter of family and friends, only then would it become the gathering place we had dreamed of for so many years.

PLANNING THE HOUSE

Despite the fact that it was our summer vacation, I was gloomy. In less than a month both of our sons would leave for college—Steve for his first year and Bob for his last. Our two sons were on the cusp of adulthood, and I realized with sadness that this might be one of the last times our whole family would be together for more than just a weekend. With the death of three of our parents, we had just lost the generation ahead of us, and now the generation after us was preparing to leave too.

We had decided to rent a house on the island so it would be easy to visit our land. One afternoon, after a picnic on our lot, we staked out the boundaries of the house. Doug and I hadn't drawn a floor plan yet, but we knew the approximate outside dimensions. Seeing those pieces of wood sticking out of the ground gave me hope that our house would stand here in the near future. I took heart in the thought that our home on Madeline would act as a lodestone to draw our scattering family together for vacations and holidays. My spirits began to lift.

"I want my bedroom to be here," announced Bob, stationing himself at the right front corner of the imaginary house.

"Then mine will be here," responded Steve, as he quickly stepped into the spot where the stakes and strings marked the left front corner. They were acting like little kids, and they knew it. Even at age eighteen Steve didn't want to lose ground to his older brother.

Doug chided them gently. "I think you're both a bit premature. We haven't even started planning the house yet."

But, the truth was, in our heads we had all been planning this house for a long time. The challenge would be to incorporate all of our ideas into one home.

A month later Doug and I stood on North Shore Road, preparing to hike into our lot in order to plot the course of our driveway. Doug had just grabbed a bundle of stakes from the trunk of our car when he saw a truck approaching. The maroon pickup slowed down, then came to a stop. The driver leaned his head out the window.

"Hi there, Spauldings. What're you up to?" It was Dave Stuart, the realtor who had sold us our lot five years before.

"We're trying to figure out where to put the driveway. We'd like to start building soon," Doug said.

"Have you thought about using the path the electric company opened up when they ran the power in? If you put the driveway through there, you wouldn't have to take down so many trees."

"Do you think the trail is on our lot?" Doug asked.

"I'm pretty darn sure it is, but if you want to be absolutely positive, you could have the property surveyed."

After Dave left, Doug and I hiked down the overgrown track the power company had made several years before. The path ended at the metal junction box containing the power supply for several surrounding lots. Once construction began, the contractor would install an underground electrical cable from the box to the house site two hundred feet away. Doug and I continued to walk until we stood beside the strings and stakes that marked the outline of our house.

"You know, I think Dave's right. It would make sense to use that trail if we can," I said.

"Yeah, I agree. But I think we'd better get the lot surveyed before we go ahead with it. I'll call on Monday when we get back to Minneapolis." Doug said.

Several weeks later, just as we were about to sit down for dinner, our phone rang. Doug answered. He leaned against the kitchen counter, then mouthed to me, "The surveyor."

"The stakes and strings?" A puzzled frown furrowed his brow. "They mark our house site."

Doug's shoulders stiffened and he stood up straight. "What do you mean they're not on our lot? How can that be?"

He listened intently, nodded several times, thanked the surveyor and hung up. By that time I was standing in front of him, hands on hips, "What on earth—"

"I can't believe it! Somehow Dave Stuart must have gotten mixed up and pointed out the wrong property irons. We actually own the lot just to the north of the one he showed us."

"How could Dave have made a mistake like that?" I sputtered.

I paused for a moment as the ramifications of this revelation hit me. My eyes widened. "What if the real owners had found our stakes on their lot?'

"What if we had started building on their property?"

I slumped down into the chair near me and didn't say anything for several minutes. I felt as if something precious had been taken from me. I said quietly, "I loved that lot. We all did." I thought for a moment, then looked up at Doug, "What if we don't like the land we really own?"

Doug put his hand on my shoulder. "I know, I know. We'll just have to go take a look at it."

About an hour later he came into the kitchen as I was putting the last of the dinner dishes in the dishwasher. "Pat! I just figured something out."

I barely had time to turn around before the rush of words continued.

"You know that missing third property iron? No wonder we could never find it. We were looking for it on the wrong lot!"

My hands flew to my mouth. "Oh my gosh! Of course! For the last five years we've been picnicking and planning our house on someone else's property!"

The news from the surveyor resulted in a frenzied trip to find out what our land really looked like. As we walked along the front of the lot, Doug spent as much time staring at the ground as he did gazing at the view of the lake. Near the center of the front lot line he suddenly stooped over and peered into the matted grass. A short piece of rusty pipe protruded from the earth. The missing iron!

Then Doug was able to give his full attention to the search for a house site. In fact we found the perfect spot right near the newly discovered iron. A broad point of land jutted out toward the lake. On one side of the point the land fell away into a deep ravine blanketed with ferns and club mosses. Huge hemlocks and several stands of white birch framed the view of the lake.

"Look," Doug said, "we can see Raspberry Island lighthouse."

I walked over to where he was standing and pushed the bushes aside to get a better view. "There it is! I'm glad we can see it from this lot 'cause that's part of what clinched the deal for us on the other land."

Doug nodded. "I would've been really disappointed if we couldn't see the lighthouse from our property."

We told ourselves this lot was better than the one we thought we owned. But by the time we got home, we couldn't remember much about what the property looked like. The vivid pictures we had carried in our minds for five years were hard to replace—pictures formed on those many summer hikes and picnics when we memorized every tree, every bush. We had even made difficult decisions about which of the stately birch trees would have to be sacrificed in order to build our house. But after a few more visits, the mental pictures of our new lot displaced those of the old, and we were ready to start planning the house.

* * * * *

As a child I spent hours playing with my set of Lincoln Logs. I liked the feel of the chunky, dark brown, wooden logs that were notched at the ends. They stacked easily, and I built one-room log cabins as well as log mansions with as many rooms as my set would allow. Little did I know that my early fascination with Lincoln Logs would one day lead to designing and building a real log house.

In order to begin the planning process, we sent for catalogs from several log home companies. I poured over the drawings of floor plans and exterior designs, trying to envision these homes on our lot. The houses were sold as kits which included logs, doors, and windows, as well as interior and exterior finishing materials. I pictured a truck delivering a giant box of Lincoln Logs to our home site. If only the process of building our lake cabin had been as simple as my childhood construction projects!

We knew we wanted a log house but we didn't realize how many decisions were involved. Did we want to use whole logs or half logs? Pine or cedar? Did we want saddle notch corners, vertical beam corners, or full log corners? We decided it would be easier to make these decisions if we visited some of the log home companies to see their model homes. Fortunately a number of the companies were located in Wisconsin, so we didn't have to travel a great distance. At first, visiting the models only compounded our confusion. There were even more options than we found in the catalogs. But eventually the fog cleared and we made a decision. We wanted a half-log house made of pine with full log corners.

We admired the look of handcrafted full log homes where each log has to be painstakingly fitted one on top of the next. When complete, they are truly works of art. But our budget prevailed, and we chose a half log home instead. These houses use standard construction and, when the framing is completed and the insulation has been installed, half logs are applied to both the inside and outside of the walls so that they have the look of a full log home.

We briefly considered building the house ourselves. That is, until we visited Bill Wellington. One of the log home companies gave us the phone number of a man on Madeline who had bought one of their kits and constructed the home himself. That was Bill Wellington. On a hot July day we stopped by to visit him.

A university professor on summer break, Bill greeted us warmly. "Come in. Come in. I'm the only one here at the moment. My wife is down at the beach with our grandchildren." He was barefoot, wearing khaki shorts and a T-shirt. A red bandana was tied jauntily at his neck; it seemed a subtle statement of individuality. Tanned and fit, he looked to be in his mid-50s. With apologies for his grandchildren's toys on the floor of the living room, he showed us around his impressive log home with its screened porch and large front deck.

Doug ran his fingers across the satiny surface of the pine cupboards in the kitchen, then turned toward Bill and asked, "So what was it like to build this house from scratch?"

Bill's shoulders sagged and he let out a low groan. "I still remember how I felt the day the truck unloaded the logs and all the other building materials in a huge pile at the end of our driveway." The corners of his mouth curved into a wry smile. "I wondered what on earth I had gotten myself into! It was the worst day of my life."

Even though he went on to assure us that in the end he was glad he had done the work himself, the words that stayed with us were, "It was the worst day of my life." And those words were all it took to eliminate any notion we had of building the house ourselves.

With that decision out of the way, our next task was to draw up house plans and find a builder.

But a few months later we almost gave up altogether on the idea of building. Doug and I went to look at a fully furnished home for sale on the island. We were lured by the idea of a completed house that could be used immediately. There would be no need to wait months or years to enjoy life on the island. The realtor told us we could sell our lot at a good profit and then purchase the house. We went back and forth about whether to buy it.

"The dock is nice, and it's the right size for our boat. Just think, we wouldn't even have to pay for a slip at the marina," I said.

"But that fireplace!" Doug said. "It's so plain, nothing more than an opening cut into a plastered wall. I thought we wanted a fieldstone fireplace."

"And the kitchen needs a lot of work." I grimaced. Then I brightened. "But the bedrooms are great. Remember how the master bedroom even has its own screened porch?"

Both of us were silent for a few minutes. Then Doug said softly, almost to himself, "It would be so special to build a home of our own with everything just the way we want it." His words turned the tide.

Little did we know that we would repeat them over and over again for the next three years—sometimes joyfully as our house took shape, sometimes sarcastically in utter frustration with the building process. "Isn't it special" became our mantra.

GENE

He was standing on the roof of Bell Street Tavern, shoveling snow, when we first met him. It was twilight on a bitterly cold Friday afternoon in mid-November, the day before the opening of hunting season. As Doug and I approached the building we could see half a dozen construction workers in tan Carhartt overalls and jackets working on various parts of the structure. They all looked alike in the dim light of dusk. We had to shout to get someone's attention.

"Hey! Is Gene Nelson up there?" Doug called out.

One of the workers closest to the edge of the roof stopped hammering and yelled over his shoulder, "Hey, Gene, some people here to see you."

One of the clones in Carhartts put down his snow shovel and walked over to the edge of the roof. "Spauldings? Meet you at the Pub. In fifteen minutes. It's down the street."

We stood just inside the door. My eyes had trouble adjusting to the darkness in the dim, smoky room that was lit mainly by two neon Leininkugel beer signs behind the bar. Once I could see clearly, I wanted to be anywhere else but there. I fervently wished the floor would open up and swallow me. It was the night before deer hunting season began, and I was the only woman in a Wisconsin bar filled with men wearing plaid flannel shirts and blaze orange vests. But I needn't have worried. None of them even noticed me. They were much too busy chugging Leinies and boisterously regaling each other with their past deer hunting exploits.

Doug and I found a table on the periphery of the crowd where we could eavesdrop on bits and pieces of the conversations swirling around us.

"Yup. My deer stand is set to go. It's 'bout 200 yards in from the road on Benjamin Boulevard."

"Had pretty good luck last season. Got three bucks and one doe. Only used four bullets."

There was a time when there were not as many deer on Madeline Island as there are today. That was long ago when the island was thickly forested and there were not enough understory plants to provide good grazing for deer. Once the old forests had been logged, the deer arrived from the mainland in droves. They swam the open waters or crossed over the ice during the winter. Deer still use these methods to travel among the Apostle Islands year round. One of their favorite foods is the Canada yew, an evergreen shrub often referred to as deer candy. The endangered yew has almost been eradicated on several of the islands with large deer populations.

In recent history Madeline has provided the ideal habitat for deer, and the island has been a mecca for hunters for several generations. One of the largest deer harvests on the island was in 1991 with just under 300 deer bagged during the nine-day rifle season.

At the end of deer season, all the hunters and their guests crowd into a local restaurant for the annual Hunters Feast, an evening of good food, door prizes, and a raffle in which the grand prize is often, appropriately, a rifle. The grand finale of the event is the awarding of an engraved trophy to the Sportsman of the Year.

Undoubtedly, somewhere around us in this dimly lit room at the Pub sat the next recipient of the sportsman's trophy.

Finally, after what seemed an eternity, a young man made his way through the noisy crowd and approached our table with a shy grin. "Hi. I'm Gene."

No, this can't be Gene Nelson, I thought. Over the phone earlier in the week when we arranged this meeting, Gene's flat, unemotional tone and laconic manner of speech had made him sound much older. I had expected to see a grizzled, sixtyish man. Instead here stood a bashful, blue-eyed man in his thirties with tufts of wavy blonde hair poking out from under his Nelson Builders ball cap. This was only the first of many surprises in our relationship with the man who became our contractor. But Gene would end up being much more than our builder. He became our resident naturalist, informing us about the flora and fauna of the island, as well as our island sociologist, telling us about the customs, attitudes, and worldviews of the people who live on the island year round. And, in the end, he became a good friend.

We talked with several other builders before we selected Gene. All of them would have done an excellent job, and there were times when we revisited our decision. But the house tour convinced us that Gene should be our contractor.

"I've been building houses since I was sixteen," Gene explained as we stood next to our car. We were going to follow his truck as he showed us several houses he had built or remodeled. He learned the construction trade by working with his uncle, an excellent builder on the island. By the time we met him, Gene had owned his company, Nelson Builders, for a dozen years.

He was one of the 200 year-round island residents about whom I had read. Like his father before him, he grew up on the island and, rather than move away to make a living, he chose to stay.

Our first stop on the tour was a house Gene had remodeled, adding several rooms. He paused on the front porch.

"This section of the house is over 100 years old," he said, running his fingers over the golden brown logs. Then, gesturing to the wall nearby, "And here's where the new addition begins." So perfectly did the logs match that we never would have guessed there was an addition unless we had been told. The same was true inside. A family room had been added and the kitchen enlarged, but the interior materials matched as beautifully as the exterior.

We climbed back into our car to follow Gene's green pick-up truck to the next home. "Did you notice how he talked about that house? And the way he touched those logs?" I asked Doug. "His houses are like his children."

The second house Gene showed us was still under construction, or rather, it looked as if the shell had been built and then construction had come to a standstill. The roof and the exterior walls were in place, but there was no siding on the outside. The plastic vapor barrier on the exterior of the house was loose in several places and was flapping in the icy wind that blew off the lake. We climbed the front steps to look around inside.

"Careful of that open space," Gene said. He was pointing at the gaping hole in the floor right behind me. "That's where the stairs to the basement will go." Then, as though the thought had just occurred to him, he said, "You know, if you two like this house, I could finish it according to your specifications."

I was trying to figure out how to respond when Gene gestured toward one of the exterior walls where a long dark line in the plywood ran from floor to ceiling. "Right here is where I cut the house in half. With my chainsaw."

"You what?" I said, eyes wide with amazement.

"This house is well-traveled. It used to be over on the mainland. When it was sold, the buyer had it moved by barge across the lake to Madeline. Years later I bought the house and relocated it to this lot."

Dumbstruck, Doug and I stood with our mouths open. Gene took that as a sign to continue. "I thought the original house was too small, so I used a chainsaw to cut it in half and then added a ten-foot section right here in the middle."

I picked up the conversation gamely, as though I didn't find it unusual to have a discussion about the chainsaw dismemberment of a house. "Well, yes, that does seem to be an improvement. The rooms are all a good size now."

We learned the whole story later. The house Gene showed us was one of four purchased on the mainland to be relocated to Madeline Island. Years before, we had seen those houses in their original location. They were part of the Port Superior development and stood near the condos we rented during our early vacations to the area. In March of 1977, newspapers around the world carried the headline "Good-Bye, Dream House" above a photograph of a two-story house tilting at a rakish angle as it sank through the ice about a mile from Madeline Island. The house followed its tow truck to the bottom of Lake Superior. Both truck and house were retrieved several months later. The owners of the remaining three houses learned from the aborted journey of the "dream house." In the summer of 1977, these houses were placed on a barge and towed to the island by the Eclipse, a diesel tug.

Our final stop on the tour was a new house Gene had built. A wooden bridge crossed a small stream on the property. Gene had decorated the sides of the bridge with a series of apple cutouts to match the apple motif that dominated the interior of the house. He pointed with pride to the ceramic tile he had installed in the kitchen and bathrooms, including the bathroom floor composed of one-inch tiles that were laid in a red and white checkerboard pattern with a red ceramic apple in the center.

Two things were clear from our tour. Gene had an unerring eye for design and detail, and everything he built was strong and sturdy and would probably stand forever. The first quality was important to me since the aesthetics of the house were my main focus. And Doug, a civil engineer, wanted a solid structure. Since we lived 250 miles away from the building site, we knew there would be times when Gene would have to make decisions without our input. We both felt confident that he would make the right choices.

"How soon could you start?" Doug asked.

Gene thought for a moment. "By late spring or early summer I should be ready for a new project."

"How long will it take to finish it?"

"Let's say we start this summer. I could finish in nine months, and your house should be ready for move-in by next spring."

He was telling us exactly what we wanted to hear, and we were so eager to start that we didn't notice the exact wording of his statement. When our house was finally complete, we realized that he hadn't exactly promised that he *would* finish the house in nine months; he'd only had said that it was *possible* for him to do so. To be fair, he probably wasn't deliberately trying to mislead us. Instead, Gene had a tendency to take on more work than he could manage, and he was always overly optimistic about how much he could accomplish.

I had a better understanding of this trait than Doug. When my husband sets a deadline, he always meets it with time to spare. He is always on schedule. I find this both amazing and infuriating. In contrast, I rarely seem to be able to come up with a reasonable estimate of how long a task will take, and as the deadline approaches I am usually rushing to finish. I am frequently late. So I was more understanding about Gene's tendency to over-promise and under-deliver.

In any case, we both agreed that Gene was the one we wanted to build our house. Several weeks after our house tour, we called Gene to tell him he was hired.

INFATUATION

How does one become besotted with a place? For besotted I had become.

After the frantic trip we'd made to look at the lot we really owned, I became infatuated with our new piece of property. Over the following months, Doug and I made numerous trips to Madeline, and we spent hours roaming across our lot during each of these visits, investigating every inch of the land, talking endlessly about where to build the house, where to place the windows so they would capture the views of the lake and the beautiful grove of birch trees. We took photos of possible house sites, of the deep ravine that led from the top of the high bank down to the lake below, of the small stream that ran through the lot. We were like new parents with their first born; we would pull out the photos and show them to anyone who seemed even the slightest bit interested. We were probably obnoxious.

Undoubtedly one reason I became enamored with our lot on Madeline was because of its beautiful natural features. I was drawn to its landscape, a place where I almost immediately sensed that I belonged.

When I traveled to Sedona, Arizona, several years before we purchased the lot on Madeline, I admired the warm-hued desert scenery and its strange red rock formations. I enjoyed the sunny, arid days followed by cool evenings. But I never felt at home there; the landscape felt alien. Having grown up in Minnesota, I longed for verdant vegetation, for lakes and rivers, for air with some heft, some substance. Those were the things that meant home. I wanted panoramas painted in hues of rich greens and translucent blues, not earth-toned shades of mocha, sage, and ochre.

With these proclivities, it is easy to understand how I fell in love with the landscape of Madeline Island and its dense green vegetation bordered by the broad blue expanse of Lake Superior.

My first truly intimate experience with our lot, the time when I learned more than I really wanted to know about its physical features, took place on a hot, humid July afternoon when Doug and I arrived at the edge of our property with wooden stakes in hand, ready to mark the outline of our driveway.

The lot that had been easy to tramp across during winter and spring was now thick with vegetation and nearly impossible to enter. As soon as we plunged into the dense underbrush, swarms of mosquitoes rose to meet us. They descended on our bare flesh and began their feast. Unfortunately we were unprepared. No long pants, no shirtsleeves to roll down, and no insect spray. Pretty stupid. Especially for people used to living in mosquito-laden Minnesota.

"Ok. I've had enough!" I said after about three minutes of swatting the voracious bugs. "Let's get out of here. We can do this another day."

"Yeah. We could wait till November. No mosquitoes then," Doug said as he swatted a fat specimen on his upper arm, leaving a puddle of blood under the smashed carcass. "'Course that'd set the building schedule back a bit."

I frowned at him. "Why must you always be so logical?"

Doug shrugged. I went back to beating down the underbrush so I could insert another stake to mark the outline of the driveway.

It was slow work. And it didn't take long to learn that we had multiple miniature wetlands on our lot. With the discovery of each new marshy area came fresh troops of mosquitoes to assault us. But we soldiered on for what seemed like days but was actually more like several hours.

All of a sudden I stepped into a deep pit. "Aaaaagh!" I yelled. "Help! I'm in quicksand!" My heart was beating wildly as I struggled to get out.

Doug dropped the stakes he had been carrying and ran to the swampy bog where I was stuck. By the time he got to me, my arms were flailing and I was up to my thighs in scummy green mud that had been invisible due to the waist-high marsh grass growing in it.

"Give me your hands," Doug commanded.

With his help I managed to extricate myself from the muck. When I was back on solid ground and my heart had stopped racing, I looked down at my legs. They were plastered with mud punctuated by numerous large red welts from the bug bites I had sustained in our driveway reconnaissance project.

"That's it! I quit!" I muttered through clenched teeth.

"We're almost through. Why don't you go back to the car and I'll finish up."

I hated that he was trying to pacify me. I hated being the weaker one. I stalked off through the underbrush without a word.

If ever there was an experience that would dampen an insane infatuation with a piece of property, this was it. Yet, looking back on that day, I can see that the driveway project was our initial investment in our land. By literally giving up some of our blood and sweat and, in my case, tears, we were furthering our commitment to this land of ours.

I remember the line from Frost's poem, *The Gift Outright*: "Such as we were . . . we gave ourselves outright to the land. . . ." Such as I was, mud-spattered and mosquito-bitten, maybe it was only then that I gave myself over completely to the land and began to earn the right to be its owner.

* * * * *

A month after we pounded the stakes into our mosquito-infested property, the driveway was completed. Bulldozers followed our guide-posts, dump trucks poured the gravel, and we arrived one weekend to find a winding trail to the front of our lot. With us were Bob and Steve, both on summer break from college. Though Doug and I had scouted out possible house sites several months before, we wanted our sons to be part of the decision too. I think we hoped it would increase their bond to the property. We had asked Gene to meet us at our lot to help make the final decision.

We heard his pickup rumble down the driveway, pause for a moment and then accelerate again. It came to a stop right near where we stood. The door to Gene's truck wasn't even closed when he blurted out, "I just saw a bear standing in the middle of your driveway! Full-grown. Must have weighed at least 350 pounds." This rush of words was startling from a man who up until now had been shy and reticent around us.

Gene's information about the bear temporarily banished all thoughts about a house site. "No kidding! A bear! Do you think he's still there?" Doug said as he took several steps down the driveway.

"No, he's probably deep in the woods by now. I think I scared him pretty good when I drove up."

Bob, Steve, and Doug all looked disappointed.

I was relieved. I was curious about the bear too, but glad that none of the men in my family were going to go off searching for him.

"Do you see bears on the island very often?" I asked.

"Not really. Mostly we see evidence that they're around—claw marks on trees, poop in the woods, bird feeders that have been knocked to the ground and emptied—stuff like that. But we don't catch sight of them very often."

Steve was looking toward the front of our lot. "You know, I think maybe there's a bear living around here. Bob, remember when we were climbing down the ravine to the lake? We saw a big pile of poop in the middle of the path. I'll bet that came from a bear."

"Could be," Gene said, readjusting his green Nelson Builders cap.

"Well, don't either of you guys go off on a bear hunt, ok?" I said with a laugh. I was trying to make light of it, but the thought of bears in the nearby woods was a bit disconcerting. I had come to the island to enjoy nature, but finding myself face to face with a bear was not exactly what I had in mind.

"That was a black bear you saw in the driveway, right?" Bob asked.

Gene nodded.

"Are there grizzlies here too?" Bob continued.

"No, only black bears—which is a good thing. Grizzlies are much meaner."

All this talk about bears was fanning the flames of my fears. I really didn't want to think about any kind of bears—black or grizzly—anymore. "I guess you didn't come out here today to answer all our questions about wildlife," I said to Gene. "Maybe we should figure out where to locate the house."

We spent the next hour walking back and forth across the front of the lot as Gene pointed out the pros and cons of various house sites. By the end of the hour we all agreed on the ideal spot for the house; it was the same site Doug and I had chosen many months before. Our home would be built close to the ravine. There was a level area with plenty of room for the house, and, by placing the sunroom on the east side, we would be able to sit on the couch and look down into the ravine.

When we had finished our discussion, without any explanation, Gene got into his truck and backed it up so that it was close to the front of the lot.

"Come on over here," Gene said as he stretched out his arm toward me. "I'll give you a hand into the back of my truck."

"What?" I shook my head slightly and looked at him with a puzzled expression.

"I'll help you up. You'll be able to see what the view from your front deck will look like."

I climbed into the back of his truck and the rest of the family followed.

We all looked out toward the lake. Doug pointed down the channel. "There's Basswood Island on the left and Hermit on the right and beyond is Oak. And, look, there's Raspberry Island. You can just make out the lighthouse."

While the rest of the family took in the view, I glanced down at Gene standing beside his truck. He was smiling broadly, clearly appreciating the whole process. He seemed to relish seeing other people enjoy the island that meant so much to him.

At that moment I was positive we had made the right choice of a contractor. His deep love for the island was contagious. Not only was I certain he would build a superb house, but I also hoped to learn much more from him about this Lake Superior island we had selected as its site.

Giving our final blessing to the house site was a far more enjoyable experience than plotting the driveway had been, and it too strengthened our ties to our land and deepened our commitment to the island.

* * * * *

"Do you want a basement?" Gene asked.

The answer to this question was just one of a myriad of decisions we would have to make before construction could begin.

Somehow we had assumed that by the time we selected a log home company and okayed the final blueprints for the house, most of the important decisions had been made. We were so naïve; we had no idea what an education the construction process would be. Actually, it was probably a good thing we didn't know. If we had been able to foresee the future, I'm not sure we would have proceeded. We were like first-time parents who decide to have a child with only a vague notion of what parenthood entails.

Sometimes ignorance makes it easier to venture into unknown territory.

* * * * *

As Doug and I peered into the gaping hole at the end of our driveway, we were glad we had said yes to a basement. Since our last visit the construction crew had been busy. A huge yellow backhoe stood poised next to a large hole in the red clay, its arm raised with the scoop dangling in mid-air, ready for the next mouthful of earth it would swallow on Monday morning when the workers returned. Our basement would root our house into this russet-colored earth.

We were lucky it was red clay the scoop was getting ready to gobble. Though generations of farmers and gardeners have railed against Madeline's compacted, reddish-brown soil because it is so difficult to till, it is better than digging into the ground and finding sandstone bedrock not far beneath the surface as is the case on several of the other Apostle Islands. The red clay breeds clouds of reddish-brown dust that form every time a car drives along unpaved roadways such as North Shore Road. Our vehicles always bring home a layer of Madeline dust as an island souvenir. After one of our trips, a friend looked at Doug's car and asked, "Where in the world have you been? Out in the desert?"

The red clay and reddish-brown dust are reminders of how Madeline Island was formed.

It was glaciers that carved out Madeline and the other Apostle Islands in Lake Superior. Before the glaciers arrived, the Apostles were simply high hills on the mainland of the Bayfield peninsula. But the powerful glacial ice widened and deepened the valleys between the hills and then retreated, flooding the valleys with melting ice and creating Madeline and the other islands. For good measure, as they left, the glaciers deposited layer after layer of thick, dark red clay till.

Looking into the large hole in front of us, it seemed as though about half the basement had been excavated. Doug pointed, "That's where I'll put my workbench." He already had a bench and a large collection of tools in his workroom at home in Minneapolis. Over the years he had acquired a table saw and various other woodworking tools and had used them to build a set of bookshelves and a handsome walnut grandfather clock. The workroom was also the place where he stored the tools he used for plumbing and electrical projects. With help from my dad, he had learned how to install sinks and toilets as well as electrical switches and outlets.

Perhaps there was something genetic in this desire for a workbench. In the basements of our childhood homes, both Doug's father and mine had built long wooden counters where they worked on various home improvement projects.

I was happy there would be a basement in our house where Doug could work on projects and store his tools. And tools we had. When Doug and I cleaned out our childhood homes, we came away with at least a dozen large plastic storage boxes filled with tools. As we stood in the basement of the small, red brick house in Mt. Prospect, Illinois, I remember Doug carefully placing each tool in one of the plastic tubs. When he discovered one particular item, he practically crowed, "Look, here's the wrench that my great-uncle used when he worked as a mechanic on the Chicago and Eastern Indiana Railroad." Doug took special care to wrap the wrench in an old towel before finding a secure spot for it in one of the boxes.

* * * * *

Once the basement was excavated and the concrete walls poured, Gene and his crew constructed the "cap." Using two-by-twelve joists to span the basement walls, they covered that framework with plywood flooring.

We arrived with great anticipation on our first weekend visit after the basement was "capped." We parked our car at the end of the driveway and approached what looked like a large, flat stage constructed in a clearing in the middle of the woods. Now it was possible to get a feel for the footprint of the house. Doug and I spent the first half hour of our visit dashing from stage right to stage left delivering impromptu lines as we imagined where we stood in our future house.

"Here's where the dining room table will go," I said as I crouched in a sitting position on my imaginary chair.

"And here's the fireplace," said Doug, rubbing his hands together as though warming them by the fire.

I grabbed Doug's arm and pulled him to center stage, "Look at the view of the lake we're going to have!" It took a bit of imagination to conjure the future panorama. The front of the lot was dense with trees. Some would have to be sacrificed if we were going to have a clear view of the lake.

* * * * *

Once the "cap" was completed, the pace of construction moved quickly. The log home company from which we bought our kit delivered the construction materials in two loads. The first included everything necessary to construct the basic frame of the house. The windows, half-logs for the interior and exterior of the house, and the interior knotty pine paneling were part of the second load of materials. After the huge truck lumbered up our driveway and deposited the first load near the building site, the crew worked hard, and the basic structure of the house quickly took shape.

Throughout the time our house was under construction, Doug and I drove to Madeline Island every other weekend to check on the progress of the builders and to make any necessary decisions about details. On the trip from Minneapolis to the island we were always full of anticipation about what had been accomplished in the previous two weeks.

As the walls rose, so did our excitement level. We started to plan our first family gathering for the coming Memorial Day, Gene's target date for completing the house.

"Bob and Steve'll be on vacation by then. We can inaugurate the house together. Boy, will they be excited to see it!" Doug said. We were in the car returning home from our most recent visit to the island.

I put down the *Log Home Living* magazine I had been perusing. "Hey, maybe Penny and Keith and their kids can come up for the Fourth of July. We'll grill hamburgers on the deck."

"Yeah, and go to the parade."

"And watch the fireworks over the waterfront."

We went on to discuss other future gatherings—which friends we would invite, how we'd hike the trails at Big Bay Park, picnic on the beach, go out to dinner at Bell Street Tavern. We were so happy to finally see our long-held dream becoming a reality.

* * * * *

It began with the land. When we first purchased it, we knew little about our property; it was a plot of undifferentiated space. But beginning on the day we signed the purchase agreement, we literally built a relationship to our piece of Madeline Island from the ground up. Our attraction deepened as we tramped across our land summer after summer, picnicked beneath its birches, and climbed down its steep cliffs to the shore. Granted, we did all this on the lot next door to the one we really owned, but it was not too difficult to transfer our affections to the new property since the features were very similar.

The process continued as we plotted the course of the driveway and as the workers excavated the basement and poured the concrete foundation.

The relationship that began with the land now extended to the structure emerging from the ground—first the flat surface of the "cap" covering the basement, followed by the outside walls and windows, then the maze of interior walls.

Each time we visited, we came to know the space more intimately. All the trips to Madeline, all the highs and lows of the building process increased its importance and value in our lives. It was becoming place to us—a special place whose meaning in our lives would grow ever stronger as we watched the house take shape and as we anticipated the time when we would be able to share it with family and friends.

BELL STREET TAVERN

We didn't know it at the time, but the months it took to build our house served an important function that had nothing to do with construction. It was during this period that we were introduced to the island and its year-round inhabitants. In the past we had spent many summer weeks there, but we were merely vacationers. We didn't yet know the character of the island and its people.

Bell Street Tavern was one venue for our island education. Our contractor Gene was both builder and part owner of the tavern, and his office was on the second floor. But food, not Gene, was our main reason for going there. It was the only restaurant on Madeline open twelve months of the year. Though hardly aware of it at first, we were ingesting something much more important than food at Bell Street. It was here that we began to learn about the island way of life.

When we first started coming to Bell Street, the restaurant was rather rudimentary. To order lunch, we walked up to a counter that consisted of a piece of two-by-ten lumber resting on a pair of wooden sawhorses. Deciding what we wanted to eat was easy. All we had to do was lift the covers of the two crockpots and pick which soup we wanted. While the choice of food was limited, there was an extensive selection of beer. The bar was stocked with the obligatory Leinenkugels, plus a dozen other domestic and imported brews.

By the time our house was finished, so was Bell Street Tavern, and the dining options had improved significantly. A thirty-foot antique bar that Gene reclaimed from a recently closed restaurant in Superior, Wisconsin, had replaced the two-by-ten counter. Dinner was served in a separate dining room with candles and white linens on the tables.

Once the era of sawhorses and crockpot cuisine ended, a professional kitchen was installed and a full-time chef was hired. Chris Martin came to the kitchen of Bell Street Tavern via an oceanfront restaurant in Florida and, most recently, a ski lodge in the Upper Peninsula of Michigan. Chris was the least temperamental and most gregarious chef I ever had met. Late in the evening, when dinner orders had slowed, Chris would come out of the kitchen to greet customers and find out if they were enjoying their dinners. He learned the guests' likes and dislikes and would even share his recipes. Chris told me in detail how to duplicate his version of one of my favorite local dishes, sautéed whitefish.

One thing that didn't change was the crowd at the bar. Doug and I usually sat at one of the surrounding tables. The stools at the bar seemed to be reserved for "regulars"—either year-round inhabitants or frequent visitors to the island who had earned the right to mingle with the residents. We sensed that there was a probationary period of sorts during which islanders would take our measure before we would merit a seat at the bar. We were still newcomers and as such we were relegated to the position of observers. We sat on the periphery of the action where we felt as if we were watching the colorful and sometimes exotic inhabitants of a fishbowl. We hoped that some time in the future we would be welcome to plunge in and take a dip.

One winter Saturday night as we sat at our table, pondering what to order, our waitress approached and said, "Oh, you're the ones getting the seafood special."

Doug looked puzzled. "I think you've got the wrong table."

"You're the Spauldings, aren't you?"

We nodded.

"Chef Chris said he was making it especially for you because you always order some type of fish."

We were stunned that Chris would take it upon himself to prepare a platter containing all our favorite fish and seafood. And there was something else that surprised us: The waitress knew who we were. Having lived in large cities all of our lives, Doug and I were unprepared for the fact that people we had never been introduced to knew our names.

We had the same experience at other times on the island. "Spauldings! How's your house coming?" we were greeted by the ticket-taker on the ferryboat. Not only did he know our names; he also knew why we were coming to the island.

On another occasion as a different ticket-taker signaled us to drive onto the ferry, she pointed and mouthed, "New car. Nice!"

We were forced to reconsider the fishbowl. We had imagined ourselves to be the outside observers. But maybe we were actually the exotic fish swimming in the bowl.

I wasn't sure I liked being the object of attention I hadn't sought. I began to realize how much I appreciated the anonymity that comes with city life. Back at home I felt I had more choice about whether I wanted to stand out as a brilliantly colored tropical fish or blend into a large school of tiny brown minnows. On Madeline, whether I liked it or not, I was conspicuous, less of a lackluster minnow and more of an iridescent neon tetra.

* * * * *

Over the months of house construction and dinners at Bell Street, we learned that, like any community, the island has its own social structure. And, as we found out, it's a rather complicated arrangement. In fact, there are really two social structures—one for those who live there year round, the other for visitors. Each has its own hierarchy.

In descending order, the hierarchies are:

Residents

1. Third and fourth generation islanders
2. First generation islanders
3. Retirees

Visitors

4. Summer people
5. Short-term vacationers
6. Driving day-trippers
7. Walk-on day-trippers

The ancestors of today's third and fourth generation islanders left their homes in Sweden, Finland, England, and Germany, arriving on Madeline Island in the late 1800s. One man dominates this period of island history. R. J. Russell, who came to Madeline in 1886, was responsible for bringing many settlers to the island. He established a sawmill, and many of the loggers who came to work for him ended up staying to homestead land, raise large families and become farmers, fishermen, and lumbermen. R. J. did things in a big way. By 1898 he and his wife owned a thousand acres on the north end of the island and had produced thirteen children, most of whom remained on Madeline to raise their own families.

It isn't simply longevity that earns third and fourth generation islanders their place at the top of the pecking order. Respected for their vast knowledge of the island and the surrounding waters of Lake Superior, they know the weather patterns, the island vegetation and wild life, and how to deal with the rigors of winter on Madeline.

I felt fortunate we had chosen to hire Gene, a third generation islander, as our contractor. He told us about growing up on Madeline—how he attended a two-room elementary school on the island and then boarded with a family in Ashland during high school, how he learned early on to fish, hunt deer, and ride a snowmobile. He provided a window into the life of long-term island residents.

There was another benefit in hiring Gene—one that we didn't realize until we were well into the construction process. Choosing a third generation islander rather than an outsider gave us a certain measure of credit with the locals. They liked us better for having selected one of their own.

On the rung below the third and fourth generation islanders are the residents who moved to Madeline as adults and have lived there for many years. Some of these first generation islanders married into life on Madeline; others came for a visit, loved the lifestyle, and never left. Many of the first, as well as the third and fourth generation islanders make their living in the tourist industry, staffing the island marina and restaurants or working in the construction trades.

The third category of year-round residents are those who moved to the island to spend their retirement years there. Some had vacationed on Madeline for many years and wanted to live there permanently, while others are newcomers.

Then there is the hierarchy of visitors. At the bottom of the pecking order—the Rodney Dangerfields who get the least respect from year-round residents—are the walk-on day-trippers, the people who walk on the ferry at Bayfield and off at the island. Unless they rent a bike or moped from the Motion to Go shop, their exploration is usually limited to the town of La Pointe. You can find them on a summer's day contemplating the colorful painted sign in the center of town, the one with the points of interest numbered on a map of the island. They usually saunter up Main Street and visit the handful of gift shops, stopping by Grampa Tony's for an ice cream cone or the Beach Club for a beer. If they venture into the Beach Club, they might be surprised at the greeting they receive. The summer wait staff at the restaurant includes a number of workers from Bulgaria. They are part of a business program that brings young people from Eastern Europe to work on the island. Easily recognizable by their Slavic accent, they have startled many a visitor with their friendly salutation: "Welcome to the Bitch Club!"

There is a subset of day-trippers who bring their cars over to the island on the ferry; they not only visit the town of La Pointe, but also drive around the island. The driving day-trippers often stop at Big Bay Park to walk along the beach and perhaps dip a toe into the icy waters of Lake Superior. I overheard the conversation of one of these driving day-trippers at a Bayfield restaurant. A paunchy middle-aged man in a bright blue polo shirt announced to his table companions, "Yup. Drove all the way 'round Madeline Island yesterday. No need to go back. Saw everything."

His comment reminded me of a similar one made by a member of another category of visitor—those who spend a week or two on the island, either camping or staying in a rented cabin. An acquaintance described her August vacation on Madeline, "We swam at Big Bay, had a picnic in the park at Joni's Beach, rented kayaks and paddled along the shore, and hiked a couple of trails." Then, she turned to me with a note of exasperation in her voice and asked, "What *else* is there *to do* on the island?"

I don't know how to respond to people who grow bored with the island's charms in a day or a week. How do I explain that I love to tramp the same trails, visit the same beaches, cruise the same shores, and dine in the same restaurants over and over again? I delight in repeating these activities both because I cherish revisiting familiar haunts and because I discover something new each time I undertake these pursuits.

"Summer people" form another category of visitors to the island. A widely circulated bumper sticker refers to them: *Madeline Island, Summer People, Some Are Not.* This sticker sounds somewhat condescending, but I have never been sure who is on the receiving end of the condescension.

Whatever the interpretation of the bumper sticker, the tradition began at the turn of the century when vacationers came to the island to escape the heat and hay fever in their home states. John O'Brien commissioned the first summer cottage on the island in 1893. Before long there was a cluster of buildings close to the ferry landing known as O'Brien's Row. The Grassie family built their family cottage known as "Merrymeet" shortly after the O'Brien's moved in. Then came Colonel Frank Woods, the first of a large contingent of visitors from Nebraska. Today the descendants of these families still make Madeline Island their vacation home.

In the past, when most families had a single wage-earner, mothers and children would arrive on Memorial Day and stay until the beginning of the school year, with fathers joining them on the weekends.

As I watched our house taking shape, I thought longingly about what it must have been like to spend the entire summer on the island. Like most dual-income families today, we'll be lucky if we can spend a week or two plus a few long weekends at our island home. Not qualifying as traditional summer people, we'll be part of a new breed of visitors who own vacation homes on Madeline. Maybe there are enough of us to add a new category to the hierarchy just below the summer people: the "homeowners-who-visit-frequently-but-don't-stay-all-summer" people.

Many of the vacation homes on Madeline are used mostly during the warmer months; a lot of them are not winterized. From the start we knew we wanted a winterized house so we could visit the island year round. What we didn't realize was that our desire to spend time on the island during non-tourist months would garner us a certain amount of respect from full-time residents.

One evening, as we stomped the February snow from our boots in the entry of Bell Street Tavern, a full-time resident seated at the bar looked up, seeming surprised to see us. "Hey, what brings you up here this time of year?"

"We came to do some snow-shoeing and cross-country skiing," Doug said.

I added, "Yeah, we love it up here in winter—so peaceful, so pristine."

The guy at the bar smiled and nodded approvingly. Then he turned to the bartender, "Hey, these people need some beer."

We had just received the island equivalent of a papal blessing.

* * * * *

There is intermingling between the categories of Madeline's social structure. Long-term friendships have developed between full-time residents and summer people. This is partly because summer people have made many contributions to the quality of life on the island. Summer people and full time residents worked together to help establish the library, the health clinic, and the historical museum.

Though there is interchange between layers of the social structure, there is also a tendency to stay with one's own kind. One of the retirees on the island commented on how difficult it is to become friends with third and fourth generation islanders: "I think they're cautious about getting too friendly because they're used to people saying they're going to live here and then pulling up stakes and leaving." One woman who had lived on Madeline for twenty years told me, "I'm still considered a newcomer. That's the way it is on the island."

Who are the insiders and the outsiders in this social system? It depends on whom you ask. Most people would agree, though, that the true insiders are those who can trace their roots back to old island families and the true outsiders are those gawking day-trippers on Main Street. The proper designation for everyone in between these two categories would likely be the subject of endless debates.

Though I would like to be an insider, I will never qualify. My roots are sunk deep into Minnesota soil, not the red clay of Madeline. Therefore I'll always be an outsider. I'm also still more of an observer than a participant in island life. I'd like to develop friendships with people in all of the above-mentioned categories, but it has been easiest to get to know other people who own vacation homes on the island. Doug and I have also made friends with some of the people who have recently retired to Madeline. Not surprisingly, we've formed friendships with the categories of people most like ourselves.

I know my position as an outsider has disadvantages. I am not privy to the thoughts and values of the insiders. I don't really understand their motivations. And I realize that much of island life is hidden from me. In fact, I have many unanswered questions. For instance, I know islanders gather at Bell Street Tavern, but that can't be the only place they get together. Where are their hidden meeting places? Also, I know that the livelihood of many residents comes from the tourist trade, and for the most part they are welcoming to visitors. But do they ever feel resentful about having to share their island with outsiders? Do they sometimes just want to lock the door and put up a "No Admittance" sign?

Being an outsider can also be advantageous. At times it's easier to see things more clearly, more objectively from the vantage point of an outsider. I've learned this in my profession as a family therapist. I'm good at analyzing the interactions of families who visit my office, but ask me to interpret the patterns in my own family and I'm often at a loss.

This description of the island social structure is my own interpretation. It is definitely an outsider's portrait of island society. Maybe my analysis is correct. Maybe not. But one thing I know for certain: Not all layers of the hierarchy would agree with me.

Besides, I know my place. I am way down on one of the bottom rungs.

CONSTRUCTION

Besides being a third generation islander, what did we really know about the man we had hired to be our contractor? Our weekend trips to Madeline began to supply some answers. One of our sources of information was the men who worked for Gene.

* * * * *

Despite the fact that he was twenty feet in the air, the young man looked perfectly relaxed as he sat astride one of the huge log beams that spanned the entire width of the house and connected the two outside walls. He was the first thing we noticed as we walked toward the house on our visit to the construction site in November of 1997.

"Hey, you must be the Spauldings," he called down from his high perch. Brett was an extrovert, the unofficial greeter at the work site. Wiry and agile, he was a carpenter who always seemed to be tempting fate as he balanced precariously on a roof joist or a second story truss.

The cast of workers changed over the months of house construction. Besides Brett there was Rich, who was stocky and good-natured. Doug and I will always remember him not only for his ready smile but also because he took it upon himself to put log siding on the closet walls in our bedroom, even though the plans called for wallboard. When Gene saw the closet, he just shook his head and muttered something under his breath. The logs stayed because it was less expensive to have log paneling than to pay for the hours of labor required to remove it.

Brett and Rich lasted only a couple of months. They were replaced by quiet, hard-working Aaron and his jovial father Fabian, who had been laid off from his job at a lumber company. We learned that there is a definite pecking order in construction. There are workers with experience as carpenters and there are "go-fers," those with no prior background who did whatever the carpenters didn't want to do. Fabian was one of the gofers and often swept up the construction debris or carried lumber and other materials where they were needed.

The fact that the workers didn't stay with the job until it was finished seemed to be fairly typical in that area of Wisconsin. Workers left because they heard of a job with better pay or working conditions. There were certainly jobs that would be preferable to constructing a house in the winter in below zero temperatures. But there may have been another reason that workers didn't stay. Gene was not an easy man to work for. He was a perfectionist, and he expected nothing less than perfection from others. Perhaps some of the men who couldn't measure up to his expectations decided to look elsewhere for work.

There was one worker who provided the supreme test for Gene's patience: Jim—or "Two Dog Jim," as he called himself. We always knew when he had arrived at the building site because his emissaries, his two large dogs, came galloping onto the lot. A few minutes later Jim, our electrician, came into view. Apparently electricians were hard to come by, especially electricians who were willing to accept a job on the island that required riding a ferry back and forth to work. Jim was a good storyteller with a mischievous sense of humor. He was fun to talk to, but he was an unpredictable electrician.

"Gene fired me, but then he let me back on the job," he confided to us the first time we met him at the house. It was easy to understand why Gene had lost patience with him. In the small main floor bedroom, Jim had placed electrical outlets every two feet all around the room. In the main room, however, there were no outlets at all along one of the twenty-foot walls. In addition, Jim had lost two copies of the electrical plan for the house. After that, Gene insisted that Jim stop at the Nelson Builders' office in La Pointe to pick up the only remaining copy of the plan before he went to the job site seven miles out of town. And Jim was required to drop off the plan each afternoon after he finished working. "I got tired of doing that," Jim told us, "and I found one of the copies I thought I'd lost, so I hid it in the chimney." Ultimately Jim got fired a second and final time, and Gene finished the wiring himself.

Though we had enjoyed the entertainment Jim provided, we were relieved when Gene decided to let him go, especially because we continued to discover Jim's wiring surprises even after the house was completed.

One afternoon after we had moved in, I slipped a CD into the stereo, sat down on the green leather couch, and got ready to relax to the strains of Mahler's First Symphony. In less than a minute I was off the couch, standing in front of the stereo system, glaring at it with hands on hips.

"What's the heck's the matter with this stupid thing! It sounds more like a quartet playing in a closet instead of the Vienna Philharmonic Orchestra performing at the Concerthouse!"

Doug heard my exclamations. When he checked it out, Doug found that Two Dog Jim had wired the whole system for monaural rather than stereo.

One worker stayed with the project from beginning to end. Pete was an excellent carpenter. His work was so good, in fact, that even our perfectionist contractor could find no fault with it. Serious and shy, Pete didn't talk much, but he beamed when we complimented his painstaking craftsmanship. It was Pete who made the intricate cuts necessary to fit the interior logs together in the corners of the rooms and carved out the logs to make space for the electrical outlets. Even now there are times when Doug and I are sitting in the sunroom and Doug will say, "Look at the way those logs are perfectly scribed over each stone in the fireplace. Pete did outstanding work, didn't he?"

With us, his customers, Gene was infinitely patient. When there were choices to be made—for example, how we wanted the interior of the windows framed—Gene would take several samples of possible trim and hold them up alongside the window to help us make a decision. One of his favorite statements was, "I can do anything you want." If Gene hadn't already won me over, that statement would have been the clincher. I grew up with a father who could build anything and fix everything. One of the last things he built shortly before my mother died was an intricate wooden arbor to shade the patio on the side of their house.

It seems only natural then that I would marry a civil engineer who not only builds things but also taught himself the basics of plumbing and wiring. I would have been very frustrated had I married a man like our neighbor, Tim. He was not a do-it-yourselfer. When Tim bought a new bedframe, he actually had to pay the department store to come out and put it together.

It also seems natural that I would be a sucker for any man who was going to build a house for us, especially from plans I designed. So when Gene said he could do anything we wanted, I found this statement endearing. However, it made Doug nervous. He was thinking about the effect on the bottom line.

* * * * *

"Geez, would you look at that place!" Doug said. It was a Saturday afternoon. We had met with Gene at the house and then decided to take a driving tour of the island. Doug slowed down to get a better look at the property on the south side of the island.

At the front of the lot were a large pole barn and a smaller shed. The doors to both stood open, and the two buildings appeared to be so full that things were spilling out of them. Piles of lumber, shingles and other construction materials were scattered haphazardly about the property. In the yard were numerous vehicles: an old RV, a 1985 Pontiac convertible, at least three trucks in varying stages of disrepair, as well as a backhoe, a Bobcat and a front end loader. The house was almost invisible at the back of the lot due to all the distractions nearer the road. It was clear that it was owned by someone who saved almost everything.

"Oh my gosh, Doug. I recognize that truck." Parked by the house was a familiar dark green truck—Gene's. We had been gawking at the home of our contractor.

In his line of work Gene's habit of saving was invaluable. When he needed a piece of lumber or hardware in a hurry, he could often find it in his shop where he stored extra building materials left over from his jobs. He rarely threw anything away. We learned that this is a common characteristic of islanders. They are savers. They have to be. If something breaks and a part is needed to fix it, the job will be finished much faster if you already have the part that's needed—or a reasonable substitute. Otherwise it will take the better part of a day to ride the ferry to the mainland, drive to a hardware store or lumberyard, buy the part—if they have it—and then catch the ferry back to the island.

Gene's assurance that he could do anything we wanted was an indication of one of his most prominent characteristics: his ingenuity. If he needed something and couldn't buy it or find it in his workshop, he would make it himself. He had metalworking equipment and would fabricate a piece of metal into the fitting he lacked. If the job required a piece of lumber in a size that wasn't available, he simply fashioned it out of lumber he had on hand. He enjoyed the challenge of figuring out how to create whatever his clients needed or wanted.

I realized that if I were going to live on Madeline, I too would need to learn some island ingenuity.

I love to cook, and at home in Minneapolis the grocery stores offer an enticing array of ingredients—arugula and mache for salads, fresh basil, marjoram, and lemon balm, New Zealand lamb, Mexican mangoes. But all it took was one trip to Madeline's grocery stores to realize that they stock the basics—pop, beer, chips—and little more. My choices were limited. I would have to learn to make do.

Several years after our house was finished, we invited some of our new island friends for dinner. As we lingered over coffee on the deck, Jan asked, "Where did you find the heirloom tomatoes you used in the salad?"

"They're not from around here. I brought them from home." I sighed. "The one thing I miss on the island is a real grocery store."

Jan's husband, Jerry, spoke up. "It's true. We don't have the best grocery stores up here. But you don't have this view back in Minneapolis," he said, gesturing toward the Lake Superior panorama in front of us.

He was right. I turned to look at the expansive vista that had captivated us from the first time we caught a glimpse of it. No matter how many times I see it, it still has the same effect on me. As I breathed in the spicy scent of pine needles commingled with lake air, I thought that perhaps doing without some of the things I take for granted in my city life is a small price to pay for the abundance of island living.

* * * * *

We learned early on that Gene enjoyed solving problems. When one of the workmen was putting up the outside light fixtures and drilled a large hole through an exterior log in the wrong spot, Gene rolled his eyes and told us, "I'll make a wooden plug for the hole, and you'll never even know it was there." And he was right. When the kitchen was finished and we realized that the electrical plan hadn't included a light fixture over the kitchen sink, it wasn't a problem. "I'll just fish the wires down from the loft." And he did. When the upstairs bathroom was finished, and I decided that I'd like a medicine cabinet on the wall, that was not a problem either. A space was carved out of the newly installed wallboard, and a medicine cabinet appeared. Gene was always eager to please and, if it involved a demanding task, so much the better.

Probably the biggest challenge we presented him with was the installation of the dark green granite tile on our kitchen counters. When I was shopping for the tile the salesman explained that it had to be installed with epoxy grout. He warned me, "This grout isn't easy to use. The installer has to work quickly because within a few minutes the grout gets as hard as a rock."

I relayed this information to Gene before I purchased the tile. "Are you sure you don't mind using the epoxy stuff? It sounds as if it's pretty tough to work with."

"No problem," Gene reassured me.

"Ok, great. I'm going to wash the wood floors, and I'll put down a tarp so that you don't have to worry about getting the grout on the floor."

When we came back the next weekend, I found hard little globs of black epoxy stuck all over the kitchen floor. The tarp was in a heap in the corner of the room. I was not thinking kind thoughts about Gene when I was down on my hands and knees cleaning the floor for the second time in a week. This time I had to use a razor blade to scrape all those little black bits of rock-hard epoxy grout off the maple floor.

Later I learned that Gene had tried using the tarp, but when the grout stuck to the tarp and then to the floor, he got rid of the tarp because it only made a bigger mess.

Several months later Doug was walking in the woods about a hundred yards from our house when he found pieces of dark green granite tile scattered in the tall grass. We pictured Gene in utter frustration pitching those pieces of tile as far as they would go.

After our house was completed and the epoxy grout was a distant memory for all three of us, we met Gene at a bar in town and joked with him about finding the tile in the woods. "How come you didn't just tell us you didn't want to use the epoxy—that it was too difficult?" I asked Gene.

His response was pure Gene. "Are you kidding?" he replied. "Just tell me something's impossible, and I'm your man!"

* * * * *

We were well into the construction process before we realized that Gene didn't read instructions; he either knew how something worked or he figured it out. I think we first became aware of his apparent dislike of written instructions when we asked him if he could install a system that removed iron from the water.

At first he attempted to persuade us that we didn't really need it. "I don't have one of those for my water. In fact, I don't know of anyone on the island who does."

But I was not going to be talked out of it so easily. "Well, I can show you my formerly white dishes that have turned beige from the minerals in the water. I want to be able to wash clothes and dishes here without worrying that everything will turn rust-colored."

"Ok then, I'll install it."

So we bought the system and gave him the booklet of installation instructions. When we came to the island a few weeks later, the booklet was just where we had left it and Gene was "still working on it." We showed him the number of the hot line he could call for further information. We even mentioned that he could take the cordless phone downstairs where the system was if he wanted to call from there. That never happened either. But, apparently using the trial and error method, within a few weeks he had the system working.

Gene's ability to figure out how things worked without reading a single word of instruction reminded me of the difference between our two sons when they played with Legos. On Christmas morning when our older son Bob got a new set of Legos from Santa, he would follow the instructions step by step, (as his parents taught him), and several hours later he would be playing with his completed Lego space ship. On the other hand, no matter how much we prodded Steve to read the instructions, he would simply look at the picture on the cover of the box and several hours later proudly display his perfectly constructed Lego battleship. Both boys ended up with good results. They simply followed very different paths to arrive at the same destination.

We heard a story from Joe Schulz that captured this trait of Gene's perfectly. Gene had built the Schulz's house several years before he started ours, and their name was on the list of references Gene gave us. Joe had asked Gene to install their garage door opener. When he went to the garage to see how Gene was getting along, there he was sitting on the floor with all the pieces of the door opener spread out around him. The only thing left in the box was the instruction sheet. Joe said he looked like a kid with a new toy on Christmas morning.

* * * * *

Our excitement level was high as we pulled into our driveway at Madeline a few days after Christmas. Bob and Steve were on break, and we had decided to make a quick trip to Madeline. Doug was easing the car into the parking area when we noticed a new structure about thirty feet from the house. It was small, about eight feet by eight feet, neatly roofed and covered in wood siding.

"What is that? An outhouse?" asked Steve as he climbed out of the car.

Bob got to the boxy little building first and pushed open the door. "It looks like a tool shed."

Inside in the corner stood a shovel, an axe, and a hand saw. On the wall was a girlie calendar featuring Miss December clad in little more than a Santa hat. Scattered across a counter that ran the length of the house were more tools, a *Wine Spectator* magazine, and a roll of toilet paper. Maybe Steve had been on the right track after all.

Back outside I noticed an attractive ceramic tile sign above the door with the name of the little house: Lunker Lodge. Just then Gene drove up. He was barely out of his truck when Doug, pointing to Lunker Lodge, yelled to him, "I don't remember this on the house plans."

Gene ambled over. "We hauled it over here for storage. It's the ice fishing house my cousin Ronnie and I share."

Here was yet another example of the inventiveness of islanders. They often seemed to find new uses for things, and Lunker Lodge was no exception. Several years later, during a conversation with Gene's wife, I learned that in its next incarnation Lunker Lodge had been transformed into her art studio.

The rest of us were still gathered around Lunker Lodge when Steve called to us, "Hey, come over here. You've got to see this."

As we approached we could see that he was watching a small white animal with shiny black eyes and short legs scurrying around the scrap pile the workers had left near the side of the house. The narrow-bodied, foot-long creature seemed unafraid of the humans peering down at him. He barely stopped to look up at us as he ran around and around the pile of wood, completing a mission only he understood. Looking over at Gene, Steve asked, "What kind of animal is he?"

Gene crouched down and pointed at the small animal that still showed no sign of fear. "That's an ermine. Their fur changes from brown to white in the winter for camouflage."

But for its constant motion and shiny black eyes, it would hardly have been visible against the newly fallen snow.

The more I learned about this man we had hired to be our contractor, the more I liked him. He was always willing to stop whatever he was doing to answer our questions—even about wildlife. Yes, he could be hard on the men who worked for him, but not out of meanness. It was because he wanted to provide us, his customers, with an excellent finished product. I could not argue with that motivation. He was always eager to please, to do "anything we wanted."

And each time we came to the island he was happy to show us what had been accomplished since our last visit. Once we had tired of watching the ermine, he proceeded to do just that on that cold December afternoon. "We've got the house all framed. And most of the roof is done."

Only the front section was roofless. Winter had already delivered a foot of snow to the island, and there were piles of snow on the floor up front. For some inexplicable reason, Steve grabbed a shovel and started pushing the snow off the floor.

Gene walked over to the side of the house and pointed at the snow-encrusted blue plastic tarps on the ground. "The half logs for the inside and outside of the house are under there, and the doors and windows are in the basement."

Gene leaned against one of the studs in what would become a bedroom. "Just as soon as we finish the roof, we'll get right on the windows. That'll give the guys a warmer place to work over the winter. Then we can start working on the inside. And I've ordered a furnace. Hopefully they'll be out here within a couple of weeks to install it—before the ferries stop running."

"Couldn't they come over on the ice road after the ferries stop?" I asked.

"Yeah, but a lot of those guys from the mainland don't like to drive on the ice road. They get pretty spooked about bringing their trucks across the lake." His tone of voice had the slight air of superiority I had noticed whenever islanders talked about the trepidation of mainlanders who did not want to travel the ice road.

I realized as we were talking that I had not yet put myself to the ice road test. Would I be a typical mainlander? What fears and trepidation was I harboring?

TRAVEL AT YOUR OWN RISK

We were poised at the crest of the hill overlooking Bayfield, ready to plunge into the town below. Spread out before us was a vast, uninterrupted vista. To the right of our car, directly beneath us, were the snowy roofs of Bayfield. Thin wisps of smoke, motionless in the still air, extended straight upward from chimneys. To the left in the distance under dusky slate skies was the dark outline of Madeline Island. In between was the flat, frozen plain of Lake Superior. The only thing interrupting the unbroken whiteness was the sinuous road that had been plowed across the snow-covered ice.

During the summer months when we summit this hill, I often catch my breath as I see the sunlight shimmering across the blue water. I feel a tingle of excitement at the first glimpse of the big lake with Madeline Island snaking long and green across the horizon. But now as I looked at the scene below, waves of fear shot slivers of cold down my back. I felt lightheaded and slightly queasy, as though I was coming down with the flu. But I knew better. I wasn't getting sick.

Our car crept down the hill. I'm sure we were going thirty-five miles an hour, but it felt as though we were traveling in slow motion. It was taking forever to reach the base of the hill. But that was ok with me because I didn't want to get there. Ever. The bottom of the hill was where the ice road began.

The ice road. It is the only way to reach Madeline Island from the mainland at this time of year. But I didn't want to drive across a sheet of ice knowing that Lake Superior was just beneath the frozen crust. I had visions of what could happen to us. I pictured the scene: a clot of people bundled in down parkas peering into a gash in the ice where moments before our car had broken through and plummeted to the bottom of Lake Superior.

I longed to be back at home in Golden Valley, safely snuggled under the blue afghan on our living room couch. Or maybe at the Powell's cabin, the one we had rented for a week in August for so many years. You didn't have to cross a frozen lake to get to their house.

Why were we building a house on an island anyway? How did Doug talk me into such a thing? What sense did it make to risk your life to get to a lake cabin in the winter? Was this house going to be worth it? Was *any* house worth it?

* * * * *

The ice road is the only way for the 200 year-round residents of Madeline Island to access the mainland for several months each winter. Ferryboats provide transportation for cars and people throughout the year except during the winter months when the ice becomes so thick that the boats can't break a path. In island parlance this is known as "freeze up" and usually occurs early in January. At freeze up the ice is too thick for the ferries, but not yet thick enough for cars. It often takes several more weeks for the ice to reach a thickness of at least twelve inches; only then it is strong enough to support car traffic. Year-round island residents look forward to the season of the ice road with eager anticipation because it is the only time of year that their passage to and from the mainland is not dictated by the ferry schedule.

Islanders rejoice when they can come and go as they please. This freedom does have restrictions, however. The restrictions come from Mother Nature whose winds, snowstorms, and sudden, unexpected warm spells can bring ice road traffic to a halt. But islanders are used to respecting the vagaries of Mother Nature and are more willing to tolerate her restrictions than those of the ferry service. They speak of the ice road with a certain reverence. In his book, *On Thin Ice,* permanent resident Charles Nelson describes the ice road as a gift. "It isn't owed to us. [There is] . . . no accurate way of predicting the size of the gift that we will receive each year or that we will receive it at all."

One winter long before we started building our house on the island, we were vacationing in Bayfield. We gazed out at the stretch of ice leading to Madeline Island and wondered whether we wanted to try the ice road. We decided to conduct an informal survey of Bayfield residents to learn their opinions about driving across the frozen surface of the lake.

The clerk at Andy's IGA told us he had driven to the island several times that winter on the ice road. He advised, "If I were you, I'd go only if the weather is bright and sunny. And be sure to come back to the mainland before dark. When you go across, just follow the trees."

"Trees? On the lake?"

"Yeah. A row of recycled Christmas trees marks the edge of the road."

The young man at the gas station told us that he had walked out on the ice road once to watch the "Run on Water," the annual foot race between the mainland and the island that is held every February. "I was out there on the road when some waves came through. The ice raised and lowered two feet. You couldn't *pay* me to drive across." The weather made our decision easy that day. Snow started falling, and we couldn't see more than three feet in front of our car.

If we had taken a survey on the other side of the ice road, on the island, would the results have been different? Yes, without a doubt. Islanders generally reassure outsiders that driving across the ice road is safe, with some reservations. But that is to be expected. They cannot exist for long on the island without access to the mainland. There is no pharmacy, hardware store, discount store, movie theater, or video store on the island. Even the basics are missing. There is no grocery store, and the only convenience store restricts both its hours and its inventory in the winter. The other establishments open in the winter are one restaurant and a gas pump. The only way to access most of the essentials of modern life is to go to the mainland.

Islanders need the ice road for another reason: Their children's education depends on it. Primary school children attend classes at the island elementary school, but beginning in junior high, island children go across the water or the ice to Bayfield High School. Instead of an orange school bus, transportation is provided by a red van. For many years two brothers, Arnie and Ronnie Nelson, have driven the van to Bayfield, and, even more importantly, they have been charged with the responsibility of making sure that the ice road is safe. Every day either Arnie or Ronnie checks the thickness of the ice with a chainsaw and, if necessary, readjusts the path of the road to avoid any newly opened cracks or soft spots in the ice.

Our contractor, Gene, proved to be an unending source of information about the ice road. "If your car does go in, it doesn't sink all at once, you know," Gene advised us.

He should know. The local paper, *The Island Gazette*, regularly listed Gene as the first person to cross the newly frozen ice at the beginning of the season and the last one across in the spring. Sometimes he was not able to complete those trips, however.

"Once when my truck went through a soft spot in the ice, I had time to get some two-by-fours out of the back of my truck. I built a walk-way over to solid ice." He got out, but his truck had to be hoisted out of the lake.

The town of La Pointe staffs an Ice Rescue Team to deal with emergencies. One day in March they got a 911 call. According to the story we heard, the voice at the other end of the line said, "A man and his vehicle went through the ice! Out here by Grant's Point. Come quick!" When the rescue team arrived, they found the man calmly fishing about thirty feet away from his partially submerged four-wheeler.

During the time our house was under construction we heard many stories about the ice road. Islanders can spot newcomers a mile away. One look at my fur-trimmed parka and Doug's hatless head as we walked through the door at Bell Street Tavern and it was obvious we weren't from the island. As we leaned against the bar, waiting for the bartender to take our order, the regulars on the stools knew they'd found a new audience for their stories about the idiosyncrasies of the ice road.

The old guy in Carhartts and Sorrels turned toward me, "Did you know that sometimes there are fish swimming on the ice road?"

I wrinkled my nose. "Fish?" I shook my head. "On the road?"

"Yep." He nodded emphatically. "When there's been a melt, you can find herring or smelt swimming around in puddles right there on the road."

"How do they get up there, on top of the ice?"

"Well, see, sometimes there's small holes in the ice, and the fish, they see light and they just swim right up through the holes."

I didn't know if I should believe his story, but weeks later when I was reading *On Thin Ice,* I found the same information as well as this helpful advice for the novice: "If the fish swim by your tires, it's ok. You just don't want to see them swim past your car window."

When Doug and I listened to islanders talking to each other about the ice road, it was as though they were speaking a foreign language. They used a vocabulary of technical terms that was unintelligible to outsiders like us. Throughout the ice road season, conversations on the island are punctuated with terms such as shove crack, expansion crack, blue ice, slush ice, candled ice, pack ice, and drift ice. This vocabulary came into being due to the need to survive winter on the island, and it has been handed down from generation to generation.

We were lucky enough to have island mentors who translated this esoteric vocabulary for us. They taught us that we should keep our car away from shove cracks or expansion cracks, which are caused by the ice expanding in warm temperatures. "Usually Ronnie or Arnie ropes off the area that has cracked and routes the ice road around it. But, just the same, you need to watch out for shove cracks."

Islanders explained that ice takes many forms. We learned that blue ice is clear as glass and very strong. Slush ice forms when slush and water freeze into a white-colored ice. And candled ice is to be avoided because it is very porous and eventually breaks down into individual candle-shaped segments.

The old guy in Carhartts was at the bar again one night and he struck up a conversation with Doug. "Do you know about drift ice?"

Doug shook his head.

"Well, I remember one day there was a guy out on the ice in his car. All of a sudden he realizes that there's open water in front of him."

Doug's eyebrows went up. "No! What'd he do?"

"Well there was open water in front of him. *And* in back of him. *And* on both sides of him. See, he was on drift ice. It's sort of like a giant ice cube floating out there in the lake."

"How'd he get off?"

"Somebody called the rescue squad."

Islanders also told us about pack ice. They explained that strong winds and high waves can propel large moving sheets of ice with tremendous force. When these ice sheets come in contact with a solid object such as a rock cliff or a dock, the ice sinks to the lake bottom and can pile up until it reaches heights of twenty, thirty, even sixty feet. This is known as pack ice. When the huge pile comes ashore, the ice often booms with a thunderous roar.

After listening to all the ice road stories, I had accumulated numerous reasons to be nervous. In fact I was scared silly at the mere thought of driving across the frozen lake. Leave that to the locals who knew what they were doing. But much to my surprise, I realized that another part of me had begun to stir, though that part was microscopic in size at first. A tiny part of me was curious: Curious enough to wonder what it would be like to drive over the ice, knowing that the waters of Lake Superior were only a foot below our tires. Curious enough to want to follow the same path that our powerboat followed in the summer. Curious enough to wonder what it felt like to be out in the middle of the ice road, where the closest land was more than a mile away. My curiosity grew and grew until it got just big enough that I finally agreed to give the ice road a try.

And so it was that in February of 1998, seven months after we had begun construction on our house, Doug and I were driving in slow motion down the hill in Bayfield. With each revolution of the tires I could feel my curiosity getting smaller and smaller and my fear growing larger and larger. We were almost at the bottom of the hill.

"Let's wait till tomorrow to go across," I said, trying to sound nonchalant.

"Tomorrow! Why would you want . . . What's wrong with today? With right now?" Doug asked.

Just then I spotted a hand-lettered sign planted in the snow next to the place where the land ended and the ice road began. In bold red letters were the words: Ice Road—Travel at Own Risk.

"No way. I don't *want* to take my own risk," I said, my voice elevating at least an octave.

"Geez, Pat. It's just a sign. Besides, look, there's a car coming across right now. It hasn't gone through the ice, has it?"

Without waiting for an answer, Doug eased the car over the frozen sand beach and out onto the ice road.

"Slow down!" I shrieked.

"I'm only going twenty miles an hour."

"Open the windows! Unbuckle your seat belt! In case we need to escape."

Doug didn't say anything. He did open his window, probably just to pacify me.

A gush of frigid wind whipped through the open windows. I pulled my hat down over my ears. With one hand I clung to the arm rest; the other hand hovered near the door handle. Just in case.

Several minutes passed in silence.

Then Doug started to laugh. "Hey, look over there. Now can you stop worrying?"

I looked in the direction he was pointing. My mouth dropped open. Less than 200 yards from our car I counted 75 pick-up trucks parked side-by-side on the ice. The occupants of the pick-ups were watching, of all things, a drag race. Six cars hurtled around an oval track plowed on the ice. Meanwhile spectators stood in the beds of their pick-ups. They jumped up and down, cheering on their favorites, pausing only long enough to take a pull or two from the beer bottles in their hands.

I closed the window on my side of the car.

After this experience I decided that the most useful attitude I could adopt when crossing the ice road was a willing suspension of disbelief. I did not allow myself to think about the fact that there was eighty feet of water underneath the sheet of ice on which we were driving. I reminded myself that islanders, including their children who go to school on the mainland, use this road every day.

By the next winter I had become much braver about traveling on the ice road. I had come a long way in one year. The weather was warm for March, one of those balmy late winter days when the air is soft and carries hints of spring. As we came down the long hill into Bayfield we noticed something we had never seen before. A few cars were crossing the ice road. As they drove, they sent huge sprays of water six feet into the air from each side of the car. They looked less like cars and more like boats cutting through rough waves.

"It looks like the warm weather is melting the ice. Should we go across?" Doug asked.

I looked at him in astonishment, "Of course! We've come this far. We're not going to let a little water stop us, are we?"

And so we drove across the flooded ice, the spray from our car shooting high into the bright sunshine, creating rainbows as we looked through the side windows. Laughing, I turned to Doug, "Oh my gosh. It's happened. I've gone native!"

Later we learned from islanders that if water collects on the surface of the ice it is a good sign; it indicates that there are not any cracks or holes in the ice. What may have seemed like a foolhardy decision at the time turned out to be a wise choice after all.

Yes, I am now much more confident about driving across the ice road, but I must admit that the first trip of the season still gives me pause. I am always tempted to lower the car windows.

MORE CONSTRUCTION

We left the Twin Cities after work on a wintery Thursday night. A heavy blanket of new snow had fallen, and, as we drove through northern Wisconsin, the landscape looked like a calendar scene of the Bavarian Alps minus the mountains. Two feet of powdery snow was heaped on the roofs of shabby taverns in the small towns, making them look like gingerbread houses decorated with fluffy, white icing. Several were gaily decorated with strings of white lights outlining the windows and doors. The warm golden light from their windows spilled out onto the snow. It was magical.

As was our custom on these trips, we spent the first night in Bayfield at the Seagull Bay Motel, which is situated high on a hill with an unobstructed view of Lake Superior. From our room we could see the lights of Madeline Island shining in the distance. We arrived around midnight and, as was often the case during the winter, we were the only guests staying there. In true small town style, the door to our room was unlocked and, though this was not a Motel 6, the owners literally left the lights on for us.

We had arranged to meet Gene at the house on Friday morning. As we drove up the driveway we were surprised to see his truck parked beside the house. Usually we arrived first and waited for Gene, but this time he was already there. At our last visit, the walls of the house had been erected and most of the roof was completed. Now, as we approached the house, we could see that a lot had changed in the last two weeks.

When we opened the door, Gene was there waiting for us. His smile broadened as we stood with our mouths open, gazing at the two-story window wall that stretched across the entire front of the main room. It framed a panoramic view of the lake. The two sets of French doors with stationary windows on either side were all there, just as I had planned them. And half a dozen additional windows filled in the peak of the vaulted ceiling. Log beams stretched from wall to wall, and the rough boards that formed the beginning of the stairway to the second floor loft and bedroom were in place. The fieldstone fireplace was partially completed.

"Ohhhhh, it's so *big*!" I gasped as I stood just inside the front door. "I know I drew the plans for the house, but I didn't realize it would be this huge."

Gene grinned. "You probably couldn't imagine what it would look like in three dimensions."

Doug and I went from room to room oohing and ahhing at everything. Gene walked with us pointing out the details of construction, but mostly he watched with quiet delight as we discovered all the changes that had taken place in the last two weeks. Doug turned to Gene and gestured toward one end of the main room, "Is this where the kitchen will be?"

Gene nodded.

"Our dining room table can go right next to it, in front of the windows," I said, feeling gleeful at the very thought of our finished house.

"That should give us a great view of the lake while we eat," Doug said.

After an hour of giddy inspection, I turned to Gene and put my hand on his arm, "You've shown us everything. You don't have to stay."

Doug added, "I'm sure you've got other things you'd like to do this morning."

But Gene made no move to leave. "There's nowhere else I'd rather be," he answered, smiling broadly. Two hours later he finally, reluctantly, said goodbye.

* * * * *

Each time we visited during those early months we were amazed at what the workers had accomplished in the two weeks since our last visit. Our house, the house we had dreamed of, was rapidly emerging from the pile of logs and lumber that had been delivered to the home site. We were delighted that our house would be completed by Memorial Day of 1998 and we were convinced that it would be a marvelous house indeed.

WINDSLED

There is a strange, nameless road in La Pointe. A block and a half long, it branches off Sunnyslope Road, goes down a steep hill, and disappears into Lake Superior. I'm sure it has baffled a number of summer visitors to the island. I know it confused Doug and me. Until islanders set us straight.

We were at Bell Street Tavern once again, the location where we seemed to glean most of our information about the island. It was early January, and the place was nearly empty. We were eating dinner at one of the few occupied tables. Realizing that our waiter had time to talk, I began to ply him with questions about winter on Madeline.

"Can you get off the island after the ferries stop running and before the ice is thick enough to drive on?" I asked. "Or do you just get stuck over here during that time?"

"Naw, we don't get stuck," said the twenty-something young man with a scruffy beard. His unkempt chin whiskers needed a trim or at least a good combing. "Haven't you heard of the windsled?"

"Sled? You go across the ice on a sled?"

"Well, it isn't exactly a sled." He pulled at a patch of particularly scraggly whiskers as though he was trying to straighten them out, but his efforts only resulted in a bigger snarl. "See, it's actually kind of a boat with wheels and a big propeller on the back. It drives over the ice but it can also float if it has to."

"How many cars can it carry?" I asked, picturing a ferry boat on wheels.

He snorted. "Cars! None. It's just for people and their stuff. When it looks like the ferries are getting close to their last run, a lot of us on the island park a car over in Bayfield. Then when the windsled starts running, we've got transportation on the other side." He was pulling at his beard again. More tangles.

"How many weeks does this windboat run?"

"Wind*sled*." He was starting to get impatient with me, this city slicker who asked stupid questions and couldn't even keep names straight.

He continued, "The wind*sled* runs a week or two before the ice road is ready and a couple of weeks after the ice breaks up." His fingers were at his chin. I couldn't watch.

"Well, is there a bus stop or a windsled stop where you catch this thing?"

"Yep. That would be the approach."

"What is . . . Where is this approach?"

"You know where Sunnyslope Road is?"

I nodded.

"Right off of Sunnyslope there's a road that goes down a steep hill. At the bottom of that hill, on the edge of the ice, that's where people stand and wait for the windsled."

I pictured a clump of people, huddled together on the ice, waiting for some kind of a crazy boat-car.

A couple of months later, I was one of those people.

* * * * *

On a blustery March day I was standing on the frozen sand of the swimming beach in Bayfield, Wisconsin. The sun warmed my back and made the wind-whipped, twenty-degree afternoon tolerable. Near me were a dozen other people. At their feet, close to the edge of ice-covered Lake Superior, were cardboard boxes packed with a week's supply of groceries. Doug had just finished hauling several large boxes of construction supplies out of our car. He set them down near the grocery boxes and then walked over to join me. We were waiting to take our first ride on the windsled.

And there it was, sitting on the ice in front of me. Finally I was face to face with the home-made contraption that I'd heard so much about. It was a flat-bottomed boat all decked out with incongruous trappings. Just as the young man at Bell Street had said, a single wheel was attached to the front with two smaller wheels in the rear. These were not car wheels; they looked like they had been removed from an airplane. Mounted on the back was a huge, four-blade propeller attached to a large engine. The main body of the boat was outfitted with rudimentary wooden benches and partially covered with a gray canvas top.

I caught snatches of conversation from the people standing nearby.

"How about those Packers?"

"They sure clobbered the Vikings yesterday night."

"Yup. They sure did!"

"They say we're gonna get hit with a real doozy of a snowstorm day after tomorrow."

"I'll believe it when I see it. That weather guy, he's sittin' over in Duluth. What does he know about what's gonna happen over here?"

Except for their loyalty to the Packers, their casual conversation could have been taking place at 7:30 a.m. at any bus stop in Minneapolis. There was no mention of the journey we were all about to take across the barely frozen ice of Lake Superior. Apparently to them it was just part of their everyday lives in winter. But not for me. The trip in the windsled was the only thing I could think about.

While their conversation swirled around me, I was having a discussion with myself. The nervous Nellie part of me had questions. "Do you really want to get into that goofy looking boat? Can it possibly transport us two-and-a-half miles across the ice to Madeline Island?" Nellie also had an answer. "I don't think I want to find out, thank you very much."

Then another part of me spoke up. "Don't be such a poop! You sound just like you did before your first trip across the ice road. That turned out fine and this will too."

With that the voices were quiet. For awhile.

I looked at my watch. 4:40 p.m. We had phoned the Winter Transportation line and the recorded message told us the departure time was supposed to be 4:30 p.m.

The fact that the windsled was not leaving on time didn't really come as a surprise. We had learned early on that Madeline operates on its own time schedule. Islanders are known for their lack of punctuality, though they would not use those words. Instead they refer to "island time." Events advertised in the newspaper are listed as beginning at 8 p.m. with the added caveat, "island time." Only when most of the people have arrived does an event begin.

"Island time" seems to be a variation of the "*manana*" attitude. It's not so much an "I'll get to it sometime, maybe tomorrow" approach. It isn't laziness or procrastination. Instead "island time" seems to be a facet of islanders' characteristic independence. It's an attitude of "I'll decide when I'm going to be there, and nobody's going to tell me when that will be."

When I learned about island time, I was overjoyed! All my life I had been apologizing for not being punctual. Finally I had found a place where I fit in! No longer was I late; I was simply on "island time."

There is one thing for which time stands still on the island—a Packers game. To Wisconsinites in general and Madeline Islanders in particular, the Packers are sacred, Lambeau Field in Green Bay is Mecca and (to mix religious metaphors) the Super Bowl trophy is the Holy Grail. Flying high in front of the Nelson Construction Office on Main Street are two flags: Old Glory and the green and gold Packers flag.

The bar at Bell Street fills up with ardent Packers fans for every game. When the game is tied in the fourth quarter and Brett Favre or Aaron Rogers cocks his arm to throw the winning pass, the cumulative holding of breath nearly sucks the air out of the room. When the pass is successfully completed and the outcome of the game is no longer in doubt, the gush of simultaneous releasing of breath is followed by noisy high-fiving, abundant back-slapping, and consumption of copious quantities of beer.

We stopped by the post office one wintry afternoon and saw the following notice posted on the bulletin board.

Choir practice at St. John's Church at 4 p.m.
or 15 minutes after the game ends. [no need to identify which game]

Just below this notice was the windsled schedule. It read:

Madeline to Bayfield: 8 a.m., 10 a.m., Noon, 4 p.m.
Bayfield to Madeline: 8:30 a.m., 10:30 a.m., 12:30 p.m., 4:30 p.m.
Except during Packers games. No windsled.

But I knew the Packers were not playing that afternoon, so the windsled's late start had to be due to "island time."

Doug turned to the man standing next to him. "Where's the driver?"

"Arnie? Oh, he headed into town about half an hour ago. I'd guess he'll be back sometime soon."

"What did you say his name was?" Doug asked.

"Arnie. Arnie Nelson. He and his brother Ronnie are the ones who drive the windsled. Been doing it for years. As long as there've been windsleds, the Nelson family's had their hands on 'em. That sled over there, Arnie and Ronnie built it themselves. And they're out here every day checking the thickness of the ice before they take people across. They take the kids to school on the windsled too. We couldn't get along without them on the island, that's for sure."

Doug and I looked at each other, but we didn't say anything. Arnie and Ronnie again. What *didn't* those two do? Nelsons seemed to be in charge of almost everything on the island.

We knew that another Nelson, Charles, better known on the island as Chuckie, had written a book called *On Thin Ice*. In it he traced the evolution of the windsled. Beginning in 1939, at least nineteen different versions of the windsled have been built on Madeline Island in order to solve the winter transportation problem. A series of ingenious island inventors produced vehicles that could transport passengers and packages over a partially frozen lake. The builders of each new version of the windsled learned from the successes and failures of their forerunners. It seemed as though islanders had been conducting an on-going scientific experiment to determine how best to transport human beings across unsafe ice.

Ten minutes later a burly bear of a man in a snowmobile suit and fur trapper's cap with ear flaps came striding onto the ice and turned the key on the dashboard of the windsled. Arnie started to lift the boxes filled with groceries and deposit them in the middle of the sled.

Doug walked over and gestured toward our boxes, "These are some construction supplies we're bringing over to the house. Will they fit?"

"Holy shit! What have you got there? Looks like everything but the kitchen sink!"

Doug pointed to the largest box, "Actually, that one *is* the kitchen sink."

Arnie started loading the boxes, leaving the one containing our sink till last. "I think I'd better make a separate trip back for this one, or else I'll have to leave some passengers behind."

The time had come. The other people started climbing over the side of the boat and finding spots for themselves on the benches. It was almost my turn. Oddly enough, what flashed through my mind at that moment was the framed print of a 1905 pen and ink drawing that hangs on the wall of Doug's office. In the center of the picture, standing at the edge of an abyss, is a woman. Wearing an elaborate hat and a long, flowing dress, she looks quite delicate and refined. But it would be a mistake to write her off as a dainty Victorian lady. There is an air of determination about her, a look that says, "You best get out of my way or I might run you over." She stands in a purposeful pose—one hand on her hip, the other raising her skirt slightly to show her front foot, which is planted squarely at the edge of the precipice. She isn't looking into the chasm below, but at the plateau on the other side. There, on the opposite bank, a man beckons to her as he stands astride a huge sack emblazoned with a large dollar sign. The woman seems intent on doing whatever it takes to reach the other side of the chasm and the fortune that awaits her. In small letters at the bottom of the drawing is the title: "Look Before You Leap."

Though not exactly at the edge of an abyss, like the woman in the drawing, I was poised on the threshold of a decision. I looked out at the partially frozen lake and then at the homemade contraption in front of me. The questions came flooding back.

Could I trust this big burly man to get us across the ice unscathed? What would happen if this Rube Goldberg machine hit a patch of thin ice or, worse yet, open water? How would I stay afloat when my water-logged down jacket was pulling me under? Would all fifteen of us and our belongings be swallowed up in the icy waters of Lake Superior?

Did I really want to leap?

I hesitated briefly, then stuck out my chin and stepped confidently over the side of the boat near the propeller and found a seat on one of the wooden benches. I sat as close as I could to the front. On the benches were several pairs of large black ear protectors. I guessed they were there to help muffle the sound of the engine once we were under way. I didn't want to use them. If I was going to ride in this thing, I wanted the full experience.

Arnie climbed in, put the engine in gear, and with a jolt we were off! The whine of the engine was deafening, but the teenager sitting across from me with his Walkman seemed oblivious. I was starting to regret my decision about the ear protectors.

I noticed that some people had brought their own seat cushions and I began to understand why. Every time we went over a ridge in the ice—and there were lots of them—it produced a bone-crushing effect.

I didn't need to worry about opening the windows in this vehicle. There were none. My cheeks stung as pellets of snow thrown up by the windsled were blown across my face. It was hard to make out our surroundings. Everything was white. Everything except the occasional evergreen tree, part of the line of discarded Christmas trees marking the path of the windsled.

I turned my attention back to the inside of the vehicle. The dashboard (was it from a car?) had a few dials. One must have been a fuel gauge, but what were the others? In the middle of the dashboard was a small cardboard circle. I looked closer and could make out handwritten letters: NSEW, apparently Arnie's version of a compass and a sample of his humor. The canvas top didn't do much to shield us from the sharp bite of the wind, but I didn't care. The ride was exhilarating!

Suddenly it was over, much too soon, and we were standing on the ice next to Madeline Island, at the approach.

* * * * *

The windsled in which Doug and I traveled is, like all the others before it, a combination of miscellaneous parts put together through island ingenuity. It is twenty-two feet long, seven feet wide, and can carry fifteen passengers. Like their predecessors, Arnie and Ronnie, inventors of this model of the windsled, improved on the previous version, which happened to be the creation of their father, Harry Nelson. The two brothers came up with the idea of adding Teflon to the bottom of the hull so that it would slide across the ice more easily. They also substituted a high performance automobile engine for the previous engine, which had been salvaged from an airplane.

Operating the windsled and maintaining the ice road give Arnie and Ronnie almost celebrity status on the island. However, their job is not all glory. It also involves starting a sometimes temperamental engine and performing mechanical repairs without gloves in below zero weather. At times they even have to free the windsled from the ice after it freezes to the surface overnight. The windsled not only provides transportation, but also serves as an emergency vehicle. Arnie and Ronnie are called on to dislodge cars stuck in the snow on the ice road or to search for missing snowmobilers.

A year after our first trip in the windsled, the town board applied for and received a grant from the federal government to build two new windsleds, as well as a floating van and a terminal building. For the first time, islanders did not design and build the windsleds; a manufacturing company did.

We overheard a conversation about the new windsleds one night at Bell Street.

"Did you see the new sleds? The bigger one, it's called the Ice Angel, it's huge."

"So I heard. And it's got a closed cabin and heat, for Pete's sakes!"

"Not only that. It's got a foghorn. And a searchlight. And even a god-damn GPS system."

"Yep. Just about everything but in-flight movies."

"But do you think the new machines are any good? What do those big companies know about what we need up here?"

"Yeah. Those first nineteen windsleds, the ones islanders built, there was nothing wrong with them. They were plenty good enough for us, all right."

Ronnie and Arnie's windsled has not been retired; it's still in use as a back-up for the new sleds. And the Nelson brothers are still the operators of the windsled service; they drive whichever vehicle best suits the conditions.

Ironically, in 2002 when the new windsleds were delivered, the weather was so warm that the ferry boats ran almost all year with only one week off. There was not much opportunity that winter to test the new sleds.

Doug and I are still waiting for a chance to ride in the new windsleds. Though I have heard that the Ice Angel is quieter and more comfortable than the Nelson-built windsled in which we had our first ride, I think I will miss some of the close-to-the-ice excitement of that first trip.

STRANDED

Only ten minutes before we had disembarked from the windsled, still giddy with the excitement of our first trip across the ice. Arnie had hoisted our things out of the sled, and we dragged them to a spot adjacent to the road leading into La Pointe. Now we stood at the bottom of a steep hill surrounded by a small mound of our belongings—two suitcases and several boxes of construction materials, everything except the large carton containing our kitchen sink.

"I'll be back in a little while with your sink," Arnie shouted over his shoulder as he revved up the windsled engine. "I'll drop it off at Gene's office."

We watched as the other passengers hiked up the hill to the parking lot where they had left their cars. This was the Madeline equivalent of a Park and Ride lot for the locals on their daily commute to the mainland.

But we were carless. Doug looked over at me. "Now what?"

I shrugged. "I don't know."

Gene had offered to let us use one of his trucks, but we hadn't thought to find out where to pick it up. One of the other windsled passengers would surely have given us a lift, but we didn't realize in time that we needed help. Now we were in a bit of a fix. It was nightfall. All the other passengers had left, and there we were, standing by ourselves at the edge of frozen, windswept Lake Superior. I was worried.

"Why don't you wait here with our stuff and I'll hike up to Bell Street and see if I can find Gene," Doug offered.

"Ok. But hurry!" I said, stamping my feet and clapping my hands vigorously, as I tried to ward off the chill that had begun in my toes and was rapidly spreading throughout my whole body. The sun had set ten minutes ago, and I could barely make out the contours of the house at the top of the hill. A stiff wind had come up and was blowing off the lake directly towards me. I didn't know the temperature, but it felt like twenty below zero. Bell Street was at least a mile away.

Doug was half-way up the hill when, hallelujah!, I saw the lights of an approaching car. A pickup rounded the corner and started down the incline. The truck slowed and then stopped next to Doug.

The driver stuck his head out the window. I strained to hear what he said. "Are you the Spauldings?"

"Yeah," Doug nodded vigorously. This was one time I was glad that islanders we had never met seemed to know who we were.

"Hop in. Gene sent me to pick you up."

Doug and the driver, a young man with long hair whom I didn't recognize, stowed our things in the back while I climbed into the warmth of the front seat of an aging brown pickup.

"Do you work for Gene?" I asked.

"Not really," he replied. "I was just handy when he needed someone."

We dropped him off at Bell Street, collected the key for the cabin we had rented for the weekend, and drove out of town. Suddenly, without warning, the truck went into a spin, and we did a 180 in the middle of Big Bay Road. Somehow we avoided ending up in the ditch.

"What the heck just happened?" I yelped.

"I don't know." Doug's hands still gripped the steering wheel tightly. "But they sure don't believe in sanding the roads up here. And I just figured out this truck doesn't have four-wheel-drive."

Still a bit dazed, we managed to find the cabin we had rented and proceeded to unload our things. Then we climbed into the truck again to drive back to town for dinner.

"I wonder if they have a fish fry at Bell Street tonight," I said. I leaned back in the seat and closed my eyes. I could already taste Chef Chris's special seasoning and homemade tartar sauce. "It seems more like six days instead of six hours since we last ate."

Doug didn't answer. I opened my eyes. He was just sitting there in the driver's seat, making no move to start the car.

"Uh, Pat. I think we've got a problem. I don't have the key to the truck."

"You *what*? What is it with you and keys? I can't believe it!"

But I could. Early in our marriage I had learned the tell-tale series of gestures. Using both hands Doug would pat down his shirt pockets, then his pants pockets, then his shirt pockets again, hoping that somehow on the first pass he had overlooked the keys stashed there. Then I'd know. He's lost his keys—again! Oh, the things I was saying in my head! But after thirty plus years of marriage I knew what would happen if I uttered them out loud. An argument would only add to our problems.

"Let's start looking," I said through clenched teeth.

We went back into the cabin and searched everywhere. No luck.

Growing hungrier by the minute, we went outside again and combed through every square inch of the truck. Still no key.

Finally there was nowhere else to look but in the snow banks surrounding the truck. That seemed like a futile exercise, but we did it anyway. To make matters worse, the cabin's outside light had burned out. The full moon reflecting off the shimmering snow gave us enough light to search. It was a beautiful night, but we barely noticed.

We were beginning to realize our predicament. The cabin was eight miles from town. The thermometer beside the door of the cabin said twelve below zero. We had no food and no phone. I was getting more nervous. I felt vulnerable. Back at home in the city there would be neighbors close by who could help. But out here on the island, away from town, most of the houses were not inhabited in the winter.

After searching for forty-five minutes, we were ready to give up. "I'm going to check the back of the truck one more time," Doug said. He crawled into the bed of the truck and felt around in the dark.

Suddenly his head popped up. "Bingo! I've got it!" In the moonlight I could see he was grinning from ear to ear.

The dusky warmth inside Bell Street Tavern enveloped us. A fire blazed in the big stone hearth, and a fiddler stood in the middle of the room playing folk songs while the crowd clapped to the music. We paused in the doorway. Gene spotted us and came over. "What took you so long? I was beginning to get worried."

When we told him what happened, he started to laugh. "Here on the island everybody just leaves the keys in their vehicles. That's probably the only time the key has *ever* been out of the ignition in the life of that truck."

That night I gained a new understanding of the risks involved in living on this sparsely populated island in winter. But I also came away with an appreciation for the trust and good will between islanders. When life is reduced to the basics—heat, food, shelter—people need each other and the bonds between them are strengthened.

STILL MORE CONSTRUCTION

Back when I first met him, Gene's hands were one of the first things I noticed about him. It was evident from looking at them that Gene used his hands as tools. Dirt was embedded in the callused palms and under his nails. Though the fingers varied, there were always several on each hand wrapped in cloth bandages. One time he extended his dwarfed right index finger and showed me the two-inch scar marking the area where he had sliced off part of it with a saw. Over the months of construction I watched him use the heels of his hands to thwack a stubborn piece of wood into place, and I saw him gently and expertly guide a jigsaw through a thin piece of wood to make an intricate cut.

One Saturday when Doug and I got to our house we discovered a sparrow had been trapped inside overnight. Over and over again the frightened bird flew toward the large front windows, banged his head against the glass, and sat stunned on one of the log beams. We tried to guide him out the door with a broom, but he only became more agitated. Just then Gene arrived. He lifted a ladder up to the beam where the sparrow was perched and gently closed his hand around the frightened bird as though he were picking up a fragile egg. In one fluid movement he carried the bird to the front door, opened his hand, and released it into the air.

* * * * *

Sometime during April 1998 it became apparent that Gene wouldn't meet his deadline for completion. It wasn't that the workers slowed their pace, it simply became more obvious to us, novices that we were, that there was still a great deal left to do, far more than could possibly be finished by the end of the spring. If I'd been smart I would have seen the signs much sooner. Gene hadn't mentioned such things as ordering kitchen cabinets, bathroom fixtures, and tile. Without those materials on hand, how could he complete our house by the end of May?

That spring some of the rosy glow of our relationship gradually wore off, and we began to see some of Gene's imperfections. The honeymoon stage was definitely over. At times when I called him from home, he wasn't as eager to help as he had been at first. His terse responses to my questions suggested that he was either preoccupied with something else or anxious to get back to work. However, the next time we talked, he would be the old Gene again, chatty and informative, talking about our project and giving me the latest news from the island.

And then, beginning that spring, something else began to happen: Occasionally Gene would disappear. I called from home and left a message that we wanted to schedule a time to meet on our next visit to the island. No answer. I left another message suggesting a specific time. Still no answer. We decided to go anyway and take our chances on meeting with Gene.

On Friday when we arrived on the island, we looked for him. He was nowhere to be found. We checked out his other work sites. No Gene. We tried Bell Street at 1:00 p.m., his usual lunchtime. No Gene there either.

"Do you know if Gene is on the island today?" I asked the patrons eating lunch at Bell Street.

"Oh, I saw him an hour or so ago," someone answered.

"Yeah, I did too," someone else chimed in.

Stonewalled.

All our other options exhausted, on Friday night at 5:30 we went to the bar at Bell Street where the locals usually gathered. Still no luck. On a small island, how could one man disappear without a trace?

He never let us down completely. Before the weekend was over, he would always show up. When he reappeared he didn't explain his absence or the unanswered phone calls. Instead he was charming and chatty and full of information about our house.

"I know you were wondering about the sheetrock for the bathrooms. It was delivered last week." Some of his wavy blonde hair had escaped from under his green Packers hat, and he tucked it back. "I have it in my truck, and first thing Monday morning the workers will get started on the walls in the main floor bath." He smiled with a boyish grin that said he had learned long ago how and when to charm people. And he was so direct and sounded so sincere that it was hard not to believe him when he said, "Your house is my number one priority."

ISLANDERS

Waving her arm and hailing us down with some urgency as she approached was a sturdy, middle-aged woman wearing an old flannel shirt and faded jeans. Doug and I had been walking down our driveway on a September afternoon, when our future house was nothing but a hole in the ground. We were in sight of North Shore Road when the woman spotted us.

"Have you seen my snow goose?" she asked, barely looking at us as she scanned the woods on either side of our driveway.

"Your what?" asked Doug.

"My snow goose. It got out of the fence and walked over this way. It's large," she held her hands about two feet off the ground, "white with black-tipped wings and a pink bill. It barks—almost sounds like a dog. I thought you might have seen it." She paused for a moment, her eyes still searching the woods behind us. Then she pulled a pen out of her pocket, walked over to a nearby birch, tore off a small piece of bark, and started writing on it. "My name's Gleason, Mildred Gleason. I live just down the road. Our place is called the Eyrie. If you see my goose, would you give me a call?" She handed Doug the piece of bark. "Here's my number."

Doug smiled and nodded. "We'll keep a look out for it and phone you if we see it."

Before we could say anything else, she had turned and was striding back in the direction from which she had come. We both stood with our mouths open in absolute amazement for several minutes. Then simultaneously we burst out laughing.

"What did you make of that? I guess she's a neighbor of ours," I said, still laughing so hard that I could barely talk. "And did you realize we said we'd give her a call? We don't even have a house, much less a phone."

"Well, if we do see her goose, I guess we can walk up the road to her house. What was the name of her place?"

"The Eyrie. I think it means bird's nest. Or something like that."

We headed back up our driveway toward the house site. We had just rounded the first bend when Doug pointed into the woods, "Pat, look over there! I think I see Mildred's snow goose!"

"Oh my gosh! It looks like a big white goose, all right!"

"Well, we'd better go see Mildred."

We had no problem finding the white wooden sign with the name Eyrie hand-painted in robin's egg blue letters. We'd only walked about halfway up the driveway when we were stopped by an eight-foot-high wire fence. It was part of a huge pen that surrounded the house and took up most of the yard. Inside this enclosure were perhaps fifty ducks and geese. And right in the center was Mildred. The birds in the pen were waddling towards her as fast as ducks can waddle as she scattered their food on the ground. Noticing us almost immediately, Mildred extricated herself from the throngs surrounding her. She hurried over to the fence.

She looked eagerly at Doug and me. "Do you have good news about my snow goose?"

"We sure do," Doug said. "Not five minutes after you left we saw your goose. And it was headed in this direction."

As Doug talked, a large smile spread across Mildred's face. "Good." She bobbed her head up and down in approval. "I expect she'll show up pretty soon." Then, abruptly, she turned and walked away and went back to feeding her flocks. Just as abruptly, she turned back towards us and said, almost as an after-thought, "Thanks."

Years later, the Eyrie was sold and the new owners hired Gene to tear down the old house and build another one in its place. One night we ran into him at the bar at Bell Street. "How's the new house coming?" Doug asked.

"Oh, it's coming right along," Gene said. "But the excavation wasn't much fun. We ran into all these buried plastic bags full of dead ducks. Must have been about 200 of 'em all told."

"What?!" Doug's jaw dropped.

"Yep. There were multiple burial sites on the property. It stunk so bad that some of my guys threatened to stop working. You know," he paused here for emphasis, "ducks don't decompose when they're wrapped in plastic."

Several years after our encounter with Mildred, a friend told me about a PBS program about the "duck lady" on Madeline Island. I'm not sure, but it sounds likely that the duck lady was our neighbor.

Mildred was but the first of many local people I met who helped endear me to the island. But more than that, Mildred's quirkiness made me think about what kind of people choose to live on an island. How does island living shape people?

I began to think about the fact that islands are circumscribed landforms. The boundaries of an island are clearly defined, and the inhabitants' lives are enclosed within these bounds. There is a sense of limitation, of restriction. This is particularly true of islands such as Madeline that have no bridges or causeways attaching them to the mainland, islands which are reachable only by boat or airplane.

Life can be difficult for those who live on Madeline year-round. During most of the year there is only a limited supply of groceries and other consumer goods available on the island. And, until several years ago, medical help was difficult to access. In the summer a doctor came from the mainland to see patients in a small office a few afternoons a week. During the other nine months of the year medical attention could only be obtained by crossing the waters or ice of Lake Superior.

The winter season on Madeline increases the sense of limitation, the feeling of enclosure that always exists on an island. Madeline becomes more clearly delimited in the winter during the ice road and windsled seasons when the mainland is even less reliably reachable.

In fact, there have been times when the island was temporarily cut off completely from the mainland due to the weather. In April 1928, Madeline was inaccessible for an extended period. There were reports that the supply of fresh food was dwindling, and several residents were severely ill. One of those suffering from illness was Edna Nelson, our contractor Gene Nelson's paternal grandmother. Newspaper articles from that period spell out the difficulties in graphic detail. The April 18th edition of the *Ashland Daily Press* called the situation "the worst in Island history" and said:

> With a number of cases of illness from influenza and gripe, which has swept nearly the entire populace of the island, and meat and flour supplies about exhausted, with no doctor, no mail for a week and no heavy supplies for three weeks, residents of

Madeline Island are helpless prisoners of the ice which is too soft to risk crossing to Bayfield and too solid for any boat.

On April 19, the *Ashland Daily Press* reported: "One woman, Mrs. Nels Nelson, is in critical condition as she requires an immediate operation for gallstones." There were numerous attempts to transport Edna Nelson over the ice to the mainland where she could get the medical help she needed. Finally, on April 23 a tugboat was able to batter its way through a mile of ice and successfully transfer her to Bayfield. When she arrived at the hospital in Ashland she was so weak from the trip across the ice that it was several days before the doctor could perform the necessary surgery.

In typical fashion, islanders tried to downplay the difficulties of this period of isolation, suggesting that mainlanders had exaggerated the problems experienced on the island. Remarks in the Ashland paper indicate they were affronted that anyone would doubt their ability to deal with adversity. Rev. Karl H. Meyers, the minister of St. John's Church on Madeline Island, was quoted in the *Ashland Daily Press* on April 21, 1928:

> Having had the plight of Madeline Island boldly portrayed in large headlines in all the leading papers of the country and various radio stations, I feel it is my duty to clarify this bit of exaggeration.
>
> Each year the stores on Madeline Island import enough foodstuffs to last all the inhabitants for months. They expect a period of at least two weeks of isolation each year and here it's only been one week and the country becomes alarmed because of the exaggeration of the newspaper. There are enough cows and hogs, chickens, etc. to last the Island people for years. The crops produced on Madeline alone would more than take care of all physical need as far as food is concerned.

I imagine him puffing out his chest as he wrote this and thinking: Puh-lease. Give me a break. You mainlanders must be wimps if you think a little isolation is going to do us in. We islanders are tough as nails.

Whatever the truth was back in 1928, life has continued to be difficult in winter even in more recent years. It takes resilient people to endure the winter season. In the diary of Otto Schroedel, then the minister of St. John's United Church of Christ on Madeline Island, is this entry for January 15, 1956:

> Walked across the two miles to Bayfield Saturday (no cars safe on the ice yet) facing a ten below wind with drifting snow all

the way and since then have been nursing two frost bitten thighs even though I had on heavy wool trousers. . . .

Even today life can feel very restricted on Madeline Island when the only way to reach the mainland is via the windsled, a snowmobile or one's (frostbitten) legs. An islander shared this piece of wisdom with us, "If the doctor tells you that you only have two weeks to live, you can hope it will be during windsled season because those will be the longest two weeks of your life."

* * * * *

As I thought about the fact that the geography of an island establishes limits, I wondered about the people who live on an island. Do circumscribed landforms lead to circumscribed lives?

It is true that islanders' lives are literally enclosed within the geographical boundaries of the landform on which they live. But my experience with the full-time residents of Madeline Island leads me to say that their lives are anything but restricted. Perhaps the limited supply of material goods and the consequent lack of materialistic pressures actually free island people to pursue other aspects of life. Madeline has a history of attracting artists and artisans of many types. Among the island's current full-time residents are writers, artists, weavers, musicians, and woodworkers. Madeline is home to a wide variety of organizations that support the arts, the island's history, and its ecology; there is the Madeline Island School of the Arts, the Art Guild, the Weavers' Guild, the Literary Society, the Film Society, Positivity Children's Theater, Madeline Island Music Camp, Madeline Island Historical Museum, Madeline Island Historical Preservation Association, and Madeline Island Wilderness Preserve.

An island breeds a different sort of people. Maybe it is because of its geographical separateness that an island heightens certain characteristics in its inhabitants. People are forced to be self-reliant, independent. Some of the best examples of this independent spirit are found in the extended family of our contractor. Through conversations with Gene we learned that the Nelsons are a large, well-established clan with a history that goes back four generations on the island. According to one estimate, they make up twenty percent of the year-round population on Madeline.

The history of the Nelsons on Madeline Island began with Nels Nelson who immigrated to America from Skona, Sweden, in 1905. He lived for several years near his older brother, Martin, who had settled in Sweden, Wisconsin, a town that has since disappeared but was located between Grandview and Drummond. Then he heard about work with R. J. Russell's logging operation on Madeline. He got the job and after a few years married the boss's daughter, Edna. Nels became a farmer, at one time owning two farms, and he and Edna raised oats, wheat, and barley and nine children—eight sons and a daughter. According to family members, the children knew they were loved; they also knew what was expected of them: Get to work on time, do the best possible job, and always show proper respect.

Once I learned about their fathers and grandfathers, I could see that the current generation of Nelsons was cut from the same cloth as their forebears. Though I am sure there may be some members of the family who are shy and retiring, many of the Nelsons we met or heard about are unforgettable, larger-than-life characters.

* * * * *

It was early evening. Doug and I had spent the February afternoon at our unheated, partially completed house. We were cold and hungry and ready for dinner. When we walked into Bell Street we noticed the old man at the bar. We had seen him here many times before and wondered who he was. He looked to be in his eighties, considerably older than most of the other patrons. Wearing old work boots and a rumpled plaid flannel shirt, he was sitting on the same stool as always. As always, he seemed to be savoring both the beer in front of him as well as the conversation around him.

We sat down at one of the tables and were just ordering dinner when Gene came in and joined us. "Who's that man over there, the one in the brown plaid shirt?" I asked.

"That's Cigar," Gene answered.

"Cigar?"

"That's 'cause he comes in at the same time every day for a beer and a cigar. He's my uncle."

Another Nelson.

Cigar, or Nels Roy, was one of Nels and Edna's eight sons. He was a legendary commercial fisherman. Even into his 80s, he was always out on the water or the ice; summer or winter, there were fish to catch. He regularly supplied fresh lake trout and whitefish for the diners at Bell Street. He also operated a sawmill several days a week, the only active mill remaining on Madeline Island. He was known as Dock-a-Day and had a reputation as one of the best dock builders in the region. The Smithsonian Institution invited him to Washington, D. C., during the nation's bicentennial festivities. He was asked to demonstrate his skills by building a log dock on the reflecting pool between the Lincoln Memorial and the Washington Monument.

I am bemused by the thought of this crusty old islander traveling to Washington, D.C., to put his talents on display for all to see. I am guessing he took it all in stride, much the way he handled the rigors of island life.

*****

Another of Nels and Edna's eight children who I heard about but never met was Arnie and Ronnie's father, Harry. He was an entrepreneur par excellence. He owned the only gas station and grocery store on the island. When more markets came along, he converted his grocery to a restaurant. He bought and flew a private plane that he used for business and pleasure. He was a herring fisherman. He purchased a single ferry and soon owned a flourishing fleet of ferries. In order to keep his summer customers, he constructed a windsled and provided transportation across the lake in winter. He owned a construction business that built roads and docks, delivered stone and gravel, and provided shoreline protection. Harry felt the island needed a small boat marina; he went to work with a dredge and a pile driver and, voilá, a marina was born. As I learned about all of Harry's accomplishments, I couldn't help but be impressed by this man who was obviously a visionary and who not only knew how to dream, but also how to turn those dreams into reality.

During the six years Harry served as town chairman, he helped establish zoning on the island as well as funding for a new municipal sewer system and airport improvement. It is clear that Harry cared deeply for Madeline Island, and I admire the fact that he found so many ways to improve life for those who resided there. Harry and his friend, Dave Strozac, started the Apostle Islands Cruise Service that is still in operation today. He opened a flying school, and three of his sons enrolled in the initial class. He became the first licensed real estate broker on the island. In 1979, when he was only fifty-three years old, his life ended tragically. Harry and four other members of the board of directors of the Washburn State Bank were killed in a plane crash shortly after taking off from the Cable airport.

Harry had six children, two daughters and four sons, many of whom inherited both his work ethic and his adventurous spirit. Arnie and Ronnie work in road and dock construction most of the year. And, as we knew first-hand by that time, during the winter the lives of islanders and visitors are in their hands as the two brothers operate the windsled and maintain the ice road.

Their brother, Wayne, has been called the "Red Baron of Madeline Island." On one occasion Wayne helped Arnie rescue an errant snowmobiler who was stranded on the ice after his sled sank to the bottom of Lake Superior. While Arnie drove the windsled, he was in radio contact with Wayne who was flying overhead in his ultra light aircraft, directing Arnie through the ice floes.

* * * * *

Gene's dad, Charles Arnold, was the youngest of Nels and Edna's children. Big Arnie, as he was known on the island, worked as a ferryboat captain for twenty-five years and then as a dock and stairway builder with his brother, Cigar, and later with his son, Greg.

Big Arnie married Joan Hagen, who also grew up on the island, the daughter of a commercial fisherman. Joan and Big Arnie attended Bay View grade school together on the island, became high school sweethearts, and married a few years after graduation. Joan worked for over twenty-five years as a waitress at The Pub restaurant on the island. When she was just twelve years old she began playing the pump organ at St. John's United Church of Christ and continued to be the church's organist for over fifty years. Joan and Big Arnie had five children, four sons and a daughter. Gene is their middle child.

* * * * *

The Nelsons are not the only islanders who are tenacious and multi-talented. That became apparent during a conversation I had one morning with Pastor Ann Larson, the minister at St. John's Church on Madeline. I was talking about an islander, a non-Nelson.

"What does he do for a living?" I asked.

"Everything," she responded.

At first I was confused by her reply. Then I understood. Out of necessity, islanders become multi-talented. During tourist season jobs are easy to come by, but in order to make a living year-round, islanders have to develop a variety of wage-earning skills. And, just as I observed early on with Gene, islanders learn multiple skills in order to avoid long trips to the mainland. They teach themselves how to repair or make the things they need rather than travel across the water or the ice to get someone else to do it for them. They are proud to be self-sufficient.

Madeline Islanders learn to live by their wits, especially when dealing with nature. And predictably, sometimes nature outwits them. In reporting on an airplane crash that took the lives of two island residents, the *Ashland Daily Press* on August 15, 1949, stated,

> Tragedy is not new to the island. In the history of many Island families is the story of death during the treacherous periods of ice-formation and ice-break-up. For "Gram" Johnson . . . it was the third time that deep personal tragedy had visited her. Her husband, Captain Russell, father of her sons, had been drowned years ago in an ice accident, and her youngest son Tommy had likewise been drowned. Now her son Jimmy was gone in an airplane crash.
>
> The residents of the Island are often close to death because of their seasonal period of isolation, and are stoical about it. In the sudden and most unbelievable tragedy that snuffed out the life of Jimmy Russell and Vincent O'Brien Jr., the Islanders retained their traditional stern calm.

Through Madeline's history and my encounters with residents, I was beginning to learn what sort of folks choose to live the island life. Hearty, creative, resilient, resourceful people.

There is another adjective that applies to a certain segment of the island population: eccentric. That eccentricity is embodied in a strange structure that stands one block off the main street of La Pointe. I noticed it during one of our weekend visits to the island when I drove into town to pick up some milk. Since it was late fall and the place was deserted, I decided it was a perfect time to poke around without interruption.

The unusual building consisted of an enormous wooden deck attached to a tiny, run-down house that seemed almost an after-thought. The deck was mainly uncovered and open to the elements, though it appeared that some attempt had been made to shelter it. Several tattered pieces of an old blue and white striped canvas tent were stretched between upright posts, but they barely provided protection for half the area of the deck. Beside the steps leading to the deck was a hand-painted sign: "Tom's Burned Down Café, Summer hours: Open 2 p.m. till whenever. Live music on weekends."

I remembered reading about this place. I dug in my jacket pocket and found the brochure listing entertainment "hot spots" on the island. It described Tom's as "The Carnegie Hall of junkyards" and a "tree fort for adults." My curiosity was piqued.

Surrounding the front steps was a jumble of objects that seemed to have ended up there for no apparent reason. An old Maytag wringer washing machine, like the one my mother had in the 1940s, sat next to an assortment of rusted wheels, a wheelbarrow full of flattened plastic drinking cups, and the four-foot prow of a skiff that had somehow become separated from the rest of the boat. Close by were a dozen sculptures made from rusted components. Another hand-made sign indicated that these were the products of an annual workshop, "Artists Wrestle Steel," in which the participants created sculptures using "Tom's amazing collection of junk."

The deck itself contained a painted plywood bar, a small curtained area that served as a rudimentary stage, and two wood-burning stoves placed side by side. Seating for the patrons consisted of a collection of old boxes and chairs as well as at least a dozen beat-up brown vinyl bus seats. The décor, if you could call it that, also included old license plates nailed to the floor and a huge assortment of hand-lettered signs tacked up in every conceivable location on and around the deck.

Some of the signs were inspirational:

"A mind that expands to encompass an idea never returns to its original size." O. Wendell Berry

"There are only two ways to live your life: One is as though nothing is a miracle. The other is as though everything is a miracle." Albert Einstein

"Leap. The net will appear."

Others were provocative:

"What are the long-term effects of instant gratification?"

"Minds are like parachutes. They only function when open."

Still others seemed to be describing the place and/or its owner:

"Don't rebuild it and they will come."

"We cheat the other guy and pass the savings on to you."

"Asylum, La Pointe"

"I used to have a handle on life but it broke."

And some simply defied classification:

"Don't make me come down there." God

Now I was even more curious. The next time I saw Gene, I peppered him with questions. "Who is this Tom? What's the story behind his place?"

"Well for starters, he's my cousin, Tom Nelson. He's Ronnie and Arnie's brother."

Another member of *that* family!

Gene told me the history of Tom's Burned Down Café and how it links two of Madeline Island's most beloved eccentrics. The first was Leona Erickson who moved to the island in 1949 shortly after her husband died. In order to support her four children, she opened Leona's Bar. Two years later she married a native islander, Emil Erickson. Her bar became the central gathering place for islanders and visitors alike. Leona was a gregarious woman with an infectious laugh that came from deep down inside her generous frame. She loved parties and hosted a variety of annual island events including a hat party, Halloween party, and a picnic held on the first weekend in August. Attended by hundreds of people, these gatherings always included music, dancing, and games. She had a fondness for animals, and her pet goats, monkeys, deer and rabbits would often wander into the bar and make themselves at home.

Leona's favorite time of year was hunting season. Year after year in November "her hunters" arrived and they became family to her. They called her "Mops," and she put on a huge Thanksgiving spread for them. The next day they all came back for the "feathers," as she called the leftovers.

Leona died in 1987. Three years later another eccentric islander, Tom Nelson, reincarnated her bar. According to Tom, he bought the building, sold the land to "someone rich," took what he could from the old structure —"windows, bar, chairs, left-over customers" and hauled it downtown where he "put a porch around it all and opened for business."

Unfortunately it was destroyed by fire on June 19, 1992, having "sustained third degree burns over 98% of its assets." It quite literally rose from the ashes to become Tom's Burned Down Café.

After many visits to the island, I came to know Tom Nelson by sight. He was hard to miss. Gray hair pulled back into a long pony-tail, wearing a crazy grin and a boisterous Hawaiian shirt no matter what the season, he looked like a burned out flower child, left over from the 60s. He could often be found at the bar at his place, inveighing against the most recent example of government injustice. The town board of La Pointe sued him to clean up the yard around his bar and complained about the noise level emanating from his open-air establishment. His response to such intrusions on his personal freedom is probably best summarized by one of the signs posted at his bar: "Obey only good laws."

My first face-to-face encounter with Tom took place one summer night at the Burned Down Café. I was standing between Doug and our friend Paul who was visiting for the weekend. One minute I was watching Tom Nelson boogying barefoot on the dance floor with some young thing, and the next minute he was hitting on me. He sauntered over and stood in front of me, then reached out, grabbed my hand, and said, "Are these two men bothering you?"

"I think I can handle them," I responded, withdrawing my hand. Unfazed by my rejection, he moved on in search of his next conquest. I was reminded of yet another of the hand-lettered signs posted near the stairs at Tom's: "On Madeline Island you can leave your keys in the car, but don't leave your wife in the bar."

Leona Erickson and Tom Nelson are not the only unique characters to have called Madeline Island home. Adrian "Ed" Valley who lived on the island in the early 1900s surely qualifies as another example of an eccentric. He built one of the first ferryboats and named it *Nichevo* which he said was Russian for "Wot th' hell." When he was diagnosed with terminal cancer and got tired of living, he hung himself over a boat-shaped coffin specially constructed for him by an island carpenter. Ed was buried according to his instructions with a gallon of moonshine and two packages of tobacco "to be enjoyed upon his arrival in hell."

Even the island's dump has a unique personality. Posted on the gate of the solid waste recycling center is this hand-painted sign: "No entry except during open hours. No garbage left on property if closed. $50 fine and bad karma."

Perhaps it is because its inhabitants have to be independent that Madeline Island has produced its share of eccentric characters. Steve Cotherman, director of the Madeline Island Historical Museum, commented on this phenomenon in his speech at the Fourth of July celebration in 2003, when he said of the island that there are "weirdos, complainers, iconoclasts, libertarians, and curmudgeons all over the place, and nobody seems to really mind.

In fact, the acceptance, tolerance, and even appreciation of all this eccentricity and diversity is one of the island's most endearing qualities."

He was not the first to notice these traits of Madeline Islanders. In 1962, Rev. Otto Schroedel, pastor of St. John's Church, remarked, "You come to the island and become eccentric, or you come to the island because you are eccentric."

I wonder if all islands have eccentric inhabitants simply because they are cut off from the mainland and therefore are separated from the mainstream. Islands are small towns with no exit. And, like small towns, islands turn inward. They must produce their own entertainment, their own drama from within. Maybe that is why they give rise to unique individuals who distinguish themselves by being different.

Doug and I overheard a conversation between a couple of eccentrics one night at Bell Street. The place was full when we came in for dinner, so we decided to wait at the bar until a table opened up. We found two stools together and ordered drinks. Doug started telling me about the pair of deer he startled on his hike through the woods earlier in the day, but I was distracted by a conversation taking place just down the bar. "Listen," I said in a low voice as I tilted my head slightly to the left to indicate to Doug why I had stopped talking.

A man and a woman, both in their 30s, were deep in discussion. Judging by their demeanor and the volume of their debate, they had been at the bar for a while. Their faces were familiar, definitely year-round islanders, though I didn't know their names. It was the topic of their conversation that caught my attention.

"Baths are over-rated," the woman said, then paused to slug down some beer.

"Yeah, showers too," the man replied.

I looked at Doug and raised my eyebrows. Doug looked down, suddenly seeming very intent on swirling the wine in his glass, trying to cover up the fact that he was eavesdropping on the conversation nearby.

"I don't get it. Why do some people think you have to take a bath every day?" the woman continued, spreading her arms and using her hands to accentuate her last few words.

The man's shoulders raised in an exaggerated shrug. "Beats me. Personally, I think it's a waste of good water."

I looked at Doug. He was smirking.

The woman nodded emphatically. "Yeah, when I get home after work, I'm too tired. I just want to sit down and have a couple of beers."

"Lots of nights I fall into bed in my work clothes." The man paused to finish off his beer. "Saves time. That way the next morning I can just get up and go to work."

"One time I went for two weeks without a bath," she offered.

I started to laugh and tried desperately to convert it to a cough. It came out as more of a snort.

"That's nothing!" the man said. "Last winter I didn't take a shower for two whole months, and nobody knew the difference!"

I couldn't look at Doug or I knew I'd lose it completely. Fortunately, just then the two unwashed-and-proud-of-it patrons pushed back their stools and lurched into the backroom at Bell Street to hang out at the pool table.

I dissolved in laughter. Between guffaws, I leaned over to Doug and said in a low voice, "What was that? Some kind of island one-up-manship? Or a strange kind of foreplay?"

* * * * *

I've come to the conclusion that it is ok to be different if you live on Madeline Island. In fact it is more than ok; it is a badge of honor. As one visitor remarked, "Everyone who lives on Madeline is a little bit off kilter, about one standard deviation off the mean."

I think Madeline would be a dull place without its eccentric characters. They add vitality and spunk to island life. I take secret delight in watching newcomers discover some of Madeline's weirdness for themselves. I love to see first-time visitors standing in front of Tom's, laughing at the signs and sculptures and enjoying its eccentricity.

I thoroughly enjoy the quirkiness of islanders. This might seem strange coming from someone who has spent her whole life trying to blend in. Actually it is probably *because* I have worked hard not to stand out in a crowd that I admire, maybe even envy, the way islanders flaunt their eccentricities. Perhaps if I spend enough time on the island, I'll loosen up a bit. Who knows, someday islanders might be describing me when they say, "Can you believe what *she* just did?"

INDIAN CEMETERY

Though I was learning about the character of present day islanders, I knew little about the first people to settle on Madeline. What had attracted them to the island, I wondered. I discovered the answer to my question as I walked along a road near Madeline's marina.

I had been focusing on a large sailboat as it quietly and majestically pulled into its berth, when the tiny cemetery across the street caught my attention. I had never noticed it before, never even knew it existed. It was filled with straggly weeds and looked disheveled and unkempt, as though the inhabitants had been deposited in their graves and forgotten. I leaned as far across the wire fence surrounding the cemetery as I dared, trying to read the time-worn letters on the headstones. As I strained to make out the names and dates engraved on the crumbling ivory markers, I noticed something peculiar about the grave sites. Next to many of the headstones stood miniature wood frame houses. Why were these quaint little dwellings located here? What were they doing in this burial ground of the Ojibway, the old La Pointe Indian Cemetery?

The Ojibway, or the Chippewa as they are called today, were the first people who chose to settle on Madeline Island. It was all because of a shell. They came to the island because of the Megis, a giant white shell that they believed provided warmth and light to the tribe. According to legend, the Ojibway left their homeland on the Gulf of St. Lawrence after the Megis disappeared from the Gulf and reappeared in the St. Lawrence River. The tribe thought this was an omen; the Megis must be followed. It led them father and farther westward until it reached Chequamegon Bay in Lake Superior, and there the Megis came to rest. During their journey the Ojibway were attacked by the Fox and Sioux Indian tribes. To ensure their safety in this new area, they settled on Madeline Island which they named Moningwunakauning, home of the golden-breasted woodpecker.

It is believed that the Ojibway arrived on Madeline sometime around 1490, but it is difficult to know for certain since the only record of their history was passed from one generation to the next through oral storytelling.

As I walked farther along the cemetery fence that kept visitors at a safe distance from the headstones, I noticed a historical marker. It explained why the Ojibway graves came to be located in a Catholic cemetery. An Austrian priest was responsible.

In 1830 Protestants established a mission and a small school for the Ojibway on Madeline Island. Not to be outdone, the Catholics sent Father Frederic Baraga to La Pointe in 1835. He arrived with only three dollars in his pocket. The lack of funds did not deter this dynamic priest, however. Within twelve days he had baptized fifty Ojibway, and they had built a church for him.

The following year he established the cemetery, and it developed an interesting mixture of cultural traditions. Ojibway custom dictated that small structures should be placed atop the graves of the deceased to protect the dead from the elements. The Indians stocked the miniature houses with food to sustain the deceased on their four day journey to the hereafter. The Christianized Ojibway in Father Baraga's mission kept this tradition but adopted the white man's style of dwelling. They built tiny houses, some complete with Victorian gingerbread trim, to protect their dead.

When it was created, the graveyard was nestled between the Catholic church the Ojibway had built and the entrance to a small lagoon. It became known as the Indian Cemetery because it was reserved mainly for Father Baraga's converts. The original log church has long since been demolished and the lagoon enlarged. Today the unlikely neighbor of the cemetery is the Madeline Island Yacht Club. When they enter the channel of the marina aboard sailboats or powerboats on their way to the boat slips, most vacationers probably have no idea that they are motoring past a cemetery, much less the resting place of a well-known figure in Madeline's history.

Buried in the old graveyard is Michel Cadotte, the man directly connected with the naming of Madeline Island. I used to wonder how the island got its name. I noticed that in the twenty-first century many Madelines live on the island. Several times when I went to island gatherings and heard someone call out "Madeline," I watched females of various ages turn to see who was asking for them. There are year-round residents, summer people, and one-time visitors who bear the name of the island. Perhaps not only their name but also they themselves were conceived on the island.

Then I learned of the first Madeline. She began her life as Equaysayway or Traveling Woman. Her father was Chief White Crane of the Ojibway nation, and her home was on the mainland near present-day Bayfield. She met and fell in love with Michel Cadotte, a fur-trader who opened a trading post on the island in 1793. When she and Michel were married, Equaysayway was baptized and given the name of Madeleine. After their marriage they lived in La Pointe, and Chief White Crane decreed that from then on the island should be called by her new name. Later on, others such as Henry Schoolcraft attempted to change the island's name, but Equaysayway's Christian name prevailed.

Michel died at the age of seventy–two. He had grown rich in the fur trade, but he shared his wealth with indigent natives and died a relatively poor man. He was buried in the Indian Cemetery where visitors who dare to lean across fences can still read his epitaph:

Sacred to the Memory of Michel Cadotte
Who Departed this Life
July 8, 1837
Aged 72 Years
11 Months
16 Days.

* * * * *

As I lean across the wire fence of the tiny cemetery and gaze at the Ojibway graves, I think about the fact that Doug and I are but the latest in a long line of people who came to explore Madeline Island, fell in love with it, and decided to stay. I am both humbled and intrigued to discover how many others came before us to this island. As I stand in front of our house and survey our property, I wonder how many other feet have trod this land. Were they in search of furs or timber, fish or farmland?

I think of this land as ours. But it is likely that someone else—Ojibway or French or Scandinavian—settled here long before we arrived and claimed it. Knowing that others preceded us, that others loved this land before us, makes it all the more precious to me.

EVEN MORE CONSTRUCTION

Over the summer of 1998 we grew more and more disgruntled with the pace of construction. Things were moving much more slowly than at first. We were still driving to the island every other weekend, but often when we arrived at the house it seemed that not much had been accomplished since our last visit. When he wasn't finished by Memorial Day, Gene had said he thought he could finish "in the fall." As July turned into August and the end of August approached, it began to look less and less likely that he would be able to make that deadline.

We were extremely pleased with the quality of construction. As the house took shape we could see the care that the workers were taking with the details of our home. It would be a splendid house someday, but it did not look as if that someday would come anytime soon.

When we returned to Minneapolis after our weekend trips to Madeline, our city lives took over and our frustrations at the slow pace of construction were soon buried under the countless voicemails and pieces of paper that accompanied our work and home lives. Back home, my friend Bonnie said to me, "What's the latest on your house debacle?"

I was taken aback by her choice of words. Debacle? Had I complained that much about the construction problems?

"It's really not *that* bad," was all I could muster in response.

We had been so naive at the outset of this process. We had assumed that if you built a house it would turn out just the way you wanted. We had a lot to learn. A friend who had been through the process commented, "It's like childbirth—painful at the time, but when it's over you're usually so happy with the result that you don't remember the suffering." I was certainly ready for the delivery of a baby house so I could get on with forgetting the pain.

* * * * *

"Have you ordered your kitchen cabinets yet? And what about the plumbing fixtures?"

Usually when we met, Doug and I had questions for Gene, but this time Gene peppered us with questions. There was a tone of urgency to his voice. It was September of 1998, and by this time it was clear Gene would not be able to finish our house in the fall.

We were heartened by his questions. Maybe our discussions with him about the sluggish speed of construction had done some good. Maybe he was going to pick up the pace. Maybe the house was back on track.

"I don't want to stop working because we're waiting for materials to be delivered. And winter is right around the corner. It would be good to have everything we need at the house before the lake freezes over." We had been through one winter of construction already so we were aware of the problems that came with the ice road.

"If you wait till the ferries stop running, you're at the mercy of Mother Nature. If she decides to send a blizzard or a sudden thaw, we won't be able to use the ice road. And if a nor'easter comes through, it'll blow the ice road to smithereens."

I was only too happy to respond to Gene's requests, and I got busy selecting and ordering materials. Within months most of the plumbing fixtures we needed were stored in the basement waiting for installation. The kitchen cabinets were delivered in November 1998, and we rented a U-Haul and brought up the stove and refrigerator right after Christmas that year. For months they sat in boxes in the middle of the main room. The only time they were moved was when one of the workers pushed them to a different part of the room in order to have more space to work.

*****

Often when I was at work, someone would ask me about the progress of construction on our Madeline home. At those moments it didn't take long for my feelings of frustration to resurface, and I launched into a tale of our most recent difficulty. One Tuesday, at our monthly business meeting, I was sitting beside my co-worker Denise, describing the latest delay.

After patiently listening to my list of complaints and nodding sympathetically at the appropriate times, Denise finally had a chance to talk. Her gray-blue eyes looked directly into mine, "It sounds like this Gene guy just keeps screwing up. Why don't you fire him?"

"We couldn't do that," I said without hesitation.

Denise didn't say anything; she just sat there, looking at me over the top of her reading glasses, waiting. Clearly she expected some explanation for our inability to get rid of the source of our problems.

"We just couldn't fire him. I guess it's an island thing," I heard myself say. My response sounded lame to me and it probably sounded ridiculous to Denise. Why couldn't we fire Gene? I wondered to myself. It really *was* an island thing.

Gene was a third generation islander; he came from one of the largest, most well-established island clans—some might say dynasties. Firing him would have a ripple effect. We would risk offending many members of the influential Nelson family. In addition, other full-time residents would feel we had betrayed Gene by letting him go.

Truthfully, I would never have been able to fire Gene, and it had nothing to do with his extended family. I liked him too much to ask him to leave. I liked him enough to forgive his weaknesses—his disappearing acts, his inability meet his own deadlines, the promises he made and broke. And he had a disarming way of owning up to his shortcomings.

When he met with us at the house on Friday mornings, he would look at us directly and with absolute sincerity say, "I know I told you we'd have the sheet rock (or the plumbing or the wiring) finished by now, but an emergency came up on one of my other jobs, and I had to send the crew over there for a few days. Starting next Monday they'll be here working on your house, and we'll be back on track in no time."

I don't know if it was our gullibility or his utterly convincing earnestness or some combination of the two, but somehow, no matter how many delays, no matter how many variations of his apologies we heard, we always believed Gene's promises for the future. In addition, he was a masterful craftsman, and the houses he built attested to that fact. They were strong and true and beautiful; and our house, unfinished as it was, already displayed those qualities. We knew the final product would be worth the wait.

And there was something else. Often during the period of construction, I felt caught between two worlds—the city and the island. My city self had different expectations for a contractor than my island self. My city self wanted a timeline and a contractor who kept a project on track according to that timeline. My island self realized that life on Madeline moved at a slower pace, with time to enjoy life, time to breathe. After all, weren't those the very things that drew me to island living in the first place? How could I be angry with workers who were living the lifestyle I longed for? I was beginning to see that I needed to change my expectations of a tightly run ship with a punctual commander at the helm.

By this time I had also learned that island living meant relationships were more important than schedules or deadlines. I had observed that the last ferry of the day rarely left on time, not wanting to leave an islander or visitor stranded on the mainland. One night the boat waited half an hour for a woman who called to say she was on the way. And when an emergency occurred on the island, volunteer firefighters and EMTs left their jobs as construction workers, store clerks, and restaurant workers to tend to those in need. Even Chef Chris at Bell Street Tavern occasionally left patrons waiting for their dinners if he was needed to drive the fire truck. I had learned to appreciate the fact that when you co-exist on a small island there is mutual benefit in cutting each other some slack. By island standards, then, if Gene failed to meet a deadline, he deserved a reprieve, not removal.

TREE FARMER

When the driveway was complete back in August 1997, Doug initiated a ritual that has become an essential part of every trip to the island; he began to take driveway walks. At first he enjoyed following the circuitous path of the road in order to appreciate its design. He had planned the road so that no matter how hard you tried it was not possible to see the house site from the end of the driveway. Privacy and seclusion were very important to him. He didn't want a house like ours in the city that was thirty feet away from the neighbors. He didn't want a house that could be seen from neighboring houses. Ideally, he didn't even want to know that there *were* any neighbors.

At the time we began the building process, the lots on either side of us were houseless. To the west of our property was the lot that the realtor had mistakenly told us we were buying. We met the Swansons, the owners of the lot to the east of ours, early in the construction process.

* * * * *

Doug and I had taken a walk and were just turning into our driveway when a car pulled up. Inside were a man and a woman who looked to be in their 50s. The man lowered the window and leaned out. "Hi! Is this your driveway?"

We nodded.

"Then we're your neighbors—the Swansons, Dick and Sue."

"Is yours the lot with the terrific sand beach?" I asked, pointing in the general direction of what I thought was his land.

"That's the one. Right now all we've got on it is a sauna. I'm Finnish and we Finns have our priorities—first a boat, then a sauna, and sometime later maybe a house. Hop in. We'll show you our lot."

We drove down a steep winding driveway to their sauna. It was perched at the edge of a broad, grassy open space bordered by a gently curving sand beach.

Pointing to a spot near the sauna, Dick said, "Eventually this is where we'll put our house so we have easy access to our boat and the beach."

Back at our driveway as we waved goodbye to the Swansons, Doug broke into a big grin. "Whew! Did you hear what they said? They're going to build down by the water." I immediately understood the reason for his elation. Since our house site was high on a bank, sixty feet above the water, we would never be able to see their home. Doug breathed a sigh of relief. It was only the west side of our lot that would need to be shielded from future neighbors.

* * * * *

His quest for privacy led Doug to take a sudden interest in the trees on our property. Our forest consisted mainly of birch, maple, and a few oaks, aspens, and coniferous trees. If we wanted our house to be screened from the neighbors to the west all twelve months of the year, Doug decided there was only one solution: We needed more coniferous trees.

In an effort to win me over to his point of view, Doug convinced me to walk over to the probable house site on the lot to the west so that we could see what our house looked like from the neighboring lot. We took this hike during the winter when our house was under construction. By this time our house had been framed, the outside plywood sheathing was in place, and the openings for the windows had been cut. As we stood on the property next door and looked back at our house, the first thing I noticed was the triple window in what was to become our master bathroom. When I designed our house I included as many windows as possible in all the rooms. The bathroom was no exception. I had planned a row of three large windows in the second floor bathroom, which would provide a sweeping panorama of the lake and the woods around our house. I hated the thought that those views would have to be blocked by shades. Planting coniferous trees suddenly sounded like a sensational idea.

But where could we buy seedlings at a reasonable price? The answer arrived in our mailbox in February. We were on the mailing list of a nursery in Hayward. On the back cover of the nursery brochure in bold, black letters was a special deal: 100 twelve-inch seedlings—50 blue spruce, 50 balsam.

On Memorial Day weekend of 1998, the original target date for completion of our house, we stayed in a motel on the island and spent the weekend hiking, biking, and planting trees. Bob joined us, but Steve was busy studying for college finals.

Early one afternoon we hauled six large boxes full of seedlings from Hayward out of our car and prepared to start the planting process. Bob and I opened packets of a special gel designed to promote root growth, emptied them into a bucket, added water, and stirred. This miraculous potion was supposed to give our little seedlings a firm foundation and then zap them into a growth spurt. The directions said that the water and gel would form a slurry. I didn't really know what a slurry was, but our mixture looked like a pail full of colorless Jello. We inserted the roots of the seedlings into this gelatinous goo. Meanwhile Doug was in charge of digging holes for the little trees on the west side of the house and along the driveway. This was not an easy task due to the hard, red clay soil and the dense mat of roots often just below the surface.

At first, planting trees was fun. Bob and I carefully removed each small seedling from the bucket of root gel, placed it into its hole, added some peat moss and fertilizer, filled the hole with soil, and carefully patted it into place. But as the afternoon wore on, we were discovered by mosquitoes.

Swat.

Swat.

Swat. Swat. Swat. Clouds of mosquitoes. Hordes of mosquitoes.

"Mom, did you bring any Off?" Bob said as he scratched his back with dirt-encrusted fingers.

"Arrgh."

The one thing I had forgotten was mosquito repellant. And the only store on the island that might have stocked some had long since closed for the day.

Bob jumped up. "Mom, I can't take this any more!"

"Me either!" I said, barely glancing in his direction as I picked up the pace of my planting. "But we've got to finish; we aren't coming back for another couple of weeks."

Bob returned to his trees. Several minutes passed as we planted in silence. Then I let out a screech. "What's crawling on the back of my neck?"

Bob came over to look. "You don't want to know."

It wasn't just mosquitoes; the wood ticks had found us too.

We were tired. We were dirty. We were full of mosquito bites, and we imagined there were ticks crawling all over us. And we were hungry. It was getting close to sunset and we had not eaten anything since noon.

We started stuffing the trees into holes as fast as we could. Unlike their pampered siblings, these trees were like the youngest children of a large brood. They would have to figure out how to survive on their own. They were jammed into place without benefit of peat moss or fertilizer.

It was nearly dark when we climbed into the car and drove back to town. The young man behind the bar at Bell Street Tavern did not seem taken aback as three filthy, disheveled people climbed onto the bar stools in front of him.

"Are you still serving dinner?' Doug asked, brushing dirt off the front of his shirt in an effort to look more presentable.

"I'm afraid not, but I could heat up some Jack's pizza for you," the bartender replied with a smile. He looked like he was in his early twenties, about the same age as Bob, though his shiny, shaved head made it hard to tell for sure.

As we scarfed down pizza and beer, we explained that we had been planting trees on our lot and that the time had gotten away from us.

"Where's your land?" he asked.

"Up on North Shore Road," Doug replied. He took several swigs of beer and then added, "Gene Nelson is building our house."

"Are you the Spauldings?"

Surprised once again to have lost our anonymity, the three of us nodded in unison.

He smiled broadly. "As a matter of fact, I helped pour your foundation last fall."

I must have looked shocked because he quickly added, "Gene rounded up a bunch of us to help. That happens all the time up here. I know Gene because he built my parents' house a couple of years ago." He reached out his hand, "I'm Ron Schulz."

Grasping his hand, I asked, "Is your mom Elaine?"

This time it was Ron's turn to look surprised. He nodded.

"I can't believe it! I've talked to her three or four times on the phone. Your parents were on the reference list Gene gave us before we hired him."

The day ended quite pleasantly as the four of us chattered on about the island and Gene and house building.

But this was only the beginning of Doug's career as a tree farmer.

* * * * *

On our next trip to the island we hauled 800 feet of hose in the back of our car—enough to stretch the full length of our driveway—so Doug could water all the newly planted trees. And he continued his tradition of driveway walks. But now the main purpose was to inspect his "crops." He continues these walks even today, sometimes to fertilize the trees, sometimes with weedwhacker in hand to clear the tall grass around the base of the trees so that they receive more sun.

Tree planting has become an annual event. Every year, usually on Memorial Day weekend, we add to our growing forest. Bob no longer joins us in this endeavor. In his words, "Once was more than enough!" We learned the hard way that 100 trees were too many. Our orders have gradually declined from seventy-five to fifty to twenty-five trees. With smaller numbers, we now can afford larger trees. To date we have probably planted at least 300 trees. Some are even growing on the neighbor's property to the west to form as dense a barrier as possible.

Recently Doug's tree farm has expanded to include several hardwoods planted in the area surrounding the house. After one of these trees died due to deer damage over the winter, Doug constructed six-foot high fortresses of chicken wire around the trunk of each tree.

In the next phase of his horticultural career, Doug began naming the trees he planted. He called the Royal Red maple with the dark auburn leaves "Red." "Hey, look at Red. He's three inches taller than when we planted him last fall."

One spring when he planted two Crimson Blaze maple trees, he decided to name them after Bob and his wife, Becky. In September he came into the house after one of his inspection tours and said, "Becky doesn't look too good. I think she'll have to be reincarnated next spring."

I frowned. "Maybe you shouldn't name them till you know they are going to survive."

Gene also augmented our stock of trees. While he was constructing our house he purchased a piece of equipment to plant full-grown trees and went into the Instant Shade business. When our house was complete he planted three thirty-foot trees—two of them on the west side of the house and one near the front walk.

"How'd you like the trees?" he asked the next time we saw him. "One is a re-po tree."

"A what?"

"A re-po tree. I had an agreement with the woman who lived across the road from Bell Street Tavern. I'd plant some large trees on her property if she'd cut the tall grass on the lot. She didn't hold up her end of the bargain so I dug up the tree. It's yours now."

Doug and I were so stunned that we were speechless. I felt uneasy about having someone else's tree growing on our property. But how could we know our contractor would give us a second-hand spruce? The next time we drove into town, I looked to see if there was a sizeable hole on the lot across from Bell Street Tavern. But there was none. Maybe the spruce's previous owner had already planted a replacement.

Every once in a while we look out the window to make sure the tree hasn't been re-poed by its original owner.

* * * *

I was kneeling in the damp spring dirt, the knees of my jeans coated with Madeline mud as I patted the soil around the base of a two-foot blue spruce. Doug was a few feet away excavating a home for the next seedling. Once again it was Memorial Day weekend, and we were planting trees. I sat back on my heels for a moment and stared off into space. "You know," I said quietly, as much to myself as to Doug, "in all likelihood, we won't be here to see these trees when they're full grown."

Doug stopped digging and leaned on his shovel. "That's true. But it makes me feel good to know that these trees will still be growing after we're gone, that we're adding to the forest on our land."

It felt right to me too. I realized that our tree planting had a different purpose now than when we began. What had started as a quest for privacy had gradually evolved into something quite different. Placing trees into the earth every May and tending our growing forest had become evidence of our desire to look after the land we owned.

It was another indication that we were beginning to embrace island values. Our city selves had wanted trees to ensure the privacy that was in short supply at home in Minneapolis. Our island selves wanted to honor the land that had been entrusted to us. Our annual tree planting weekends were a sign that we were learning to be responsible land owners.

But ownership is temporary. We are merely caretakers of this piece of property. Our role as stewards of the land is like that of a museum curator

—it is our job to preserve and protect the land, to maintain and improve its condition until it is passed on to its next owner.

Someday Doug and I will be gone, and after that our children and then our grandchildren. But the land will still be here. And the lake. And the red clay cliffs. And the eagles, bear, and deer. And the scent of the earth and water rubbing shoulders.

It will all pass into the hands of others. May they be good stewards.

WHEN WILL CONSTRUCTION END?

One Friday in mid-November 1998 we drove down the driveway without our usual eagerness. We were concerned. Over the last month construction had once again slowed almost to a standstill. We had talked with Gene, and he acknowledged that things had been sluggish but reassured us that the crew would "get right on it and work hard till they're finished."

As we approached the house site we were surprised to see that there were no workers' trucks anywhere. When we opened the door to the house we were greeted with utter silence.

"Do you think the guys are on a break?" I asked Doug.

"I don't think so. It's three in the afternoon, and they usually quit around 4:00 so they can catch the 4:30 ferry."

"Well, where *are* they then?"

"Maybe they ran out of materials. We'll have to talk to Gene about that."

"Speaking of Gene, I thought he was planning to meet us here right about now."

"You know Gene; he's always at least a half an hour late."

Half an hour passed. Then an hour. We were getting colder and colder. And crabbier and crabbier. We didn't know what to think.

"I believe we've been stood up," I said.

"It sure looks like it."

"I have just one thing to say. Isn't it special?" I was being sarcastic but I couldn't stop myself. We had repeated those words with delight so often over the last fifteen months. But at the moment they seemed to make a mockery of our current situation. Right then I fervently wished we *had* bought a house.

Though we looked for him, we didn't see Gene all weekend. We were angry!

On the drive back to Minneapolis, we talked for almost the entire four hours about what to do.

"This is the last straw!" Doug pounded his fist on the steering wheel.

"Hey! Watch what you're doing or we'll have another problem to deal with," I sputtered. "Let's think about all our options."

The conversation I'd had with my co-worker Denise just two months before was going through my head. Once again I felt caught between two worlds. My city self agreed completely with Doug. But my island self knew I should take into account Madeline's slower pace and cut Gene some slack. However, my Minneapolis self was on the verge of overpowering my island sensibilities.

By the time we drove into our driveway in Golden Valley we had decided to write Gene a letter. If that failed to produce results, we'd have to think about other options. We mailed the letter the next morning.

> Dear Gene,
>
> We were disappointed and frustrated to visit our house this past weekend and find that nothing had changed since we were there three weeks ago. We had planned to meet with you to discuss the progress on the house, but you never showed up.
>
> First you promised that our house would be completed by the end of spring, then the Fourth of July, then in time for our family vacation in August, and, most recently, by the third week in September. Those dates have come and gone. We've worked hard to be patient, realizing that you had other projects in addition to ours. But we have run out of patience.
>
> We have been very happy with the quality of your work. You have built a beautiful house. There is just one thing wrong with it. IT ISN'T FINISHED! We'd like to end the building process as satisfied customers, and we'd like to continue to highly recommend you to others. In order to do that: 1. We would like our house to be your top priority until it is finished. 2. We would like a firm completion date in writing and your absolute commitment to meet that date.
>
> Please contact us with your response.

We received no response to our letter. In fact, Gene never mentioned it at all. There wasn't a dramatic change, but in the next few weeks the pace of construction picked up, and by our next visit a lot had been accomplished. We breathed a sigh of relief.

* * * * *

There was another delay, but this one was not Gene's fault. We had ordered granite tile for our kitchen countertop from a store in Duluth. Early in February we arranged to pick it up on our way to the island. When we got there our salesman was not in the store, and no one could find the tile he had promised would be waiting for us. We were told they would look into what had happened to the order and we should call the salesman the next day.

The following afternoon we were at the house with Gene. He offered to make the phone call. We only heard one side of the conversation, but that was enough.

"Hey, Ned. What size shirt do you wear?"

Gene paused. Apparently Ned asked why he wanted to know.

"We were wondering how big to make the noose."

Ned personally delivered the tile to the building site within the week.

A SMILE SOUTH OF WASHBURN

The ancient mariner caught our attention. Standing twenty feet from the edge of Highway 13 just outside of Washburn, Wisconsin, he was a striking figure. Over six feet tall, with a long mustache and flowing beard, he stood with one arm outstretched, holding an illuminated lantern. Doug slowed down so we could get a better look at him. It was then that we began to notice the other carved wooden figures that crowded around the mariner. The property contained several low-slung buildings, but mainly it was filled with fanciful wooden creatures. Intrigued, we decided to stop.

The lot extended farther back from the highway than we had guessed from the car, and it was carpeted with a dense layer of sawdust. The scent of freshly cut wood filled the air; a chainsaw lay on the ground. Near the saw stood a four-foot tall chunk of wood that was being transformed into a gnome. His pointed hat had already emerged from the log, and he had an impish grin on his partially carved face.

There were bears of different sizes; all were standing on their hind feet. One stretched its arms upward, obligingly holding a circular table over its head. These were not the life-like replicas of actual animals that are the usual products of woodcarvers. These bears were mischievous, and each displayed its own unique personality. Next to the bears stood a forest of totem poles, some as much as thirty-five feet tall. In addition there were trolls, fish, turtles, mushrooms, and signs carved with the names of homeowners as well as commercial establishments.

"Howdy! Where are you folks from?"

Startled, we turned to discover that the deep voice originated from a short, sawdust-covered man who resembled one of his own elfin creations. With his long, white beard and rotund figure, he looked like an abbreviated Santa Claus. He introduced himself as Bill Vinneaux and offered to show us around his place.

As we followed him along the narrow path bordered with his creations, he pointed out the sign he had carved with the name and address of his place. It read: "The Wayward Wind Studio, Located a smile south of Washburn, Wisconsin."

He led us farther away from the highway toward the back of his property, showing us the little village he had created for other artists. The miniature houses looked like they were straight out of a fairy tale. Each cottage displayed the creations of a different artisan. One house contained wood spirits, the name the artist had chosen for the intricately detailed faces that she carved into pieces of bark. A sign on the wall described her work. It said that as she carved, faces would appear in the wood, each with their own unique personality. I found one of the spirits irresistible, and we decided to buy it even though our house was not yet finished. It now inhabits the screened porch of our home on the island.

In the center of the little village were a dozen massive, eight-foot tall tree trunks standing upright in a circle like a wooden Stonehenge. A fire blazed in a fire pit in the middle of the circle, adding to the mystery of the place and providing welcome warmth on a drizzly, gray day.

Bill's philosophy of life and work were carved into various signs scattered around the place. "I do it for the pure enjoyment of it all," read one sign. And near the circle of tree trunks, or Woodhenge, as he called it, a sign announced reassuringly, "Around here there are only friendly spirits."

"This is where I work in the winter," Bill told us as he opened the door of one of the small sheds toward the front of his property. Like the ground outside, the floor of the shed was cushioned with a thick layer of sawdust. But the creations indoors were far different than the rough, chain-saw items outside. Inside were several fine, hand-carved pieces of furniture. In the corner sat a grandfather clock decorated with a tiny mouse perched on the scrollwork at the top of the piece. A large mirror with an intricately carved frame was adorned with a bear peeking over the top and into the mirror as though looking at his reflection. Below the mirror sat a dresser with a curved front and a series of small drawers, each one carefully fashioned by hand. The most charming pieces were part of a collection. There was a bed frame, a dresser, a table and a set of four chairs; all were embellished with ornately carved sunflowers. Bill pointed to a book on the table that had provided his inspiration for this collection. It was a handsomely illustrated edition of *Goldilocks and the Three Bears* and was open to a picture of Goldilocks waking up in a large wooden bed covered with carved sunflowers.

"Are you interested in anything in particular?" Bill inquired as he brushed a clump of sawdust out of his beard.

Doug smiled. "We really stopped in just to see your place."

Bill's eyes twinkled. "Well, I'll carve just about anything you want unless it's ugly. I won't carve ugly things."

Laughing, Doug offered, "We do need a wood mantle for the house we're building on the island." He glanced at me for a sign of approval.

I nodded. Now that construction was underway again, I agreed that it was a good time to shop for mantles. I turned to Bill. "I've seen a photo of a mantle carved with an attractive north woods scene. Could you do something like that?"

"Come on over here. I have a book with photos of some of the things I've made. There are quite a few pictures of mantles in there. Maybe something will catch your eye."

We paged through the book. We saw a number of appealing mantles. We were hooked.

We began in earnest to discuss some possible designs. Instead of a generic outdoor scene, Bill suggested that we think of family stories or experiences that could be depicted in a scene on the mantle. We liked that idea, but realized we needed some time to think.

Bill led us to the back of his property and showed us several huge pieces of a forty-five-year-old red cedar tree that he thought would be suitable for a mantle.

I could see that Doug was getting excited. "Actually we're going to need two mantles because our fireplace is double-sided," he explained.

Bill looked thoughtful. He smoothed his rough hopsack tunic over his round belly. "If you cut this cedar into fourths, one piece of it could be your second mantle. See this part with all the whorls and knots and indentations. If I smooth the surface and stain it a rich reddish brown, it would make a magnificent mantle."

As it turned out we purchased two mantles from Bill. Both are magnificent. One is the massive piece of cedar with all its natural markings. The other is a carved mantle. After much family discussion, we unanimously decided to have Bill depict our first picnic at the Raspberry Island lighthouse. In the center of the mantle is the lighthouse, nearby, our small Smokercraft boat, and on the horizon, the setting sun. There is also an eagle carrying a fish in its mouth, a reminder of the bird Gene pointed out to us the day we all stood in the back of his pickup as we tried to imagine the view from the deck of our house.

I'm glad Bill suggested we choose a mantle design with family significance. Visitors often want to know about the scene carved on its surface. Doug is always eager to tell guests the story of our first trip to Raspberry Island.

On my birthday in 1999, Doug surprised me with a gift that could not be wrapped. He led me blindfolded to the entry porch of our house. There, next to the front door, stood the ancient mariner. And there he still stands, his raised lantern welcoming family and friends to our home.

MOVING DAY

"I'd like to schedule the moving van sometime in May. Does that sound do-able?" I asked.

"Sure," Gene answered. He was measuring the floor of the bathroom in order to decide where to place the first piece of ceramic tile.

I didn't trust his answer. He was concentrating more on the job in front of him than on my question.

"No, really. I don't want to schedule a date that isn't realistic."

Gene looked up. "I'm sure I can get everything finished by the middle of May."

Why didn't I believe him? Could it have anything to do with the many other completion dates he had given us during the two years of construction—promises that may have been well intentioned but were not kept?

"Ok, I'll call and see if I can reserve May 20. That'll give you a few extra days."

"We'll be finished; no problem."

It was March of 1999, and the end of construction was in sight. The kitchen cabinets which had been sitting in boxes in the middle of the main room for over six months were finally installed. Gene had epoxied the dark green granite tiles to the kitchen counters and finished the tile backsplash above them. The exterior logs had been stained "Spanish Moss," and those on the interior were coated with clear urethane to preserve their mellow honey color. Doug and I had spent several chilly weekends applying "Misty Mica" paint to the interior sheetrock walls. It was only about forty-five degrees in the house at the time, but by closing the door to the room we were working on and setting up several space heaters, we were able to get the temperature up to about sixty degrees so that the paint would adhere.

There were still some major projects left to complete, however. The ceramic tile had to be installed on the floors of both the first and second floor bathrooms, the plumbing fixtures in the bathrooms and the kitchen had to be connected, and a number of light fixtures had to be mounted on the walls and ceilings.

Once these projects were out of the way, the house would be finished. Doug and I were looking forward to occupying a completed house during the coming summer rather than merely visiting a half-finished structure filled with workmen.

* * * * *

On May 19 we arrived at the house to sleep overnight so that we could be there early the next morning when the movers arrived. We were so excited by the time we boarded the ferry at Bayfield that our level of exhilaration had inflated to the size of a giant, helium-filled balloon. But when we walked through the front door, the balloon burst with an almost audible bang. The first thing we saw was a bare electric cord dangling over the spot where our dining room table would sit the next morning. The light fixture was still packed in its cardboard box in the corner. Other unpleasant surprises followed.

As I glanced into the main floor bathroom, I stopped short. "The toilet isn't hooked up in here. It's sitting in the middle of the floor."

"I'll check out the other bathroom," Doug said.

He ran up the stairs to the second floor.

"Guess what! The toilet's installed up here, but the faucets for the sinks are still in the boxes." A minute later, "The shower works though."

"Great!" I shouted from below. "We've got a total of one working bathroom. It just happens to be separated by a flight of stairs."

We also discovered that we had closets, but no closet rods or shelves. We had window screens, but they were piled in a corner of the basement. We counted our blessings, however, when we discovered that everything in the kitchen was installed and in working order.

The next morning, exactly as promised, the moving van rumbled up the long driveway, and two husky, young men began carrying the furniture into the house. Through the front door came a green leather couch and two plaid easy chairs for the main room. Next came the dining table and chairs and the beds for all three bedrooms. We hardly remembered what some of the pieces looked like since we had ordered them almost a year before, when Gene was promising that the house would be completed in the fall of '98.

When the movers were finished, it was our turn. Up the stairs came all the things we had been storing in the basement in anticipation of this day. There were the treasures we had purchased at antique stores over the last two years: the oak carpenter's chest that was as finely crafted inside as out with its many compartments for tools, the brass ship lantern that would hang from a hook below our mantle, the walnut dresser with two handkerchief drawers for one of the main floor bedrooms, and the oak Frost Kist ice chest that Doug was proud to have discovered in an antique store in Cannon Falls. In addition, we unpacked some of the family treasures we had saved from our parents' houses. Glass cake pans and brightly colored ceramic mixing bowls that had belonged to Doug's mother found a new home in our kitchen cupboards. The blue enamel coffee pot that my mother always used to make egg coffee for large family gatherings had a place of honor above one of our kitchen cupboards. On the fireplace mantle we placed the one-hundred-year-old wrench that was used by Doug's great uncle, a mechanic on the Chicago and Eastern Indiana railroad. A small pewter candy dish that used to hold my father's favorite Chocolate Nips found its way to one of the end tables beside the couch in the main room.

I stood back and looked around. Despite the fact that things were not finished, it felt great to have everything else in place.

"Oops! I almost forgot something important," I said as I made a beeline for the basement. I came back upstairs carrying a small box.

"What on earth is in there?" Doug asked.

"You'll see," I replied as I walked over to the window above the kitchen sink. I opened the box and took out a small piece of sandstone.

Doug moved closer to get a better look. "What's so special about that rock?" Doug asked.

I rubbed my finger across it, remembering its oval shape and rough, fine grit surface. I turned it on its side to see layer after layer of different shades of sandstone. I stroked the surface several more times before I gently placed it on the windowsill.

"It's a rock I found on our beach the day we learned that the lot was ours," I told Doug.

"Then I guess it deserves a place of honor in our new house."

Since that day, many new rocks have joined my honored piece of sandstone. Now the windowsill is filled to overflowing with rocks picked up from beaches on Manitou or Raspberry or York or Stockton islands as well as additional rocks from our own beach. But I'm always careful to rearrange the jumble so that my first rock, the one with layers that remind me of our many experiences on Madeline, sits at center stage.

* * * * *

"Let's eat lunch. I'm starving!" I said, tugging open the refrigerator door. The fridge was bare except for several cans of Budweiser and the pre-made sandwiches we picked up the day before at a Super America station in Hayward.

We sat down at the new dining room table for our first meal in our (mostly) completed house. "Here's to Birkenloch!" Doug said as he raised his can of Bud.

"And here's to Gene! He finally finished—almost," I added as I clinked my can against Doug's.

"When we get through with lunch, let's go find him and invite him over for a beer," Doug suggested.

As we pulled up in front of Bell Street Tavern, we spotted Gene's truck parked right in front of the entrance. "It's funny there aren't any other cars around. Where's the lunch-time crowd?" I asked as I climbed out of the car.

When we got to the front door there was a large, hand-lettered sign taped to the glass. "Bell Street Tavern is closed for two weeks. See you again on June 3rd when a brand new Bell Street opens!"

"Why would they close over Memorial Day?" I wondered. That was always a busy weekend at Bell Street since many people came to the island to open their cabins for the season.

"And what's this business about a brand new Bell Street? It's only been open for about two years," Doug said as he pulled on the handle of the front door.

"Let's ask Gene when we find him. He has to be in here somewhere," I said, following Doug through the door.

It didn't take long to discover Gene's whereabouts. There he was, twenty feet in front of us, chainsaw in hand, cutting a large opening in the sheetrock wall that divided the bar from the restaurant. He had his back to us, and with the roar of the chainsaw he didn't immediately realize that we were there.

"Hey! You snuck up on me! How're you doing?" he said as he shut off the chainsaw.

"*What* are *you* doing? is the real question," I said, gesturing toward the newly cut hole in the wall.

"Now that I'm finished with your house, I decided to do some work here." He readjusted his Nelson Builders cap. "I never liked the layout. So I'm cutting a big doorway right here, putting up a wall over there, and installing some more lighting." He surveyed the room and then grinned. "I think it'll look much better once I'm finished."

I tried to smile, but I wanted to throttle him. Finished with our house, my foot! What about the bathrooms, the lighting fixtures, and all the other things that remained undone? I was trying to calm down enough to think of what to say when Doug took over.

"This is a pretty big project. Are you going to have time soon to finish things at our house? Like the bathrooms?"

"Sure. I'll get right on it. I figured you'd be ok for now with one working bath."

"Not really! The problem is that we have to run up and down a flight of stairs to use all the working parts," I said.

"That's true," Gene responded, looking down at his feet, like a kid who just had been scolded. Which he had. He looked up sheepishly, "I really will get over to your place as soon as I can."

Driving back to the house I fumed and fussed about Gene. I was usually the one who stuck up for him when Doug got upset about how long it was taking to finish the house. But this time even I had had it with him. I was unhappy that he hadn't completed what I considered some of the essentials of our house, but what put me over the edge was finding him at Bell Street starting a huge new project with not even a glance backward in our direction. When I finally calmed down, I said, "Well at least he had the decency to look remorseful when we pointed out what was left to be done. Maybe he actually will come out soon and do the work."

Even as I uttered the words, I knew better than to believe them. By this time we realized we couldn't necessarily take Gene at his word. He would probably plan to get over to our place soon, but then he would get caught up in his new project and postpone our house till later.

As it turned out, it was Doug who installed the toilet and the faucets, Doug who put up the shelves and rods in the closets, and Doug who hung the light fixtures. By this time Gene had learned that Doug could handle such projects, a fact that probably made it easier for him to put off the work he had agreed to do on our house. He may even have been hoping that Doug *would* finish those jobs so that he didn't have to. We came to realize that Gene enjoyed starting new projects much more than he liked finishing them.

At the end of moving day we were exhausted and tumbled into bed. I woke once during the night and was totally disoriented. It was pitch black in the room, and I couldn't even make out the contours of the furniture. I stumbled out of bed and walked to the window. There was no moon, but the stars were startlingly bright in the infinite black expanse. How different from our bedroom at home in a first ring suburb of Minneapolis where the stars are barely visible in a sky often colored an unnatural shade of peach by the reflected lights of the city.

The next morning we got ready to leave for the drive back to Minneapolis. As I packed my suitcase, I complained to Doug, "I don't want to go home. It just seems wrong to leave. So anticlimactic. After all these months—no, years—of planning and waiting, when we finally move in, what do we do but pack up and leave. I want to stay here and enjoy it. I don't want to go back to Minneapolis."

Doug looked somewhat surprised by the intensity of my unexpected outburst. "Well, I don't know about you, but I have to get back to work to help pay for this place."

I made a face at him. "You're always so practical! Don't you wish we could stay here a few more days and just enjoy it?"

"Of course. But don't forget we'll be back in less than a week for the Memorial Day weekend. And Bob and Steve will be coming too. It'll be their first chance to see the finished house and stay here."

"Ok, ok, I'll go. But I don't have to be happy about it," I said, feigning a pout. It was wrenching to leave. All those years of tramping through the tall underbrush on our lot, eating picnic lunches at our house site, motoring past the waterfront in our small boat. Followed by months of poring over house plans, touring log home companies, and countless trips to Madeline while the house slowly took shape. And all the while imagining what it would be like to have a completed home, to invite family and friends for the weekend and, most of all, to be able to enjoy island life. Now our dream was finally a reality, and what did we do but pack up and drive away.

* * * * *

Memorial Day weekend didn't turn out quite as we had expected. Bob and Steve were both home from college for the long weekend. As the four of us drove up the driveway, Bob said, "There aren't any spruce seedlings hiding in the back of the car, are there? Because I'm not planting one more tree. Ever."

"No, no. We might have some indoor projects for you to help out with, but no trees. We promise. You've done your tree duty," Doug answered.

The weather was unseasonably warm for Memorial Day weekend. It was hot and humid, and there was no wind to bring cooling breezes off Lake Superior. The mosquitoes were out in full force.

"Let's open some windows," Steve suggested once we'd unpacked the car.

Doug frowned. "We can't. The screens aren't up yet, and the bugs would drive us crazy."

"I'll turn on the ceiling fan. At least that will keep the main room cool," said Bob as he flipped the switch. Nothing happened.

Doug groaned. "Great! One more thing to add to Gene's punch list."

We discovered that the TV didn't work, and neither did the stereo. And with only one bathroom, in two pieces, the stairs were well traveled that weekend.

In spite of the unfortunate new surprises, our first family weekend at Birkenloch was a success. We ate all our meals on the porch, climbed down the ravine to the shore, and took a quick dip in icy Lake Superior. In the evenings, accompanied by the music of the peepers and tree frogs, we played Hearts and Pictionary on the porch by the light of the antique kerosene lantern. Finished or not, we were finally in our house, enjoying time together.

SWEET AIRS

From the time I was a very young child, my father sent me off into the world with two pieces of advice. It was always the same whether I was a three-year-old on my way to the swing set in the back yard, or an eight-year-old going over to a friend's house to play Candyland, or a teenager off to the Sno Daze dance with a date: "Have fun," he said, and "Be careful." Never one without the other. His first dictum was easy to follow; I had no difficulty figuring out how to have a good time. However, his second piece of guidance was problematic. The trouble was I never knew what it was I was supposed to be careful *of*. He never explained. So I did my best to be on guard for anything that might bring harm. Naturally I ended up being something of a worry-wart. I was cautious about anything unknown or un-familiar, definitely *not* a risk taker.

As a child I gave no thought to why my father so often told me to be careful. But I do remember looking through his childhood photo album and asking about the pretty girl whose round face was surrounded by dark ringlets—the pretty girl, eight years older than he, whose arm encircled his waist as he held his teddy bear, his pretty sister, Marion, who died of consumption at age sixteen. It was not until I had children of my own that I fully understood what her death must have meant to his parents. I am sure little Bobby, the precious, only surviving child, was admonished to "be careful" about many things by his grief-filled parents. And, as often happens, so began a chain reaction extending through several generations of parents.

My father experienced that early loss at an age when most children barely understand that death exists. To know the loss of a dear sibling at so young an age must have pierced the protective veil of childhood and made him aware that terrible things can happen in this world. No wonder when he had children of his own, he worried about our safety.

But if the first important man in my life counseled caution, it was perhaps inevitable that when searching for a mate I would, at some unconscious level, seek out a man who would encourage me to take a few of those risks my father warned against. And I found one.

Doug is hardly a wild man, throw-all-caution-to-the-winds type. He is a civil engineer, after all. But, unlike my father, he would bring me to the edge of a risk and, instead of putting a protective arm across the path, he would give me a gentle push. When I stood on cross country skis at the top of a hill I deemed too steep, he would not listen to my whining. He would shoot down the slope ahead of me and then yell from below, "Come on, Pat, you can make it! No sweat!" And then I would find myself at the base of the hill, having enjoyed the trip down. Or if we were driving on a narrow mountain road with no guard rail, and all I could see was our mangled car at the bottom of the valley far below, he would point out the glorious snow-covered peaks up ahead that I was missing.

So when we were looking at sites for a lake cabin, I suppose it was unavoidable that they would all involve some amount of danger—or what I considered danger—which was pretty much anything other than a cabin with a kiddie wading pool out back.

Our final choice came with its own assortment of potential perils. There were the milder sorts of risks such as being late and missing the last ferry of the day or running out of milk in the winter when the grocery store was closed for the season and having to pour orange juice on the breakfast cereal. And then there were the more serious hazards such as driving across a frozen stretch of Lake Superior to get to our house or getting caught in a sudden squall with five-foot waves in an uncovered sixteen-foot boat that probably shouldn't have been out on the big lake in the first place.

One winter while our house was under construction I planned a vacation to Costa Rica. The travel agent who helped us with our bookings called our trip a "soft adventure." I poured over the guide books, trying to decide what to see and where to stay. One of the books described an idyllic spot that I couldn't stop thinking about. It said, "If your vision of the perfect tropical hideaway is a luxurious little open-walled cabin overlooking a secluded beach backed by dense tropical jungle, then Rainbow Adventures may just be your pot of gold." It certainly did sound like a place for an adventure. A little risky perhaps, but, what the heck, that's what made it sound like fun. At the time my father's voice in my head had quieted to a barely audible whisper. When I made reservations for our trip, I included Rainbow Adventures. It would be the final stop of our vacation and we would stay for five days.

During the early part of the trip I found myself thinking a lot about the rustic little open-air cabin described in the guidebook. I thought about it with equal measures of excitement and dread. The closer we got to the end of our trip, the more the dread eclipsed the excitement. By this time my father's voice was screaming in my head: Open walls? What were you thinking? That place sounds downright hazardous!

When we arrived at Rainbow Adventures we found that our cabin overlooking the Gulfo Dulce (Sweet Gulf) sat by itself at the end of a fifty-foot trail near the edge of the jungle. It had four-foot walls and, true to the guidebook description, between the top of the walls and the roof was nothing but open air. No windows, no screens, nothing. Definitely risky. Especially when we were told to wear knee-high rubber boots on any jungle hikes so we would have some measure of protection from the poisonous coral snakes and boa constrictors that lived in the jungle surrounding our cabin.

But, despite the dangers, I was determined to appreciate the natural world surrounding our cabin at Rainbow Adventures. One of the lodge's proprietors encouraged us to listen to the early morning sounds of the jungle each morning when we awoke. He described it as hearing the jungle wake up.

I awoke in the middle of our first night there to hear the initial sounds —the faint notes of nocturnal birds buried deep in the jungle. I smiled. But the smile vanished from my face when I heard the blood-curdling cries of some wild animal.

Doug sat bolt upright. "What was *that*?"

"I don't know," I whispered as I grabbed his arm and squeezed it tightly. I clung to Doug and held my breath as the horrible sounds drew closer and closer. I was sure some huge jungle beast was approaching our cabin and would tear us apart limb by limb. I lay frozen in bed until finally the sounds moved farther and farther away from our cabin.

The next morning at breakfast I tried to act nonchalant as I asked one of the guides what creature was making those horrible sounds. We learned that roving bands of howler monkeys used their terrible shrieks to warn away competing groups of monkeys.

The second night the sounds were still awful but at least I no longer feared for my life. The howler monkeys apparently were the wake-up call for the rest of the forest creatures. When their cries died down, and the first light of dawn began to glow in the sky, all the birds in the jungle seemed to wake simultaneously and call out to each other, creating a chaotic cacophony of exotic bird songs. This jungle symphony repeated itself each morning of our stay, and we became more skilled at distinguishing the individual melodies of the various birds. I began to look forward to lying in bed and listening to this amazing jungle alarm clock.

*****

We moved into our house at Madeline three months after our trip to Costa Rica, when our experiences at Rainbow Adventures were still fresh in our minds. On the island we were surrounded by forest rather than jungle. On warm nights we opened the bedroom windows so that in the morning we could listen to the sounds of the forest waking up. At first I had no idea which birds were singing their lyrical ballads in the early morning hours. But after attending several birding hikes on the island I was able to distinguish the voice of the oven bird from that of the hermit thrush and the chickadee. I learned that a pair of ravens flying overhead were the source of the raspy, raucous exchange that sounded amazingly like an old married couple arguing.

I liked to listen to the night sounds too. There were often noisy choruses of frogs as well as soft rustlings in the grass when the small animals of the forest searched for food. But sometimes I got more than I bargained for. One night the stillness was broken by the piercing shrieks of a terrified animal that had become the prey of some larger beast. The cries were clearly those of a creature in its death throes. I put the pillow over my head to block out the sounds. It didn't work; I could still hear the terrible screeches. Suddenly they stopped. The stillness was deafening. Whatever it was, the animal had been devoured by its predator.

Did an owl swoop down on a field mouse? Or did a fisher snatch up a hapless red squirrel? I didn't know. I didn't really want to know. I had to remind myself that this death was part of the endless cycle of life. Whether I liked it or not, I realized that the nocturnal cries of the hunted are as much a part of nature as the melodic morning birdsongs.

I recalled a conversation I'd with Gene several weeks before. He was sitting on the floor in the hallway, repairing our washing machine. "It was a hard winter for the deer," Gene said, threading together two brass plumbing fittings. I frowned slightly and tilted my head to one side.

As he tightened the fittings into place with a sharp turn of his wrench, he continued, "With all the freeze/thaw cycles, the snow formed a hard crust on top. The deer couldn't run very fast. They just sank into the soft snow beneath the crust. But the coyotes and wolves—"

"There are *wolves* on Madeline?" I blurted out.

"Yep. At least a couple of them. Anyway, the wolves and coyotes could stay on the crusty surface of the snow, and the deer couldn't get away from them." He stood up and reached behind the washing machine using his fingers to thread the new fitting onto the hose.

I was silent for a moment. "Poor deer." I stuck out my lower lip in sympathy.

"Well, that's how it goes in nature. A good year for coyotes, a bad year for deer."

Gene knew the ways of the natural world. Besides being a keen observer of nature, he came from a long line of ancestors who lived close to the earth; and he had not only absorbed a great deal of factual information about nature, but had also become resigned to the laws of the natural world.

I know of only one island where these laws don't apply—Prospero's island in Shakespeare's *The Tempest*. In Act 3, Scene 2, is this description: "The isle is full of noises, sounds and sweet airs, that give delight, and hurt not." But this was a mystical isle ruled by Prospero, a magician. Sweet sounds. No harm. A magical isle indeed. But Madeline is a real island, and real islands are governed by the laws of nature.

I was beginning to understand that the natural world was not only a source of enjoyment, a place to have fun, but also a place to exercise caution, to be careful, as my father advised so long ago. I realized that in order to reap some of nature's rewards I must also be willing to take some risks. And once again I was forced to recognize the two faces of nature—one bright and benevolent, the other dark and indifferent.

FOURTH OF JULY

Far down at the other end of Main Street, half a dozen blocks away, the fire truck bleated its horn repeatedly. It wasn't on its way to put out a fire. Instead, this was the signal that the Fourth of July parade was about to begin. Kids playing in the street were shooed back to the curb by their parents, and we all peered down the block trying to catch the first glimpse of the chartreuse fire engine slowly making its way toward us.

People of all ages lined the streets; most were clustered in extended family groups and wore patriotic garb of some sort—everything from straw bowler hats encircled with red, white, and blue bands to glittery, flag-embellished T-shirts. Several young girls wrapped in white sheets and wearing gold Statue of Liberty crowns cavorted along the sidelines.

I was almost as excited as the young children along the curb because this year our whole family was here and, for the first time ever, my sister, Penny, and brother-in-law, Keith, were able to join us. This was the kind of family celebration on the island I had longed for during the many months of construction. I stood on my tiptoes. "I see it! It's only half a block away."

Finally the fire engine pulled up in front of us. Children broke free from their parents' grasp and dashed out into the street to scoop up candy tossed by volunteer fire fighters seated on the truck.

Doug was already focusing on the next vehicle in the parade. "What the heck is that pickup hauling?" he asked.

"I don't know," Penny answered, "but it's one of the weirdest things I've ever seen."

I shaded my eyes to get a better look at the sunshine yellow contraption. "I know! It's one of the old windsleds."

A sign on the truck said that this windsled was last used during the winter of 1957. Proudly waving to the crowd from the bed of the truck where he sat on a lawn chair was Elmer Nelson, the inventor of this version of the windsled.

A little girl led the next group of marchers. She carried a sign: The Kelly Family Drill Team. Following her were two dozen Kellys dressed in bright red T-shirts, each carrying a collapsible metal lawn chair with patriotic colored crepe paper streamers woven through the seat and back. The Kellys were singing "The Star Spangled Banner" in unison.

A middle-aged Kelly male at the head of the pack came to a sudden stop and loudly blew the whistle attached to a lanyard around his neck. "Ten hut!"

Twenty-four Kellys came to an abrupt halt. Twenty-four Kellys simultaneously raised their chairs.

As the Kelly leader walked backwards, barking out orders, his clan raised and lowered their chairs on cue while marching in intricate formations. In their final maneuver the Kellys formed two lines facing each other, raised their chairs to form an arch and then one by one lowered their chairs and promenaded beneath the family arch. The crowd roared in approval.

Next came floats and marchers sponsored by businesses and community organizations.

I tapped Doug on the arm. "Hey, look at the members of the Wilderness Preserve." I recognized some of the people I had met at the annual meetings, but they looked a lot different today. They were dressed as bees in black and yellow striped shirts. Making buzzing noises as they wove in and out of the crowd, they attempted to "sting" people with their pointed cardboard noses while their leader toted a boom box playing what else but "Flight of the Bumble Bee."

I was still watching the bees when Keith started laughing. I looked down the street to see what he found so amusing. Members of the Yacht Club had taken the term "drill team" literally. Wearing florescent orange life preservers, they carried power drills with the electrical cords trailing along behind.

The aroma of roasting hot dogs wafted through the crowd, compliments of the Bell Street Tavern float. Standing on a huge flatbed trailer decorated in red, white, and blue, Chef Chris tended hot dogs on a charcoal grill. He plopped frankfurters into buns and reached down to hand them out to the crowd. His two assistants, one dressed in red, the other in yellow, walked behind the float, dispensing catsup and mustard.

Then the twelve-member Madeline Island Band came into view. They are an ad hoc group with different membership each year; they only practice for a few minutes before the parade, their single annual performance.

During a pause, I filled Penny in on the history of the final segment of the parade. The last marching unit is always the product of the Live Art Theater Project sponsored by Tom Nelson, owner of Tom's Burned Down Café. It usually includes a number of huge papier-mache puppets used later the same afternoon in a show on the ball field. For a month before the Fourth of July, people of all ages come to a work area adjacent to the Café to help build the ten-foot-tall puppets.

Fliers had announced that this year's theme would be Pirate Island. Making their way down the street were two enormous wood and papier-mache ships—one British, the other full of pirates. The pirate ship boasted a live woman as the figurehead. With long frizzled black hair and a toothless grin, she leaned off the front of the boat, leering and hissing at the crowd. The pirates on board sang lusty songs boasting of their prowess in battle. To prove their mettle, the pirates periodically leapt from their ship onto the British galleon and used their cardboard swords to do battle with the patriots. The crowd got into the spirit of the fray, booing the British and goading on the pirates.

When the last float disappeared around the corner, we joined the rest of the spectators as they made their way to the lawn of the Madeline Island Museum to wait for the program to begin. Everyone spread out blankets or set up lawn chairs facing the raised wooden platform draped in patriotic bunting. After reciting the Pledge of Allegiance and singing "The Star Spangled Banner," we listened to Steve Cotherman, director of the Madeline Island Museum, give this year's patriotic speech.

Steve called Madeline Island "a case study in diversity." He explained that the people who live there are "rich and poor and everything in between; upper class, lower class, middle class, and classless; educated formally or schooled through experience and hard-knocks; gay, straight, Protestant, Catholic, Buddhist, nativist, vegan, belly-button gazers, and agnostics" . . . and they "never disagree over the basics, like the benefits of decent phone service, the absolute beauty of the place, their love of a tall cool one, and their disdain of the Vikings, or the liberating feeling of driving the ice road—whenever the hell they want."

Steve closed by saying that the people of Madeline Island "adore Benjamin Franklin, who way back in the eighteenth century wrote the words that islanders live by: 'It is the first responsibility of every citizen to question authority.' By those revolutionary standards, I challenge anyone to find an island—a community—with more patriots than we have here on Madeline Island."

I nudged Doug. "He sure got that right, didn't he?" The crowd agreed. They rose to their feet and delivered a thunderous standing ovation.

People finally sat down again for the presentation of the parade awards. "Wait till you see the prizes," I said to Penny. "They're old bowling, softball, and hockey trophies with new nameplates attached." When the judges announced that the first prize for the marching unit went to the Kelly family, the crowd cheered.

The program ended with the audience singing an adapted version of the Woody Guthrie song, "This Land Is Your Land." They belted out the last stanza:

As I went walking, I saw a sign there,
And on the one side, it said "No Trespassing,"
But on the other side, it didn't say nothing.
That side was made for you and me!

The verse reminded me of a bumper sticker I had seen a couple of days before on a car obviously owned by a year-round islander. It said, "I don't give a shit how they do it on the mainland." Both sticker and song captured the spirit of stubborn independence so typical on the island.

Steve Cotherman was right; Madeline islanders are uniquely equipped to observe this holiday. In fact, I think the American virtue of independence is celebrated on this island all year long.

A few days later as we started packing the car for the drive back to Minneapolis, I realized that a shift was beginning to occur within me. Even though I was only a part-timer and even though at times I still felt like an outsider, I was starting to identify myself as a member of the island community.

Now I not only embraced the slower pace of life on the island, but also the independent spirit and quirkiness of islanders as well as their tolerance for diversity. I even looked forward to traversing the ice road and climbing aboard the windsled.

I was becoming one of them.

NATURE'S WILL

At home in Minneapolis I sit at the kitchen table and look out into my garden. Here is nature that I have snipped, shaped, and tended into a landscape of my design. Steve built limestone walls of varying heights to give structure to my hilly garden. A cedar arbor stands on one side with a stone pathway leading to the arbor seat. I planted dozens of perennials and filled in any open spaces with bright blossoming annuals. I spend hours weeding, fertilizing, and watering my backyard flower garden.

At the table in our house on Madeline Island I look out onto an untended landscape of nature's design. We have deliberately chosen not to grow grass around our cabin, though swaths of green lawn surround many island homes. We don't want the upkeep a lawn requires. At this house we prefer to spend our time enjoying nature, not manicuring it.

After construction, the area immediately adjacent to our island house consisted chiefly of the reddish-brown clay typical of the region. There was no discernable vegetation. We decided to wait and see how nature would landscape our property. She responded with abandon.

The spring after our house was finished I was delighted to find patches of wild strawberries, blue forget-me-nots, and white flowered bunchberries surrounding our house. A profusion of daisies followed in July. Even our driveway was edged with bouquets of daisies. Penny gave me a wildflower identification book, a thoughtful gift. Now I could learn the proper names of all the flowers sprouting around our house. I discovered that the tiny white blossoms covering a hillside in early spring are starflowers. The bright orange blooms that mingle with the daisies are orange hawkweed. And the masses of bold yellow button flowers that dry to an attractive brown are tansy.

But nature saved her best gift for August and I didn't need a plant book to identify it.

Doug and I had just arrived for the weekend and were carrying our suitcases up the path to our house when he suddenly stopped in the middle of the walkway.

"Pat, look." He pointed to a large flat rock bordering the path. A bushy plant leaned over the surface of the rock, displaying its rosy harvest for our perusal. Wild raspberries! Right at our doorstep! And this was not the only raspberry bush; we discovered masses of raspberry bushes reaching their fruit-laden branches onto our entry porch and front deck.

Doug teases me that there are skid marks across Wisconsin caused by sudden stops after I have spotted a roadside stand selling raspberries. Raspberries are my favorite fruit, and I can never consume enough of them during their impossibly short harvest season. So it was a delightful surprise to find that, unbeknownst to us, nature had deposited a raspberry patch quite literally on our doorstep. Somehow it doesn't seem quite right to enjoy nature's bounty without any work on my part. It seems as though I am defying the Midwestern work ethic that was such an important part of my upbringing.

But I am learning. It is not about deserving. Nature does her will without paying heed to the efforts of human beings. Sometimes she brings unexpected gifts. And sometimes, just as inexplicably, she takes them away.

* * * * *

A storm was coming.

We were sitting on the deck looking down the channel of the lake toward the Minnesota shore some forty miles away and listening to the thunder rumbling and grumbling in the distance. The sky and the lake were both a deep leaden gray. Even the distant tree-covered islands were a dark grayish green instead of their usual brilliant emerald. Only a power boat heading toward the marina with its long, white wake streaming behind stood out in bold relief. It was almost jarring in the otherwise monochromatic scene.

It was July 5, 1999. All of our holiday company had left that morning. Only Steve and Doug and I were able to stay on a few more days.

"Seems like it's been thundering off and on almost all afternoon." Steve got up from his chair and walked over to the railing at the edge of the deck.

"If it's going to rain, I wish it would just get it over with," I said, shifting position in the recliner where I had been ensconced most of the afternoon. I was pouting because we had been planning a boat trip, and the foreboding skies had kept us at home. Instead we idled away the afternoon sitting on the deck, reading.

"Careful what you wish for," Doug said. "I just heard on the radio about a big storm yesterday over in the Boundary Waters."

It was too soon to have all the details, but later we would learn about the blowdown. On July 4, 1999, a storm with wind speeds in excess of ninety miles per hour swept through the Boundary Waters Canoe Area and mowed down over 350,000 acres of trees. At least sixty people were injured by falling trees, and hundreds of campers were trapped in the woods in the midst of the ferocious storm.

I went back to my book. The next time I looked up, things were changing. Fast.

"The wind is coming up," I said, hurriedly getting up from the recliner. Until just moments before, the air had been almost still. Now gusts of wind were blowing bits of dried leaves and pine needles across the deck.

The alarm in my voice got Doug's attention. He stood up so quickly that he knocked over his chair. "Oh, my gosh! Look out there," he said pointing toward the lake. As we watched, about half a mile from shore the waves began to change direction, and the wind shifted from west to northwest. Suddenly huge waves topped with whitecaps were coming straight towards the shore in front of us. A vivid flash of lightning, followed almost immediately by a loud crack of thunder just off to our right, left no doubt that the storm was upon us.

"I'll close up the porch. You two get inside," Doug yelled as he bolted across the deck.

Before Steve and I could reach the French doors ten feet away at the front of the house, the rain started. Huge drops pelted our faces and arms, and our T-shirts and shorts were drenched by the time we got inside. Steve and I each got behind one of the doors and pushed as hard as we could, but we were no match for the wind. I was using every ounce of strength I could muster to get the door closed, but it was still inches away from the latch. Doug came in from the porch and, adding his force to ours, we finally managed to close the doors. No sooner had we securely latched the doors than horizontal rain began to pour over the tops of the uncaulked door frames onto our heads. Within seconds we were standing in puddles of water.

"Towels," I shouted over my shoulder as I ran down the hall.

We wadded up the brightly colored beach towels to form a dam at the top of the doors, then started to mop up the water at our feet. The next moment a huge gust of wind hit the windows in front of us. We looked up in alarm. Just then we heard a searing crack and, as we watched, the top six feet of the pine tree to the left of the house was shorn off and sent spinning into the air. It landed with a loud thud just below the stairs at the end of the deck.

"The basement! Get to the basement!" Doug yelled, grabbing me by the arm.

It wasn't until I was at the bottom of the stairs that I had time to think about being frightened. Now I was trembling. Were we in the middle of a tornado? I didn't even know if the island had warning sirens. Would our new house still be standing when the storm was over? I tried to remember what we were supposed to do in a storm. The only thing I could think of at the moment was that you were safe if you were lying down in a bathtub. But there was no tub in the basement. Would we be secure down here or should we move under the stairs?

When the horrible din from the wind had ceased, we climbed up the stairs to survey the destruction. Fortunately, other than leaves and small tree limbs covering the ground, the main damage was the water on the floor and the decapitated pine tree outside.

As we learned later, the remnants of the huge storm system that had caused the blowdown in the Boundary Waters had traveled across Lake Superior and hit Madeline just hours later.

This was but the first of numerous storms we have watched from our house on Madeline. Many of them were ferocious. Each time a huge black cloud is bearing down the channel towards our house, I am humbled by the power of nature. Nature, the same force that can stir up storms and tear down trees, can also create a wildflower garden where before there was nothing but bare earth. Nature has the power to hurt and heal, to destroy and delight.

BEARS

Despite the heat, Steve had decided to go jogging. Forty-five minutes later, when he came through the door, he was breathless. I assumed it was due to the sweltering temperature outside. He stood just inside the front door panting.

"That was . . . a run . . . I won't forget!"

The tone of his voice got my attention. "What happened?" I stood up and hurried over to him.

"I was about a mile down North Shore Road. . . . All of a sudden I spotted a black bear tromping through the bushes. . . . Only about thirty feet away from me." Steve was still panting, though not as much as before.

"Holy cow! What did you do?"

"First I slowed down to a walk. Then I got really scared, because the bear stood up on his hind legs. Then he started sniffing the air."

"Steve!"

"I made sure I didn't look him in the eye." Steve was breathing almost normally now. "I stood up straight and tried to look as large as I could. Then I started talking to him. Quietly I said, 'Hello, Mr. Bear. I'm not going to hurt you. Maybe we can just be friends.' The whole time I was slowly backing away from him."

"Did he come after you?"

"No. He just stood there sniffing. After a while he got back down on all fours. By that time I was pretty far away from him. And then he just sort of ambled off into the woods."

It came as no surprise to learn that there were bears on the island. Residents as well as tourists had told us about bear sitings. But Steve's description of his encounter, and of how nonchalant the bear seemed, took me by surprise. It was unsettling to think we might bump into a bear at a time or place we least expected it.

We had also heard stories of bears on Stockton Island, one of our favorite boating destinations. Stockton is estimated to have 2.1 bears per square mile, one of the greatest concentrations of black bears in North America. Stockton is the most visited island in the Apostle Island National Lakeshore, making human interaction with bears almost inevitable. On one occasion, as we were docking our boat, we watched several bears frolicking on the beach at Quarry Bay. A few brazen bears have been known to climb aboard sailboats moored in Stockton's harbors; they have been lured there as they tried to find the source of the delicious scent of human food wafting from the decks.

Some bears cause too much trouble for their own good. Skar, an infamous bear, named for the large wound on its flank, staged numerous raids on Stockton's campgrounds, threatening campers and causing property damage. After trying every available nonlethal method to discourage Skar's aggressive behavior, park rangers were forced to put him down.

* * * * *

After Steve's encounter, I bought several books about bears. In *The Great American Bear*, author Jeff Fair describes the experiences of Lynn Rogers who spent years in the woods studying black bears. Rogers believes that most human fears about bears are over-blown. He regularly visited bear dens and fed the big furry critters from his hand without experiencing any problems. He even named the bears he studied. Rogers acknowledged that cornered bears have been known to charge humans, but he advised that most of these are fake charges and are designed simply to frighten.

Yes, sir, a fake charge would certainly have the desired effect on me!

The other book, titled *Bear Aware*, was more to my liking. Bill Schneider, in my estimation the more sensible of the two authors, indicated that black bears do pose a threat to human beings. He included information about "Hiking in Bear Country" and "If You See a Bear Charging You." He seemed to take these bear-to-man incidents much more seriously than Jim Rogers.

After reading this information, my morning walks were not so relaxing any more. I was constantly scanning the woods along the driveway and North Shore Road for furry, black shapes. By then I had learned what to do if I saw a bear. The Schneider book advised: Look as large and dominant as possible. Make loud noises. (Banging pots and pans was suggested. Not too practical for a walk.) Carry pepper spray. Be prepared to use it if a bear starts charging and gets within twenty feet of you.

I had memorized all the information, but I seriously doubted I would have the presence of mind to use it if the need arose.

* * * * *

The November issue of the *Island Gazette* was in the pile of mail on our dining room table in Minneapolis. Usually Doug and I fought over who would get to read it first, but he was away at a meeting that night. I settled into my favorite chair in the family room and put my feet up on the ottoman.

It was only a small advertisement on page thirty, but it caught my eye immediately.

BEAR GUIDE SERVICE

Bears shot during 1998 Season by:

Pat Gleason (rifle) 350 pounds, field dressed

Chris Frank (rifle) 550 pounds, field dressed

The estimated live weight of Chris' bear is 680 pounds. This bear tied the second largest bear taken in the State of Wisconsin. It also tied for eighth largest in the nation and for the thirty-first largest in the world.

In 1999, a total of eight hunters were assisted with getting their bear.

Jeff Larson (rifle)
Tyler Larson (rifle)
Don Zimmer (rifle)
Todd Freeman (rifle)
Brian Dawson (rifle)
Mike Gardner (pistol)
Barb Wyler (rifle)
Deb Wyler (bow & arrow)

IF YOU'RE INTERESTED IN SIGNING ON FOR THE 2000 SEASON, CALL US!

I was certainly glad to hear that the 680 pound bear was no longer roaming the island, and I was amazed that a woman had killed her bear with a bow and arrow!

Once again my interest in black bears was piqued. I wanted a chance to see *Ursus americanus* for myself.

* * * * *

Doug and I were driving home from town one evening at dusk. Twenty feet ahead something moved in the ditch beside the road. A dark shape hurtled out of the ditch and into the woods.

"Was that—"

"A bear?" I finished Doug's sentence.

"What else could it be?"

I *did* want to see a bear. I mean *really* see one. Not just some dark shape along the road. However I preferred to be in our car or house when the sighting occurred. I definitely did not want to find myself up close and personal with a bear.

* * * * *

One warm August day I woke suddenly at 6:00 a.m. Almost immediately I realized what had startled me out of my sleep. Through the open window came the sounds of branches breaking under heavy footsteps. I leapt out of bed and went over to the window. A bear! Just a few feet from the house, foraging for food. I was thrilled!

I had read that black bears go on a feeding frenzy at this time of year before six months of hibernation. This single-minded eating mode is called hyperphagia, and bears often feed for up to twenty hours a day. They stuff themselves with as many insects, berries, plants, and nuts as they can find. And now here was a bear cramming his mouth full of berries from *our* yard.

"Doug, Doug, wake up!" I whispered. I wanted to get Doug's attention without scaring away the bear. Groggily he raised his head off the pillow.

"Quick! Come over here!" I motioned to him, without taking my eyes off the bear. He joined me at the window.

"Let's go downstairs where we can get a better look at him," Doug said in a low voice.

We dashed down the stairs to a first floor window. Now we could tell that this was a full-grown bear, probably weighing at least 250 pounds. I could feel my pulse quicken despite the pane of glass that separated us. From this perspective the bear was a lot more intimidating than he had seemed from our second-story bedroom. But mostly I was fascinated.

There was nothing graceful about this massive mammal as he lumbered through the brush looking for food. Then suddenly he stopped. He had found a Juneberry bush—a sought-after delicacy for this furry gourmand!

I sucked in my breath when I heard the loud snap of the Juneberry bush as the bear pulled it over to reach as much of the ripe purple fruit as possible. The bush definitely suffered during this encounter. Hungry bears don't seem to possess good sense or to be ecologically minded. They tend to trample their food source. During bear-gorging season, it is easy to observe many slumped-over Juneberry bushes along North Shore Road.

I giggled with delight as the bear crammed handfuls of Juneberries in his mouth, all the while snorting with pleasure. I could practically see the grin on his face as he stripped the branches bare with gluttonous glee. He feasted for at least fifteen minutes until all the berries had been devoured. Then he tipped back on his haunches. I fully expected to hear a loud belch emanate from his bulging belly. But there was none. After a few moments he dropped back down on all fours and shambled off into the woods.

I finally had *really* seen a bear!

GOLDEN BIRCH TIME

Visitors are drawn to the windows at the front of our house and, in good weather, to the deck beyond. The view is a broad expanse of Lake Superior with seven of the Apostle Islands scattered across it. On a clear day we can look down the shipping channel and see all the way to the shores of Minnesota, forty miles away.

"Which island is that one off to the right?" someone invariably asks.

"That's Hermit. The locals call it Wilson's Island. It's named for John Wilson who was banished from Madeline Island after he lost a fight with John Bell, the territorial governor. He lived alone on Hermit Island until his death." Doug is glad for the chance to provide bits of lore about the islands—glad also to point out the lighthouse on the shores of Raspberry Island, ten miles away.

The views from the windows at the sides of our house are also appealing, but often overlooked. Our house is set in a forest; beautiful white birch trees crowd the house on both sides. Most people like the view of the lake the best. But I am different. It is the birches I love.

Birches are elegant, womanly trees with white skin and long, slender limbs. I especially like to look at them from the windows of our second floor bedroom. As a child I grew up in a single story bungalow. Maybe that's why I've always been fascinated by the view from second story rooms. I feel as though I'm in a treehouse, a secret place high above the ground where I can observe the world around me from a new perspective. I'm at the same level as the pileated woodpecker; I watch as he searches industriously for lunch. And I glimpse the red squirrel in his afternoon play, leaping from branch to branch. Best of all, from my second story perch, I can see deep into the surrounding birch forest.

When I wake in the morning, one of my favorite sights is the birches. If I look to the east I can see them through the bedroom windows and to the west through the bathroom windows.

If the sun is shining, I need no clock. I can tell the time of day by noticing which part of the trees is illuminated. The birches west of our house are awash in the morning sun while those to the east are set aglow by the warmth of the afternoon rays. When the wind blows, I need no wind gage. I have only to look at the birches to know the direction of the wind and to estimate its speed. A faint southerly breeze barely sets the leaves aflutter, but when a gale sweeps off the lake, the birches bend in submission.

One afternoon as we hiked the land surrounding our house, we came upon dead birches fallen on the forest floor. On close inspection, we noticed something strange. The bark shell of the tree was perfectly intact—but empty. The pristine white cylinder of skin remained in one piece long after the center had rotted away and disappeared. There was no way to distinguish between the long-dead warriors on the ground and their newly fallen comrades. Even after they die, birches possess a certain mystery, a mystery that haunts me.

Though I love to look at the birches any time of day, there is one especially magical hour when they are at their prime. I call it "Golden Birch Time." On summer evenings Doug and I carry our wine glasses outside to the chairs on our deck to toast the arrival of Golden Birch Time. I tilt the recliner to just the right angle and let my body sink into it. I lift the glass of chilled Sauvignon Blanc and inhale its crisp, fresh aroma before I take the first sip. The only sound is the soft murmur of the tree frogs.

Near the horizon, the billowy, white clouds appear incandescent, as though lighted from within. They remind me of the Sunday school folders of my childhood which always pictured Jesus standing with arms outstretched in front of brilliant clouds like these.

We watch as the blue sky near the highest part of the islands begins to turn a soft shade of pink. Gradually the features of the islands become indistinguishable. Their forests and beaches fade and then disappear. Slowly the islands are transformed into dark purple outlines against the peach-colored horizon and the pale blue waters of the lake.

Everything so far has been prologue, setting the scene for what is to come. Now it is time for the birches to take center stage.

As the sun drops closer and closer to the crest of the high hills on the mainland, it focuses its intensity on the birches surrounding our house, burnishing the trunks until they glow like rich, golden honey. The warm amber color envelops everything. Our faces are luminous in the soft, reflected light.

Nothing moves; everything is preserved in a state of suspended animation. It seems as though the golden stillness will last forever.

I long to stop the progression of the sun at this moment when the whole world seems to be motionless and everything is bathed in a golden glow. If I could, I would preserve this moment the way insects were preserved in amber, the resin that oozed out of ancient trees and fossilized living organisms. My wish is not so different from that of two-year-old Steve, long ago on Raspberry Island, when he begged Doug and me to stop the sun from setting.

Like the poet Keats in "Ode on a Grecian Urn," I long for permanence in a world of change. Keats describes the "happy, happy boughs" of a tree pictured on the urn. Boughs "that cannot shed your leaves, nor ever bid the Spring adieu." For Keats it was the Grecian urn that embodied a realm in which time stood still; for me, it is those few moments just before sunset when the sun gilds the birches.

But the sun does not heed my wishes, and little by little it slips behind the hills of Bayfield and eventually disappears altogether, leaving behind a russet glow atop the ridge line. As Doug and I watch, the birches gradually recede into the gathering dusk. Soon darkness blankets everything—blackest of black, that time of night before the moon rises, before the stars appear. Is it truly darker or does it only seem so because the light of day departed only moments ago? Yet even nighttime cannot completely erase the silver sheen of the birches. Their pale white trunks stand like ghostly apparitions in the dusky forest.

A cool breeze wafts up from the lake, tempering the warmth of the day. I shiver. A whisper of sadness wraps round me, dampening the joy I felt only moments before. But I am not like two-year-old Steve. I know the sun will return tomorrow morning. And tomorrow Golden Birch Time will come again. If not tomorrow, one day soon.

Besides, there is a price to be paid when humans try to achieve permanence. Toward the end of the poem, Keats calls the Grecian urn "Cold Pastoral" and tells the "bold lover" who is leaning toward his fair maiden: "never, never canst thou kiss, though winning near the goal. . . ." The lovers will be forever frozen in clay. Though tantalizingly close to one another, they will never know the bliss of fulfilling their desires.

And that other symbol of permanence, those intriguing pieces of amber with organisms forever preserved within them? Their immutability is costly

On Island Time | 167

too. They were created when insects walked on the surface of the sticky tree sap and their legs became trapped in the gooey liquid. The more the insects struggled, the more firmly they became stuck.

Perhaps because the golden light fades, because it does not last forever, it becomes more precious. I remember the words of a friend in her eighties: "I love the lilacs when they bloom. I love their fragrance, their pale lavender color. It seems I savor the lilacs more each year because I don't know how many springs I have left."

Because of the darkness that follows, I savor the golden light.

WILDLIFE SUPERHIGHWAY

Long before our house was on the land, long before the land was ours, long before any human owned the land, there was a deer path extending parallel to the lake.

For many years the heart-shaped hooves of deer have flattened the ferns and tall grasses to create a narrow track close to the edge of the high banks overlooking Lake Superior. Other animals—coyotes, fishers, bear—shared that path. These days Doug and I sit on our deck and watch the procession continue.

* * * * *

One bright July afternoon I was working at the picnic table on our deck. Had I looked up, I would have noticed sailboats catching the soft breezes as they cruised regally across the lake. I would have seen power boats skimming across the water, darting in and out among the islands. But I was so preoccupied with my writing that I didn't lift my head. Gradually a soft rustling in the grasses penetrated my consciousness until finally I looked up. There, not ten feet away, stood a lovely caramel–colored doe, studying me. She stopped her afternoon grazing to ponder this strange being, this intruder on her centuries-old territory. She looked at me shyly with soulful brown eyes. Poised on her slender legs, she seemed ready to flee in an instant.

Many times had I seen her friends and relatives bounding into the woods as our car approached, their white tails held high like flags as they leapt out of our path. But never had I been so near one of these graceful animals.

Fascinated, I waited to see what she would do. We gazed at each other for several minutes. When she did not move, I took a risk, rose from my chair and walked slowly to the railing of the deck, narrowing the space between us. "You are a beauty," I said softly. "Lucky for me that you came close so I can admire you."

Without so much as the ripple of a muscle, she stayed to consider me. What did she make of this human staring at her? Could she tell from my gentle conversation that I meant no harm?

We continued our quiet communion until she decided I posed no threat. Then she lowered her head and went back to her lunch.

I thought of a conversation I had with Gene when he was working on our house. "It's hard to spot deer," he told me. "They blend in with the surroundings so well that they can be just a few feet away and you never notice them." Remembering his words made me feel even more fortunate to have such an intimate encounter.

After that I became attuned to the sounds of the natural world. I learned to be still and listen. I began to hear the smallest rustlings in the bracken ferns, the slightest crunching of a twig, the faintest footfall landing on soft earth. Once I began to hear the music of nature, symphonies surrounded me.

* * * * *

On another summer day on the same deck, Doug and I were sitting at the picnic table finishing our dinner. Suddenly a spotted fawn dashed across the deer path. I couldn't believe an animal could move as fast as this tiny deer. "What on earth . . ." I started to say.

Suddenly a blurred black shape with a long tail bolted across the deer path in hot pursuit of the fawn.

"What was *that*?" Doug asked.

"I don't know. I've never seen anything like it."

The next day we happened to be at the Apostle Islands Visitor's Center in Bayfield. Doug described what we saw to the ranger on duty.

"Most likely a fisher," she said.

"A fisher?"

"It's a carnivorous animal, a member of the weasel family." She picked up a book, *Mammals of North America,* and showed us a drawing. We looked at a picture of a smallish animal resembling a house cat with a long thick black tail, round ears, short legs, and a wedge-shaped snout.

"Fishers weigh between six and twelve pounds," the ranger said. "With needle-sharp teeth and claws on both their front and hind legs, they feed on small mammals and birds, even porcupines. You can spot them on the ground and up in trees, looking for prey."

"Who do you think won, the fisher or the fawn?" Doug asked.

The ranger closed the book. "I'd bet on the fisher."

I didn't like her answer. It was one thing to be within a few feet of an elegant deer, it was something else entirely to witness predator chasing prey. I had the same reaction as I used to have to the TV show *Wild Kingdom* that was popular when I was growing up. I loved the segments showing wild creatures cantering through open fields or sauntering through the jungle, but when animals started killing other animals, I left the room. Though I knew animals ate other animals, I didn't want to watch.

The evening we saw the black streak that turned out to be a fisher, I didn't have a chance to be afraid. It all happened so quickly. But what I learned about fishers the next day gave me pause. The ranger said nothing about them attacking humans, but still, I didn't like the idea of them skulking around in the forest or lying in wait in the treetops.

After the evening we saw the fisher, Doug began referring to the deer trail at the front of our lot as "the wildlife superhighway." As we waited to see what animal would amble or barrel down the path, we came to think of watching the superhighway as part of our evening entertainment.

* * * * *

Same deck. Same summer. Slightly different cast of characters.

In the center of our front deck, seven stairs lead down to the ground; the bottom step is about twenty feet away from the wildlife superhighway. I was sitting on the highest of those seven steps with Doug and Becky, Bob's girlfriend. We were husking sweet corn for our dinner that night and talking about the day's boat trip to Devil's Island. Bob was inside taking a nap.

"The view from the top of the lighthouse was really spectacular. I had no idea that you could see Two Harbors, Minnesota, from . . . "

Suddenly Doug lowered his voice. "Don't move. Look over there. To the left. A black bear just climbed out of the ravine." Slowly, very slowly, Becky and I turned to see a large black bear starting to tramp toward us on the superhighway.

At the sight of this huge creature coming closer and closer, I turned to ice. I tried to speak, but no words came out of my mouth. I tried again. "What . . . What do we do now?" I whispered. "Corn? Could we throw him some corn and make a dash for the door?"

Instead the three of us froze into place and watched as the bear lumbered across the path directly in front of us. This was no cub or yearling.

He was easily 300 pounds. Covered with glossy black fur except for his tan snout and the area around his eyes, he looked as if he was wearing a mask. Not once did he turn his head to look at us. It was as though we were invisible. His trek along the trail seemed to last forever, yet it was over in no time at all. Finally he disappeared into the woods to our right.

After he was gone I let out my breath in a long whoosh and scrambled up the steps into the house. From this position of safety I had to admit that I was thrilled to get such a close look at this magnificent animal. If I could be sure the outcome would be the same, I knew I would gladly repeat the experience.

Since then, when Becky, a preschool instructor, teaches her classes, the children often beg her to "tell the bear story again." Though they have heard the tale many times before, they listen each time with rapt attention. They especially like the part about Bob taking a nap and missing the bear. After Becky finishes the story, the children sit quietly for a moment. Then, inevitably, at least one child will say, "I don't want to take a nap today. I might miss the bear."

* * * * *

Once I had become aware of the presence of wild creatures all around me, I took my newly acquired sensibility with me wherever I went on the island. And there was plenty of wildlife to observe, though not all of it traveled on the superhighway.

One night on the drive back from town, our car lights caught what looked like a medium-sized dog loping along the side of the road. As we drew closer we could see that it was not a dog at all, but a coyote. He had a coat of mottled gray and a long bushy tail. We slowed down, staying about thirty feet back, so that we could watch him. After a minute or so of being illuminated by our headlights, he began to veer into the center of the road, forcing us to slow our speed to a crawl.

The coyote trotted smugly down the middle of the road as though he owned it. (I don't know why I assumed it was a *he*. Maybe it was the attitude of machismo he projected.) Every once in a while he bounded over to the ditch beside the road and pounced on some unseen prey. These hunting expeditions never seemed to produce any trophies; the coyote always came up empty pawed.

After a succession of these forays, he resumed his sassy prancing down the center of North Shore Road. We weren't sure if he was aware that we were following him until he paused to look over his shoulder at us. His yellow eyes glowed in the light from the car's head lamps, and I could swear I saw a slight smile—or was it a smirk—as he turned his head. He seemed to revel in the fact that he had an audience, saying, "Hey, you humans, why do you suppose I'm out here in the middle of the road? I want to make sure *I'm* the center of your attention."

As we neared the spot where our driveway turned off North Shore Road, I prepared to wave goodbye to our cheeky little friend. But instead, amazingly, as though he knew just what he was doing, he turned into our driveway and continued to lead us down our own road. Halfway to the house, something attracted his attention along the side of the drive and he pounced and then pounced again and again until he disappeared in the brush.

I laughed aloud several times at his chutzpah as he led our little parade. From the safe enclosure of the car, I thoroughly enjoyed his antics. Had I been on foot when I noticed him, I am sure I would have given him wide berth, and, sadly, I would have missed his whole performance.

* * * * *

We also heard reports about wildlife that others observed. Animals were often the topic of discussion at Bell Street as people passed along information about their latest sightings. One winter night I overheard a conversation between two old guys who were leaning against the bar just a short distance from our table.

"Did you hear about the two cougars out on the ice over in front of the Bayfield Inn?"

"No way! Cougars? Didn't know there were any around here."

"Me neither. Oh, I heard folks over in Bayfield talk about seeing cougars in the National Forest nearby, but I thought it was just talk. Then the other day I saw those two big cats with my own eyes. Right in the middle of the afternoon. There they were, about fifty feet off the ice road. Just playing around like a couple of kittens."

"Did ya get up real close to 'em?"

"Naw, I kept my distance. Whad'ya take me for, a damn fool?"

I was fascinated at the thought of seeing cougars on the ice. I wished *I* had seen them. The only place I had ever seen a cougar was at the zoo, certainly never in the wild.

I was fascinated but also frightened. What would I do if I saw a cougar on one of my island walks? Or a bear? Or a fisher? Maybe I shouldn't even go out walking by myself. I didn't want to have these fears. I wanted to enjoy the natural world and its creatures. My experience with the doe could almost seduce me into forgetting they are wild animals. Cougars might act like playful kittens, but they are still predators, still worthy of my apprehension. I hoped I could learn from the two islanders at the bar. They knew when to be intrigued and how to take the necessary precautions to deal with nature's potential to harm.

My growing awareness of the wild creatures surrounding me led me to a new realization. In the same way as I was learning to live among and learn from the human community on the island, I realized I was also finding my place in yet another community, the community of wild creatures with whom I shared this land.

Long after I am gone, long after some other family occupies our Madeline house, I hope the imprints of heart-shaped hooves will still be found on the path along the high banks of Lake Superior. I hope those who follow me will also treasure close contact with nature's creatures.

THE LAKE IS THE BOSS

WARNING. Dangerous Waters.

Lake Superior waters are dangerously cold and sudden storms arise. The lake's history is replete with shipwrecks and violent storms. Small boats, canoes and kayaks should be used with extreme caution on Lake Superior. Just off-shore, 50 degree F waters can cause even strong swimmers to suffer hypothermia in 15 minutes. Swimming is not recommended in Lake Superior. Keep an eye on the weather even on calm days.

On one of our early summer vacations to the area, I read this warning, printed in a brochure published by the National Park Service for visitors to the Apostle Islands. It had the desired effect. I was afraid. I realized that the lake was no place to take chances.

For one thing Lake Superior is not a small swimming hole; it is enormous. The world's largest inland body of water, it contains ten percent of the world's fresh surface water and is sometimes referred to as an inland sea. The big lake holds three quadrillion gallons of water, half the water in all of the Great Lakes combined, and enough to cover Canada, the United States, Mexico, and South America with one foot of water. It is so large that it affects weather patterns. When air masses collide with air cooled by Lake Superior in the summer or warmed by the lake in winter, huge amounts of energy are released, creating intense storms. Some say Superior makes its own weather.

Its size is not the only thing that makes me uneasy; it is also the fact that Superior is extremely deep; in places it is deep almost beyond human comprehension. When we visited the Marine Museum in Duluth, I was intrigued by the contour map of Lake Superior. The bottom of the lake was not smooth and flat. Instead it was rough and uneven, filled with rugged peaks and yawning valleys. The crenated surface of the map reminded me of the tall tale Garrison Keillor told one Saturday evening on *A Prairie Home Companion*. He described how enterprising developers drained Lake Superior and made scads of money selling choice lots on the newly revealed mountainsides. But what made me catch my breath at the museum was the placard beside the contour map. It said that at its deepest point, Superior is 1330 feet deep and its average depth is 483 feet.

We've noticed those peaks and especially the valleys as we've traveled between the Apostle Islands. We were half a mile from the shore of Stockton Island when the depth sounder on our boat registered 365 feet. I gulped. A silent shiver ran down my spine. Logically I know if your boat is afloat, it really doesn't matter how much water is under it. I also know it's possible to drown in a few feet of water. But I find it unnerving to be close to land and realize that the bottom of the lake is hundreds of feet below me. I just don't like it.

Another reason the National Park Service warning gave me the jitters was the mention of shipwrecks. Lake Superior has been known to rip huge boats to shreds and fling their occupants into the frigid water. I had heard the stories—stories such as the sinking of the *Edmund Fitzgerald*, a 729-foot steamer, probably the most famous shipwreck on Lake Superior and a potent reminder of the awesome power of the big lake. The ship, which was two blocks long and several stories high, sank so quickly during a heavy storm in November 1975, that the crew didn't even have time to send up a distress signal. There were no survivors and no witnesses to the tragedy, and the potential causes of the disaster are still being debated today. It was a small comfort to me that the *Edmund Fitzgerald* went down out on the big lake, a long way from land. I reassured myself that we are always within sight of one of the islands or the mainland when we take our boat out on Lake Superior.

However, the reassurance I drew from that fact began to diminish when Steve was a grade-schooler and became fascinated with shipwrecks. On our annual summer vacations to Madeline Island we stopped at area bookstores so he could search out books about shipwrecks on the Great Lakes. The first volume he discovered was *Ghost Ships, Gales and Forgotten Tales: True Adventures on the Great Lakes* by Wes Oleszewski. It was soon joined by *Ice Water Museum: Forgotten Great Lakes Shipwrecks* by the same author and *The 100 Best Great Lakes Shipwrecks, Volumes I and II* by Chris Kohl. He eagerly relayed the stories of these shipwrecks to the rest of us, and I soon learned that many of them took place close to land. When Steve found *The "Unholy" Apostles: Shipwreck Tales of the Apostle Islands* by James Keller, I had to forfeit all notions that I was safe on our boating trips among the Apostles. Steve read the *Unholy* book from cover to cover and on family boat trips he became our resident expert and guide to shipwreck sites in the area.

* * * * *

One summer afternoon we were all peering over the edge of our sixteen-foot Smokercraft into the crystal clear water, attempting to distinguish the outlines of old timbers or pieces of steel on the lake floor twenty feet below us. We were within sight of Sand Island, trying to see the remains of the steamer *Sevona*.

"Over there. I think I see something." There was high excitement in eleven-year-old Steve's voice as he pointed to a spot five feet in front of the bow.

Bob moved close to where Steve was standing. "Looks like a rock to me," he said to his younger brother in a voice seasoned with sarcasm.

Steve ignored this remark. "Well, this is where the *Sevona* sank in a huge gale on September 2, 1905. The ship was 373 feet long; it was trying to seek shelter on Sand Island, but instead it hit these shoals."

"September?" I said. "I thought the big storms on Superior were usually in November."

Steve nodded. "That's true. I guess this one came early."

Poof. There went another of my reassurances. I had told myself that we would never have to face any of Superior's big, ship-wrecking storms. They always happened in November, long after we had taken our boat out of the water for the season.

Glancing toward the brownstone lighthouse in the distance, Doug asked, "Did the lighthouse keeper notice that the *Sevona* was in distress?"

"Yup," Steve puffed out his chest a bit, looking pleased to be able to tell us the story. "Emmanuel Lueck was the name of the lighthouse keeper. He could see the ship through his binoculars, but he couldn't do anything to help. He had no radio, no signal. Nothing but a rowboat. He saw the *Sevona* hit the shoals. Then it split in two. Some of the sailors made it to shore in lifeboats. But the keeper watched the captain and six others get killed. The high waves tore up their life raft."

Steve went on to tell us that this was not the only shipwreck caused by that fierce storm. On the same day John Irvine, the lighthouse keeper on Outer Island, watched as the *Pretoria*, loaded with ore and riding dangerously low, began to sink. Ten men got into a lifeboat, but it took on water and began to flounder. As Irvine hurried down to the shore, five of the men aboard managed to cling to the sunken lifeboat. The waves catapulted the boat ashore and then threatened to sweep it and the men back out into the churning lake. Irvine reached into the furious waves, grabbed hold of the boat and didn't let go. Because of his courage all five men survived.

Steve's stories reinforced how important the lighthouses and their brave keepers were and still are to boaters in the Apostle Islands.

Listening to those shipwreck stories brought back memories of our family's first trip around Madeline Island with waves pouring over the sides of our small boat. When we traded in our sixteen-foot Smokercraft for a twenty-four foot boat, I felt much more secure.

* * * * *

On an overcast September morning we loaded a picnic basket and four friends into our new boat for a trip to Stockton Island. Despite the drizzle, we enjoyed a hike along the mile-long beach at Julian Bay which is famous for its "singing sands." We laughed when our shoes squeaked as they landed on the rounded quartz sand grains. As we prepared for our trip back to Madeline, the winds were calm and the weather radio predicted stable conditions for the rest of the afternoon. The trip was uneventful until we were less than a mile away from La Pointe. Suddenly, without warning, we saw a ten-foot-high wall of water approaching. Out of nowhere a squall had sprung up, and we were headed straight into it. There was nothing to do but try to ride it out. Our new boat, which had seemed such an improvement over our small Smokercraft, struggled against the six-foot waves. Doug turned the boat away from our destination so that we could run with the storm. The waves continued to pour over the boat, making it all but impossible to see through the windshield.

"I hate to do this, but I'm going to have to unzip the isinglass curtain that's keeping us dry. Otherwise I can't see where we were going," Doug warned us.

I glanced at Roger. He looked worried. "What time is it?" he asked.

Mary checked her watch. She stiffened. "Five-thirty."

I knew why Roger was asking.

Doug knew too. "I think we'd better turn around and head back into the storm while we still have enough light to see," he said in a strained voice.

As Doug began to turn the boat, the waves slammed against it. He held onto the wheel so tightly that his knuckles protruded in sharp white lines. We all watched nervously as water cascaded over the starboard side of the boat.

"Pat, you'd better get out the life jackets." Doug said. He spoke in an even tone, but his brow was etched with fear.

The look on his face made my heart pound faster. Up until now I had been concerned about the squall, but not really afraid. I had been counting on Doug's ability to handle the boat and get us through the storm. But now if *he* was afraid, I was downright terrified.

Without a word I scrambled to the back of the boat, slid the cushion off the seat and reached inside. Solemnly we all donned the bright yellow jackets. Somehow, with waves crashing into the windshield and water streaming through the isinglass, Doug guided our boat and its six drenched occupants back to the marina and safety.

Days later, I was able to think about this experience with a clearer head. Though I have been a city person all my life, during our stays at Madeline I was learning the joys of being close to nature. But as I relived our recent encounter with the sudden squall, an involuntary shiver ran through my body. I realized that sometimes in a boat or on the ice road there is no margin for error. If you make a mistake out on the big lake, it could kill you.

Why, I wondered, do human beings choose to live on the shores of huge, unruly bodies of water where in a split second you may find yourself face to face with a life or death situation? Why would year-round residents of Madeline choose to live on the edge of this unpredictable inland sea? Why do I choose to live there part time?

There is no doubt that Lake Superior sculpts the lives of those who live on Madeline Island. Surrounded by water, cut off from the mainland by two-and-a-half liquid miles, islanders rise to meet the challenge by building ferries, windsleds, and ice roads to maintain their connection with the rest of civilization. But they have learned that the big lake sometimes takes umbrage at human attempts to control the environment. Superior can whip up waves that render watercraft useless and destroy highways built on ice. Humans are left to salve their wounds and wait till the lake chooses to calm itself and let them pass freely again. A retired commercial fisherman, Julian Nelson, summed it up when he said, "The Lake is the boss. Make no mistake, the Lake is the boss."

Extreme geography seems to attract people. Simon Winchester writes about this phenomenon in *A Crack at the End of the World*, the story of the 1906 San Francisco earthquake. He says that humans often build their homes in beautiful but dangerous places. As he points out, natural beauty frequently goes hand in hand with risk. If people want to live somewhere absolutely geologically stable, he suggests they move to Kansas or Nebraska. Instead, many people choose dramatic beauty, even if it is accompanied by the potential for danger.

We too had chosen to build our house on Madeline in a beautiful but dangerous place. We perched our house on the edge of a high bank, facing northwest, looking straight into the path of the strongest storms that sweep across Lake Superior.

Ah, but the beauty. From the moment we unlock the door at the beginning of our visits until we reluctantly leave, we are drawn to the lake. We never tire of our view of Superior and its many moods—one minute smooth and serene, the next stirred up into roiling, agitated waves.

But simply looking at the lake is not enough for us. Refusing to watch from afar, we want to open ourselves to the full experience of the lake. Inevitably we find our way down the steep bank, clamber aboard our boat and confront the power of Lake Superior head on.

* * * * *

Simon Winchester's comments reminded me of the conversation we had as we traveled through Austria with our friends Alex and Volker, both native Austrians. "The mountain can kill you if you don't know what you're doing," Alex said from the front seat of the van. He paused, turned in his seat so he was facing Doug and me, then added, "but if you're careful, it's not a difficult climb."

We were driving on the road the guidebook described as the "most splendid alpine highway in Europe," the Grossglockner Road. Earlier that morning when we left the valley below, the highway before us slithered up the side of the mountain like a long garter snake. The hikers mounting the slopes above us were insignificant black specks scattered like freckles across the brilliant white face of the mountain. Now it was almost noon and the sinuous highway had transported us to a panoramic point where we stopped to view Austria's highest peak, the Grossglockner. As we got out of the car, we saw that the specks had metamorphosed into climbers garbed in brightly colored clothing. Despite our sunglasses, as we gazed toward the highest peak we had to shield our eyes from the over-powering whiteness. For a few moments we stood in silence, awed by the view.

Then the mountain climbing stories began.

When they were young, Alex and Volker had learned the art of scaling mountain peaks from their fathers. They described the thrill of climbing the Grossglockner. But it was evident that what was vital was to have successfully reached the summit of the mountain. That was the big achievement. It was a rite of passage, an accomplishment worthy of their Austrian heritage. Volker shared some of his hard-earned wisdom. "It didn't take me long to learn that when you're climbing as a group, you're only as strong as your weakest link."

Alex chimed in, "That's true. There are always some idiots up there who don't know what they're doing and they can cause problems—even death —for the other climbers." Early on Alex and Volker had learned not only the joys of climbing but also respect for the mountain and the knowledge needed to climb it successfully.

When nature provides mountains, lakes or forests, people learn the potential risks as well as the pleasures that accompany such terrain. Inevitably people respond to the invitations presented by nature. Mountains dare people to scale their heights, lakes beg to be mastered, forests to be explored. Human beings long to conquer the challenges posed by dramatic geographical features.

*****

Back on Madeline, Gene had talked many times about the risks he was willing to take in order to live on the island. But one story in particular stood out. As Doug and I sat at a table with him at Bell Street Tavern, Gene described a November trip several years back when he had taken his boat from La Pointe over to Bayfield. When it was time to return home, Gene headed out into a fierce storm.

"The waves were over ten feet high. As high as this ceiling," he pointed. I tilted my head back. From this perspective, ten feet seemed very high indeed. I felt tiny as I looked up and imagined ceiling-high waves coming toward me.

Gene continued, "When I finally got back to La Pointe, there was blue water over the top of the dock."

"Blue water? What is that?" I asked.

"It means that the water flows over the dock instead of breaking over it. The wind is so strong that it pushes the water to one side of the lake and raises the water level. Instead of waves breaking, the water rises."

My eyes widened at the very thought of it. "Oh," was all that I could manage in response. Then after a minute I asked, "Weren't you scared?"

"No," Gene grinned. "That was back in the days when I was invincible."

His smile faded, and he was silent for several moments as he stared into his empty glass. Then he looked up. "I'm not afraid of the lake." He paused, then added, "I respect it."

There it was. That is what separated me from islanders. They had gained hard-earned knowledge through their own experience with nature as well as through the lore passed down from previous generations. This understanding gave them great respect for nature, and it also helped mitigate their fear. I had the fear, but I lacked their erudition.

I wondered, do islanders feel humbled in the face of nature? Gene's comments seemed to suggest that they do. Or does nature make them more determined to prevail? Perhaps both are true. As I watched the expression on Gene's face when he told his story, I saw the same combination of bravery and humility that I had witnessed in the faces of Alex and Volker as they described reaching the summit of the mountain. In Austria it is the power and beauty of the Grossglockner; on Madeline Island it is the allure of Lake Superior. Both mountain peaks and inland seas tempt humans to conquer their majesty. Both offer rewards for those who dare to take life-giving risks. And, to my surprise, I realized that I was becoming one of those people.

Life on Madeline Island had begun to have its effect on me. I was still by nature a timid soul and the echoes of my father's "be careful" still pulsed through my veins. But I was learning the rewards that could be mine if I accepted the invitation to take a risk, to step outside my cocoon of comfort.

Now I knew the thrill of being fully alive and the sense of accomplishment that accompanied me when I drove across the ice road, or stepped into the windsled, or dared to stay still and watchful in the presence of wild creatures, or rode out a Lake Superior storm in our boat. Now that I had begun to accept invitations to take life-giving risks, I was not about to turn back.

UNINVITED GUEST

"Doug, help!"

Standing at the kitchen sink I heard a loud whoosh followed by the sound of rushing water, lots of rushing water. I rounded the corner just in time to see water cascading down the side of the washing machine and spreading across the hallway floor. Doug came running, took one look at the flooded floor and reached in back of the washing machine to turn off the water valve. He tinkered with the machine while I mopped the floor.

"We have another problem with this machine!" Doug said. "This time a fitting broke. Better call Gene. He'll be able to fix it." Within minutes of our call, Gene was there. He discovered the source of the problem, promised to order a part, and had repaired the washer by the next time we came to the island.

Emergencies brought out the best in Gene. He was good at handling a crisis and enjoyed being a hero. As I had guessed back when we first met him, the houses Gene built were like his children, and he was quick to answer calls of distress from the owners. And besides, I think he disliked the idea of someone else making a mess of his workmanship.

Gene's repair skills were not limited to washing machines. He could repair almost anything—including furnaces. When the temperature in our house falls below fifty degrees, the security system is alerted and the caretaker is called. Our furnace quit twice in the middle of winter, and Gene, our caretaker, received the calls. Both times he immediately went to the house, assessed the problem, and crafted a temporary repair until he could purchase the part needed for a permanent remedy.

We felt fortunate to have a resourceful repairman so close at hand, and we knew how difficult it could be to find someone from the mainland who was willing to come to the island to fix an appliance or a furnace. "We don't do repair work on the island" was a common response to an inquiry about service. If the repairman was willing to travel to the island, it could be a week or two before he was able to fit the job, and the ferry rides it required into his schedule.

Perhaps Gene's ability to deal with homeowners' emergencies was a trait he learned from the man who taught him construction skills: his uncle, Elmer Nelson. Though Elmer did not build the cabin owned by Paul and Roberta White, he was the one they called in emergencies. Their son, Mike, a friend of mine, told me this story from the White's family history:

One Sunday afternoon a crack developed in the bowl of the toilet at the White's house. Water began to pour across the bathroom floor. Paul turned off the water and called the man who repaired everything for them, Elmer Nelson.

As he was kneeling in front of the toilet, preparing to fix it, Elmer turned toward Paul and Roberta who were standing in the bathroom doorway, "God put me on this island just for people like you."

Gene might have uttered a similar statement to me one afternoon in December. Doug was at home in Minneapolis, and I had invited three of my friends to our house for a weekend visit. We had enjoyed Christmas shopping in Bayfield and evening conversations in front of the fire. On Sunday afternoon we were packing the car to leave when I heard a strange noise in the sunroom. As I entered the room I was greeted by the shrill cry of a red squirrel who sat on the fireplace mantle, loudly scolding me for invading his territory. I screamed, backed out of the room, and slammed the door, trapping the squirrel in the room.

"What are we going to do?" I shrieked to my three friends who had hurried over to the door of the sunroom when they heard my screams. Terry and Karen, who were braver than Mary Ellen and me, grabbed brooms, went into the sunroom, and opened the door leading out to the front deck. They swatted at the squirrel and tried to sweep him out the door, but the frightened squirrel ran behind the couch as he scolded them in his high-pitched voice.

I knew there were only two hours until the last ferry of the day, and I also knew we couldn't leave with the squirrel in the house. There was only one person I could think to call: Gene.

I don't know what he thought when he heard my hysterical voice at the other end of the phone asking if he would please help us get a squirrel out of the house. All I know is that he immediately agreed to come, despite the fact that he was watching the fourth quarter of the Packer game. In addition, he was taking care of his one-year-old son and would have to find a babysitter before he could leave.

Within thirty minutes Gene was at our house, a rifle slung over his shoulder. He quickly assessed the situation, grabbed a broom and started swatting at the squirrel. The squirrel took a twelve-foot flying leap from the mantle to the other side of the room where he clung to the window ledge. Gene was behind him in an instant, and, with one stroke of the broom, he sent the squirrel flying out the door and onto the deck. Gene dropped the broom, grabbed his rifle, and took off into the woods chasing the squirrel. He returned several minutes later empty handed. Despite the uproar the squirrel had caused, my friends and I were secretly relived to hear that he was still alive.

Gene grinned from ear to ear as my three friends and I thanked him profusely for coming to our rescue. Then, ever the island naturalist, he began to educate us about red squirrels. "They are very territorial, you know. Each male squirrel stakes out his own territory and defends it. I'm sure your squirrel thought it was really nice of you to build this house for him. How do you think he got in anyway?"

"That's what we've been trying to figure out. We didn't leave the door open or anything," I answered.

Gene looked thoughtful. He surveyed the sunroom and then went outside and scanned the front of the house. I watched as he scrutinized the roof overhang where six canister lights dangled by their electrical cords from the soffit. We had moved into the house the previous spring. For months Gene had been promising to come over and finish installing the soffit lights. When he noticed me looking up at the lights, Gene grinned sheepishly.

"Hmm. I wonder if the squirrel got into the soffit through the openings for the lights and then found his way down to the joint between the wall and the chimney. There's room there for him to crawl through. I've been meaning to caulk that opening. I'll be over next week to do the caulking and take care of those lights."

True to his word, by the time Doug and I returned the next weekend, the lights had been installed and the caulking as well as several other odds and ends had been completed. As we looked around the house, amazed at all Gene had accomplished in a few days, I turned to Doug, "If I had known that's what it would take, I would have invited that squirrel into the house months ago."

ISLAND CONTROVERSIES

Arguments were a rare occurrence in my family. In fact, I can count on one hand the number of times I heard my parents raise their voices with each other. Of course my sister, Penny, and I had the usual sibling spats, but even we managed to tolerate each other fairly well. Consequently when I observed noisy outbursts in other families, I assumed the worst: Parents would divorce and family members would never speak to each other again. I had no experience with this type of conflict.

I do remember heated conversations about politics when Pop, my grandfather, and Florence, my great-aunt, joined us for Sunday dinners. But at an early age I realized that everyone at the table was on the same side. Since former Presidents Roosevelt and Truman, the main targets of my family's political ire, were not invited and neither were any of their supporters, I knew I was only hearing half the story. I'm sure my family had no idea what effect these discussions would have on me. In order to learn the other side of the argument I had no choice but to become a Democrat.

My background didn't prepare me for the impassioned disagreements I observed between Madeline Islanders. I was somewhat taken aback but also very curious when I witnessed their fiery exchanges. I soon learned that conflict is a participatory sport for many residents of Madeline Island and a spectator sport for the rest. Maybe conflict is inevitable among islanders because they live in close geographical quarters and exhibit a hearty, sometimes even fierce individualism. I've come to the conclusion that many of the residents of Madeline Island take pride in their skill at disagreeing with one another.

Doug and I heard a number of heated disputes about controversial topics at Bell Street Tavern. The bar was often a venue for earnest discussions of politics, both national and local. And when we began to subscribe to the town paper, we found that it provided another forum for debate. A glance at the minutes of Town Board Meetings and committees such as ZAP (the Zoning and Planning Committee) and CAP (the Community and Public Works Planning Committee) which are published in the island newspaper, gives plenty of evidence of the contentious arguments that are a common occurrence.

A proposed bike trail was a hot topic one night at Bell Street Tavern. A guy at the end of the bar opened the discussion. "Why do we need a bike trail anyway? It's just for the tourists. They're the only ones riding bicycles on our roads."

Mid-bar, a younger man clad in Carhartts nodded his head in agreement. "Yeah, it's the tourists on the roads all right. It takes me twice as long in the summer to drive to the dump because they're pedaling three in a row along Big Bay Road. We've got to do something about that."

"Could snowmobiles use the bike trail?" asked a woman seated next to the Carhartt man. "If they could, I'd support it."

"Not from what I've heard," said an older man in a faded Packer sweatshirt. "They're saying that snowmobiles would rip up the path."

"So the trail would be mostly for the tourists, no snowmobiles would be allowed on it, and the town would have to pay for part of it? Forget it!" This was the final statement from the end-of-the-bar guy who started the conversation.

Doug and I supported the idea of a bike trail. We regularly used the trails in the Twin Cites, and we had also biked on Madeline Island. But it was not very relaxing to ride on the narrow island roads with cars whooshing right next to us.

Mentally I was formulating comebacks to many of the arguments I heard that night at Bell Street: *Hey! Your livelihood depends on the tourists. Put a trail through the woods, and then bikers won't slow you down on the roads.* But being conflict avoidant, I was not about to utter any of these statements out loud. I got knots in my stomach just thinking about speaking up. I certainly didn't want to be the focus of attention and have to take on most of the patrons at the bar. So I kept my mouth closed and listened to the discussion. For weeks, conversations like the one we heard at Bell Street were repeated wherever people gathered on the island.

Aware of the strong feelings about the bike trail, the town board wisely called a special town meeting to discuss the issue. At stake was a $624,000 federal grant awarded to the town. As far as many islanders were concerned, the main problem with the grant was that it would necessitate spending $115,600 of local money.

A packed house of year-round residents attended the meeting. As soon as the chairman called the assembled citizens to order, a tall, forty-ish man wearing a Harley T-shirt and a full beard stood up. "I move that we scrap the whole idea of a bike trail. For at least five years."

"I second that," called out a younger man from the other side of the room.

The town chairman got to his feet. Looking unruffled, he said, "The floor is open for discussion of the motion. I suggest we begin with a presentation of the facts of the project."

His words had a calming effect, and people settled back into their chairs. An hour later a new motion was made to scratch the plan for the proposed bike trail through the woods and instead work with the county board to design a trail alongside one of the main roads on the island. After a short discussion, the crowd voted unanimously to accept this motion. Doug and I were impressed by the lively community debate about this issue. It seemed as though this was democracy at work as the framers of the Constitution intended it.

Ultimately the people of Madeline Island were heard, and the shoulders of County Road H were widened to accommodate a bike lane. To me this seemed a partial solution at best. As a bike rider, it put me only a few more feet out of harm's way. I would definitely have preferred the woods. But the decision had been made, and the discussion at Bell Street moved on to other controversies.

It was not long before the debate focused on a new topic: the proposed noise ordinance. Residents of downtown La Pointe had complained for years about what they called the "excessive noise" late into the summer nights caused mostly by outside live music. The chief source of much of this noise was the open-air tent bar, Tom's Burned Down Café. Walking around La Pointe on a summer evening, Doug and I had noticed that the music at Tom's permeated the small downtown area. I enjoyed most of the bands and never considered their music a problem, but I could imagine that the people who lived close by and heard it every night into the wee hours might have a different opinion.

In order to address the noise issue, the town board purchased a decibel meter, trained officers of the police department to use the machine, and took readings at various locations, day and night, in order to determine the normal ambient sound levels. They also measured the sound levels that were the cause of some of the complaints. Using the data they collected, the town board drew up a detailed noise ordinance that was passed on February 12, 2002. From what we could gather, most patrons at the bar at Bell Street Tavern didn't think the noise in town was excessive and therefore felt the noise ordinance was unnecessary.

The conversations we heard at the bar were a preview of those that took place at the town meeting in April 2002. The island's annual town meetings are patterned after those held in the early settlements in New England, and they allow citizens to make their views known on topics related to town governance.

According to *The Island Gazette,* a "record breaking, standing-room-only" crowd attended the Annual Town Meeting on April 9, 2002. Most people attended to voice their disapproval of the noise ordinance passed two months before. The official minutes of the meeting recorded some of the comments voiced that night:

> "I've got a list here of all the ambiguities in the Noise Ordinance and there are a lot of them! I don't think we should have an ordinance that isn't clear." (This statement was a bit self-serving considering that the source was Tom Nelson, owner of Tom's Burned Down Café, the acknowledged origin of much of the "excessive noise.")

Other people had somewhat different perspectives.

> "There are such things as *walls* that lower decibel ratings."

> "La Pointe is a resort town. People come here to have fun and fun is noisy."

> "Should we really support an ordinance that outlaws other important island events? According to the ordinance, the library 'Jazz Night' fundraiser would be illegal."

At the end of the discussion a motion was made and passed to repeal and rewrite the noise ordinance. The town clerk recorded the vote while reminding the assembled crowd that their motion was advisory only and that it would take a two-thirds majority of the town board to officially repeal the ordinance.

The town chairman described his reaction to the meeting in his column in the *Gazette.* "This was the first town meeting that I chaired. As soon as it started I realized that I hadn't dressed properly —I should have worn my son's ice hockey goalie equipment."

Though recent island disagreements certainly generate plenty of heat, there are some historical precedents for these modern-day conflicts. In fact, current controversies pale in comparison to several from the past. One of these disputes lasted for over ten years. It arose from the competition between two ferry lines for passengers traveling between La Pointe and Bayfield. One company was owned by Harry Nelson and the other by Howard Russell who, as it happens, were related. In the spring of 1966 the *Duluth News Tribune* reported on this feud:

> Battling bow to bow, the "Nichevo II," piloted by Captain Harry Nelson, and "Gar-How II," piloted by Captain Howard Russell, raced to be the first to make the spring crossing to Bayfield. Asked about what old-timers call a bitter rivalry, Nelson says, "There's not a lot to do up here, and they've got to have something to talk about. . . . Of course I haven't talked to Russell for ten years and he hasn't talked to me, But you can't make much of that. He hasn't said a bad word about me."

My friend, Mike White, whose family spent summers on Madeline during those years, explained that the battle between the ferry companies affected the general public as well. People who were regular passengers on the boats had to choose which ferry line they would support. Once you declared your allegiance to one of the ferry companies, you dared not set foot on the boats run by the rival company. I don't know if you would have been ordered off the boat if you dared defy the rules, but I was certainly glad that I didn't have to confront this situation.

The fierce competition ended in 1970 when William P. O'Brien, an attorney residing on the island, mediated an agreement between Nelson's Nichevo Ferry Line and Russell's Apostle Island Ferry Service to form the Madeline Island Ferry Line, the ferry service that is still in operation today

Probably the mother of all conflicts between islanders culminated in the fight between William Wilson and Judge John Bell on Madeline Island in October of 1847. Both men were larger-than-life characters. Wilson was a celebrated and rugged woodsman who lived in La Pointe. Bell at one time or another held almost every office in La Pointe and was known as "King John." Bell and Wilson had been feuding for years. Things came to a head one day when Wilson threatened to kick Bell's dog. They set a date to fight, agreeing that the loser would leave Madeline Island forever. Bell knocked Wilson out cold, so Wilson took all his worldly possessions and paddled across Lake Superior to an uninhabited island. There he built a cabin and lived out the rest of his years alone on what came to be known as Wilson's or Hermit Island, one of the Apostle Islands. In the end, however, Wilson prevailed over Bell. He died in 1861 and was buried in an unmarked grave in the old mission cemetery on Madeline Island.

Has my immersion course in island conflict had an impact on me? Yes and no. Witnessing some of the impassioned debates on Madeline has made me more comfortable in the midst of a fiery exchange. I'm now more apt to see an argument as an honest exchange of differing opinions rather than the beginning of World War III. In fact, for a time in my professional life, I worked with divorcing couples, serving as a mediator for child custody disputes. Often this required the ability to maintain Gandhi-like calm in the face of a paroxysm of frenzied verbal fireworks.

But I guess my early upbringing still prevails. Because when I hear those contentious debates at Bell Street, I'm still more apt to be a spectator than a participant.

ISLAND GENEROSITY

Late in the afternoon on a gray November Saturday, Bob and I decided to go into town. Our family had been spending the long Thanksgiving weekend at our house on Madeline Island, and we were tired of watching football.

We wandered into the Dockside gift shop that sat adjacent to the ferry dock in La Pointe. We were the only customers, and Henry Goodman, one of the proprietors, was in a talkative mood. Henry, a man in his early 70s, had a wide smile and an easy way with people. Somehow we got onto the topic of the ice road, and Henry launched into a series of stories. He told these tales as all good storytellers do, with relish, enjoying the effect they had on a new audience. Bob and I were still relative newcomers, and we had not heard any of these anecdotes before.

There is one story in particular that I have often repeated because it captures the spirit of the island so well.

Henry's tone of voice shifted and he became more serious as he began this narrative. "One day in February, I don't remember the year, it was sunny and mild, and lots of people decided to drive over the ice to Bayfield and Ashland and Duluth. Then, all of a sudden, just before nightfall, the weather changed. Out of nowhere, a terrible blizzard came up. On the ice road you couldn't see a thing. It was a white out."

Henry gazed out the window at the lake, remembering.

"In the midst of the snowstorm all those people who had left for the day tried to get back to the island. What a mess! Here on the shore we could see headlights going every which way. Cars were heading off in all the wrong directions. Some of the islanders decided to go out on the ice and try to guide the lost cars back to shore. People helped folks they normally weren't even speaking to."

Henry paused and shook his head slowly back and forth. Then he said softly, "Lots of lives got saved that night."

Bob and I were quiet for several minutes, imagining the events of that day. "After the rescue, what happened with the people who hadn't been speaking to each other?" I asked.

I was hoping for a happy ending to that part of the story too.

"The next day they just went right back to giving each other the cold shoulder," Henry said with a grin.

Several years have passed since Henry told this story on that gray November day. I'm not so new to the island and its people any more. I've had time to reflect on his narrative, and I've come to believe that it reveals several prominent traits of Madeline islanders—their penchant for feuding as well as their generosity and compassion for those who need help. Despite their ornery individualism, there is a strong sense of community among residents. They are loyal to one another. Even sworn enemies will readily help each other in times of need. The same sense of geographical separateness that forces people to be self-reliant also encourages them to depend on each other.

When there is trouble they have no one to turn to but each other. Madeline Island has a volunteer fire department and a crew of EMTs. If you have a heart attack or your home is on fire, it will be a friend, a neighbor, another islander who comes to your aid. The *Gazette* regularly publishes letters of thanks to the fire crew or EMTs who have saved lives or homes.

The need to rely on one another in emergencies is heightened by the geographic isolation. When a fire is so large that it is difficult for the Madeline Island firefighters to control, they may have to call neighboring fire departments for assistance. That aid is always a boat ride away, however, and the ferry service must be notified that a special run is needed. The same is true for a medical emergency that requires more intervention than the EMTs are able to provide.

We have heard many stories of islanders helping not only each other but also strangers in times of need.

This short article appeared in the January 20, 2004, issue of the *Gazette* under the heading "Thank You From Lorraine:"

> I'd like to thank the good Samaritan who pulled my little red truck from the brink of my ravine on Thursday the 15th while I was in Ashland for a stress test. As of yet I haven't heard who it was so. Thank you, thank you, thank you.

In the same issue a first-time visitor to the island writes of her appreciation for the kindness extended to her. A portion of her letter reads:

> On Friday we took the ferry out to Madeline Island. We drove halfway around the sparsely populated island, way out to Big Bay on the northern tip of the island. After we had stopped for a garage sale, we got back in the car to find that the starter had gone out. From here on, the entire day should have been a disaster. Our well-being was totally in the hands of strangers, but what kind hands they turned out to be! . . . The quality of these people will bring me back again and again; . . . I will remember [them] on winter nights. They restored my faith in the goodness of strangers.

In her letter, this visitor names one person as being particularly helpful that day—Lorraine Motisi. Is it the same Lorraine who owned the little red truck and wrote the first letter? I don't know, but I hope so. I'd like to believe that in a short span of time one kindness engendered another and linked these strangers with gratitude.

Doug and I have also been recipients of Madeline generosity. One Sunday afternoon we stopped at the marina to check on our boat. When we climbed back into our car, Doug put the key in the ignition, turned it, and nothing happened.

"What's wrong with this thing?" I asked.

"Nothing, as far as I know," Doug said.

He tried turning the key several more times. Still no response.

After making a number of unrepeatable statements about the car, Doug said, "We're probably going to have to get this blasted thing towed off the island to the dealer in Ashland to get it fixed."

"Well that will take care of the car, but what about us? How are we going to get back to Minneapolis? We both have to work tomorrow."

We decided to walk the eight blocks to Bell Street Tavern to make a couple of phone calls. Ron Schulz, the same young man we met after our first tree planting weekend, was tending bar that day. I started to explain. "Our car broke down over near the marina, and we'd like to use the phone to call Gene. We're hoping he has a car we can borrow to drive to Ashland so we can rent a car there."

"Sure, you can use the phone," said Ron. "But just hang on a couple of minutes. I'll be right back." During the short time he was gone, the patrons at the bar sympathized with our predicament.

"Hey, good news!" Ron said as he returned to the bar. "You can use my parents' car; it's just sitting in their garage up here. I called them down in Florida, and they said it would be fine. You can drive it home and return it in a couple of weeks when you come back."

"Oh, we can't do that," I protested. I was not used to such kindness from people I hardly knew.

"Sure you can," said Ron. "Lots of people up here have helped me out. Now it's my turn."

Over our continued protestations, a man at the end of the bar spoke up. "Go ahead. Let him help you. That's the way we do things up here on the island. And that's one of the main reasons I live here."

FISHERMAN

Something was amiss. As Doug and I were driving down North Shore Road on a frigid January afternoon, we noticed a man striding down the middle of the road. He was wearing a snowmobile suit, carrying his helmet. But there was no snowmobile in sight.

"Should we stop and ask if he needs a ride?" Doug asked.

"Sure. I wonder if he's had some kind of mishap," I responded.

If we had been at home in Minneapolis and encountered an unfamiliar person walking along the road, I doubt that we would have stopped to see if he needed assistance. But this was different. This was Madeline. Here on the island people did not fear strangers, they helped them.

Doug opened his window. "Want a lift?" he asked. The young man had tousled brown hair and cheeks reddened from exertion.

"Thanks, I sure could use a ride to town, if you're going that direction," he said.

Once settled into the back seat of our car, he explained his predicament. "I was over near Stockton Island, getting ready to check my nets, when I hit a patch of thin ice and my snowmobile went in. I managed to get off before it sank."

"Wow! And you walked all the way back to Madeline?" I asked.

"Yup. I got over to the island and then hiked along the shore till I found a spot on the bank where I could climb up."

"That's quite a distance!" Doug said.

He nodded. "It's about four miles from Stockton to Madeline and then another two to three miles along Madeline's shore."

"Didn't you run into thin ice anywhere on your trek?" I asked.

"Not till I got close to Madeline. Along the shore the ice was pretty rotten in places so I gave those spots a wide berth."

"Too bad about your snowmobile," Doug said.

196 | On Island Time

"I think it'll turn out ok. I know the spot where it went down. I'll get some friends to help me retrieve it tomorrow or the next day."

"You mentioned checking your nets," I said. "Fishing nets?"

"Yup, that's right. I'm a commercial fisherman from Bayfield. My family's been in this line of work for three generations. I went out on the lake to check my nets for whitefish and lake trout."

After we dropped him off at Bell Street Tavern, where he said he could find someone to give him a ride over the ice road to Bayfield, we realized we had never learned his name. That mystery was solved in the next issue of the *Island Gazette* which featured an article about the man we had christened "our fisherman." We learned that Craig Hoopman's snowmobile sank in 207 feet of water and had not been retrieved.

Several winters later, we had a ring-side seat for a performance by commercial fishermen. They had set their nets on the ice about 300 feet from shore directly in front of our house. We peered through our binoculars and watched with fascination as they arrived on four-wheelers and began the task of pulling up their nets. One man attached a rope to the end of the net that protruded from a hole in the ice. Then he climbed on his ATV and drove slowly across the ice as he drew the net up to the surface. The second man removed the fish as the net came up through the hole. One by one he tossed the day's catch into a huge bucket.

The final scene was enacted by a bald eagle. Just moments after the fishermen climbed astride their four-wheelers for the trip back to Bayfield, the eagle swooped down and gobbled up the remnants of the catch left behind on the ice. Then, for a long time, he sat on guard beside the open hole as if waiting for dessert.

* * * * *

I had seen John Hagen's photo in a book about Madeline families. He stood on the wooden dock, pipe in his mustachioed mouth and a solemn look on his face as he held a huge fish by the gills. Born in Finland in 1881, he came to the United States at the age of two. By the time he was fifteen his career as a commercial fisherman had begun. Before long, he and his younger brother, William, operated a thriving commercial fishing business on the south side of the island at Hagen's Cove. I learned about these two fishermen from William's grandson, our contractor, Gene Nelson.

In the early years, William and John lifted their nets by hand from depths of 150 feet or more. Many of the fishermen of that day used gill nets, long strings of netting which were suspended like curtains in the water. Schools of fish swam into the almost invisible nets. Smaller fish slipped right through, but the gills of larger fish became entangled in the netting. Because the early gill nets were made of cotton or linen, they would rot if left in the lake too long. Huge wooden net reels sat on the bank at Hagen's Cove. Here the brothers wound their nets on the reels to dry in the sun. If they weren't careful as they performed this task, they would have to spend hours untangling the net. The brothers took good care of their nets in other ways too; they owned at least twenty cats that prevented mice from chewing up the nets.

The Hagen brothers fished during the 1940s and 1950s when commercial fishing in the Apostles was in its heyday. Lake trout and herring were the big catches, and the Hagens netted as much as twenty-one tons of herring in one day and twenty-five tons of lake trout in a good season.

Fish camps dotted the shores of several of the Apostle Islands during this time; many had been there since the late nineteenth century. Starting in 1888, Booth Fisheries used Rocky Island as its base, supplying Lake Superior whitefish and lake trout to customers in St. Paul, Milwaukee, and Chicago. South Twin and Rocky Islands as well as Little Sand Bay on the mainland were sites of other fishing operations.

* * * * *

Our little boat headed toward Manitou Island. At first the only thing Doug and I could see as we approached the shore was the wooden dock. Slowly the outlines of several small wooden buildings appeared. A haphazard collection of rough buildings clings to a narrow strip of flat land in front of the dense hardwood and coniferous forest which covers Manitou Island. These are the remnants of a fish camp, preserved by the National Park Service so that twenty-first century visitors can imagine what life was like in the camps many years ago.

As we tied up our boat, a sturdy man with bronze weathered skin and bushy white eyebrows approached and offered to give us a tour. A retired Ojibway fisherman from Red Cliff, he had been a regular at this fish camp for many years. Now he worked for the National Park Service.

Beginning in the early 1900s, this assortment of weathered buildings served as a poor man's fishing camp. Like our guide, most of the men who stayed here were not permanent residents. Instead they often were looking for a place with stable, thick ice for winter fishing. Artifacts in the main cabin gave a glimpse of daily life at the camp. A pair of long underwear was hanging on the wall next to a cast iron frying pan and a black, six-foot long, snaggletoothed saw, used to cut holes in the ice.

In recent years Manitou Island has been the site of several archeological digs. Thousands of fish bones were discovered in prehistoric sites, evidence that people have fished the waters around the Apostle Islands for centuries.

But the size of the catches has been dwindling in the last fifty years. Over-fishing is one reason for the decline of the Lake Superior fishing trade; the other is a nasty-looking serpentine fish, the sea-lamprey. This parasite first arrived in Lake Superior after the Great Lakes were opened to ocean traffic and ocean predators. Sidling up to native fish with its toothy suction-cup mouth, the lamprey eventually decimated Superior's lake trout population. Today less than a dozen commercial fishing boats ply the waters among the Apostle Islands.

I'm glad there are at least a few left. Sometimes when I'm busy in a back room of our Madeline house, I hear the distinctive guttural chug, chug, chug of a fishing boat engine. I drop what I am doing, grab the binoculars off the kitchen counter, and station myself on the front deck to see the fishing boat go by. It moves slowly, so I have plenty of time to watch it make its way regally down the channel in front of our house. Low to the water, the wooden hull is painted white with a single red stripe punctuating its plain exterior. Trailing the boat in the air is another stripe, this one white. A line of snowy seagulls flutters behind the vessel, anticipating the fish detritus that will be tossed into the wind by the fishermen.

I linger on the deck. I no longer see the boat but can still mark its progress by the deep resonant rumble sliding off into the distance toward the mainland. I stand still, listening until the sound has faded away completely, swallowed up by the gentle lapping of the waves.

NIGHT WALK

We turn off the 10:00 news: talk of war with Iraq, a nuclear threat in North Korea, smallpox vaccinations. As I switch off the lights to go upstairs, the moonlit landscape outside the windows catches my attention. "Let's go for a walk," I suggest to Doug. He checks the thermometer. "Five below. We'll have to bundle up." We layer on parkas, scarves, hats, two pairs of gloves, insulated boots.

Late night walks in the winter are a family tradition at our island cabin. Sometimes it is just my husband and me, sometimes it is the whole family. Every New Year's Eve we take a walk after the annual Trivial Pursuit game is over. Some years our walk has been lit by the bright light of the moon; other times it has been so dark that we've had to use flashlights to make sure we are staying on the road.

Tonight the landscape around our cabin is transformed by the full moon. This morning an inch of powdery new snow fell. The white bark of the tall birches gleams in the moonlight. This is not the warm golden glow produced when the late afternoon sun burnishes the birch trunks; instead the moon turns the bark a cool, unearthly white. On the glittering snow, the trees cast long black shadows, dark sentinels standing guard over our property. As we walk along the driveway, the tree branches glisten as though strung with tiny white Christmas lights. The day was warm, but the evening cold froze the melt. Each branch, each twig is covered in ice that shimmers in the bright moonlight.

As we walk we look for the small fir trees we have planted along the driveway every May. I tease Doug that he is inspecting his "crops." The oddly misshapen little balsams remind us of the lesson we learned the winter after our initial planting. The deer relished our balsams and regularly snacked on our little trees during the winter, creating irregular, surreal sculptures. Since then we have planted spiky-needled blue spruce trees that the deer avoid.

We notice few animal tracks along the way. The deer, rabbits, squirrels, and coyotes who are regular winter visitors seem to have stayed away, perhaps due to the cold. We follow the only set of tracks we find; some animal seemed to suddenly leap off the roadway into the woods. Was it fear that caused that leap? Or an animal leaping on its prey? Was the animal being pursued or was it the pursuer?

Somewhere along the way, as he almost always does on our walks, Doug says, "Nice driveway." He is proud of the path he planned to our house site. His comment brings memories of the hot July day when we bushwhacked through the chest-high underbrush, swatted at clouds of mosquitoes, and sloshed through unseen puddles in marshy areas—all this in order to pound three-foot stakes in the ground to mark the 800-foot path of the driveway. We plotted a sinuous trail with multiple twists and turns, all the while trying to spare the stately old maples and oaks on our land. For a moment we are warmed by the memories.

At the end of the driveway we stop. Often this is as far as we go. We breathe in the chill air. It is so raw it hurts our lungs to inhale, so icy it makes our nostrils temporarily stick together. It is still. No wind. Utter, absolute silence. To our city ears the quiet is almost unnerving. At home in Minneapolis our house is near a highway and we live with its constant hum as the background of our lives. But here in the stillness it is easy to imagine that we are the only human beings outdoors on the island on this night.

Without discussion, we continue on. Despite the cold, neither of us wants to turn around and go back just yet. The beauty of this hushed moonlit night pulls us onward. We walk down the county road until we see lights from the first dwelling along the way. The glow is coming from curtained windows of an old gray school bus that has been converted into a house. On warm days I can envision living in this funky little dwelling. Tonight I imagine only the chilliness inside. We have heard through island gossip that the owner is planning to build a house on her land next spring.

Eventually we turn back, retracing our steps toward home. As we near the house I stop. I don't want to go back inside. Inside is the TV with its reminders of the turmoil in the world. Out here, in this pristine white wilderness, Iraq and North Korea seem very far away. Our life here is reduced to the basics. Our concerns are simple ones. Do we need to go to town for milk? Is it time to bring in more wood for the evening fire? Life on this island seems safe and remote from the world where heads of state contemplate war. I am reminded of the only tracks we saw in the snow. In the world of man as well as in nature, it often seems difficult to distinguish between the pursuer and the pursued. And I wonder more often these days whether I could trade my busy city existence for a simpler life here on this quiet island.

LEAVING

The rush of packing was over. It was 10:10 a.m. and we had to get to the dock for the 10:30 ferry or we'd have to wait an hour before the next boat left. We'd loaded our car with suitcases, a cooler filled with leftover food, and two bags of garbage. As Doug and I motored down the driveway, I turned around in my seat for one last look at the house. The dark brown logs glowed, and the windows reflected the abundant sunlight.

"Goodbye house," I said wistfully.

"Goodbye Bearnard," said Doug. He was addressing the wooden bear holding a welcome sign that stands on our entry porch.

This is our ritual. We know our lines. We utter them each time we leave.

We rounded the first bend in the driveway and then the second. I could no longer see the house. I turned forward in my seat and watched as we passed the clumps of wild daisies bordering the drive.

Doug stopped the car at the end of the driveway near our Birkenloch sign and got out to attach the chain between the two wooden posts. As he climbed back into the car I asked, "Why is it always a lovely day when we leave?"

"I know. I hate to leave too. Maybe we should just sell our house in Minneapolis and move here full time."

As we drove down North Shore Road I read the signs at the end of the driveways, "James, Birch Bluff, Lewis, Nelson," watching as we passed the stands of maples and birch with deep green bracken ferns at their feet. The lush foliage was set off against the backdrop of a brilliant blue sky.

We drove onto the ferry dock in La Pointe at 10:28 and gave the ticket-taker our coupons. "Go ahead and drive right on. I think there's just enough room for you and the car behind you."

The ferry worker in the red jacket was starting to unwind the thick rope from the dock post. He noticed us and directed our car to one of the two remaining spaces. "You just made it—again. You sure like to cut things close, don't you?"

Doug pointed at me, and I nodded sheepishly.

I breathed a sigh of relief and removed my seat belt. The "regulars" on these trips had already pushed back their seats and were sipping coffee while scanning the newspaper. Or else they were settling in to catch forty winks, ready to be lulled to sleep by the gentle rocking motion of the ferry.

"Shall we act like tourists and go out on deck?" I asked. Doug already had his car door open.

We stood at the railing and watched as the ferry slid out of the harbor and headed into the waters of the bay separating Madeline Island from Bayfield. The brightly colored Beach Club restaurant and the large windows of the Dockside gift shop grew smaller and smaller. We watched as the island became a sliver of green riding low on the water. I pointed toward a spot halfway up the length of the island.

"Is that where our house is? Just to the left of that sailboat along the shore?"

"Pretty close. Just a little farther to the left I think."

"Goodbye house. Goodbye Madeline," I murmured softly.

* * * * *

As my friend Mike White is fond of saying, "Leaving the island is always like a little death." I know just what he means.

Back when our children were small and the end of our week-long vacation to the area drew near, I hated the thought that it would be a whole year before we would return. As the dream of building our own place grew closer to reality, I told myself that when we had a house of our own we would be able to come often and stay longer. Then it wouldn't be so difficult to leave. Or so I thought. In truth I don't think it has gotten any easier. No matter how many days or weeks we've stayed, no matter how soon we will be returning to the island, I am always reluctant to leave.

It only gets worse on the drive home. As we near the city, I have a re-entry reaction. I feel as if I am a cat falling into a bathtub full of water. Like the cat, with his fur standing on end and all four legs stiffened, I fight against the inevitable. When I see the skyline of Minneapolis coming into view, I want to make a U-turn and head straight back to Madeline. In the city there is too much traffic, too much noise, and there are too many people. Everything seems too fast, too loud, too crowded. It is all too much. I long for the peaceful sanctuary we have just left where the closest thing to a traffic jam occurs when the ferry unloads the twenty cars on board.

* * * * *

In the back hall of our house in Minneapolis are colored pen and ink drawings of two houses. One is the two-story, foursquare brick house where Doug grew up in Mt. Prospect, Illinois. The other is my childhood home, the small, brick bungalow in Golden Valley. I lived in the same home throughout my childhood; for all but the first four years of his boyhood Doug's family occupied the house in Mt. Prospect. Our families lived comfortably yet frugally in these homes. Owning a lake cabin or a second home was not part of my early experience or Doug's. Such a luxury was beyond the means of our middle class families.

Because of my background I find I am sometimes uncomfortable that we have two houses. It doesn't seem right. It seems as if I should choose one or the other. But that would be difficult.

How could we sell the house we have lived in since 1970, the house that contains all the memories of raising our sons? I would miss the doorframe in the hallway where a series of pencil marks charts the progress of their growth. I would miss walking by the stairway to the second floor where I can still picture the two of them as preschoolers sliding down the steps on their stomachs on Christmas morning in a hurry to see what Santa had left in their stockings. I would miss their small handprints in the cement sidewalk, the same one on which they raced their Big Wheels.

Our second home is still too new to hold a storehouse of memories. But it has qualities that are not found in our house in Minneapolis. Our second home is neater, cleaner. All the unwanted stuff that comes to our main place of residence through the mail doesn't follow us to our island dwelling. We only bring things to our second home that have significance to us. This is probably because it is an effort to carry things there. If we bother to pack it into the car, transport it 250 miles and lug it into our island house, it must have some meaning, some value, some purpose in our lives.

Our second house is like home without all the distractions. Or maybe it is a house with the best parts of home. It is the place where we have more time to enjoy nature, more time to think, more time to be together, to enjoy each other's company.

At our island home, we are content to simply be. We have noticed how infrequently we think about taking the ferry to the mainland. And it is easy to put off trips to "town," which is only ten minutes away. At home in Minneapolis, I think nothing of driving fifteen minutes on the freeway to the grocery store or to the mall or to Target. And it is not unusual to make several of those trips in a single day.

There is something elemental about our life on the island. In many ways our days are reduced to the basics; they are not cluttered with so many things, so many decisions. Because of this we have time not only to notice but also to revel in a long summer sunset, an approaching storm, or the fireflies rising in the sky with the moon. I think that by nature we human beings seek a retreat, a place to think about our lives, to contemplate life itself. That is what I find at our island house.

* * * * *

We were at a party on the island at the home of friends. Gene built their house soon after he finished ours. I was talking to Gene's wife. "Do you think you'll live here full time some day?" she asked.

I paused, looking down at the drink in my hand as though somehow it held the answer to her question. "Doug would move in a minute. He could easily do his work from the island. But it wouldn't be so simple for me. I don't think my clients would be willing to drive 200 miles to see me." I hoped I sounded sincere but I was hedging and I knew it. I was using my work as an excuse. I didn't really know the answer to her question.

I've been asked the same thing many times before. When islanders inquire, there is a subtext. They're really wondering: How much of a commitment are you willing to make to this place? How seriously should we take you?

Back home in Minneapolis people often pose the same question, but I have detected different inferences behind that query depending on who is doing the asking. Some people think we would be crazy to live on the island full time; others think we would be crazy not to.

Even if we did move to Madeline, I think we would always be outsiders. Or would we? The full time island population has always been an amalgam of different types of people. Early on it was the fur traders, lumbermen, farmers, and fisherman who were welcomed to Madeline. In the twentieth century islanders have made room for developers, merchants, proprietors of restaurants and lodgings, and artists of many types. The island has always taken in outsiders.

Maybe it wouldn't be so difficult to make a place for ourselves among Madeline's full-time residents. But the question remains: Do we want to make that choice? My husband and I have different answers. Doug's response is an emphatic "Yes!" At times, especially on a sunny July day, I'm also ready to move there permanently. Other times I'm not so sure.

Doug loves the island and feels he could easily do without the distractions of big city life. He grew up as an only child, and I wonder if that makes it easier for him to contemplate living a more isolated life than in the city. I think it would be more difficult for me. In my work as a psychologist I spend all day in the company of other people, and, though I value time to myself, I don't think I would like having less contact with people than I do now.

I also ask myself how I would make it through the winter, especially during ice road and windsled season. Would I miss living in close proximity to the array of theaters, museums, and music venues so close at hand in the Twin Cities? How would I feel about not seeing my children and good friends as often?

I think of a comment made by a friend: "If you lived there, you wouldn't feel the same way about the island." If we were permanent residents would the island provide the same sense of escape, retreat, peacefulness that it holds for us now? Or is it the comings and goings that make it so precious? Is it the contrast between the serene island and the hectic city that makes us value our time there? Would we grow tired of too much peacefulness?

So far these are unanswered questions. Fortunately for us we can remain undecided. A definite answer is not required right now.

SEPTEMBER WEDDING

I was standing on the front deck wearing my fleece bathrobe, the one with bright red reindeer set off against a forest green background. I held a hose in my hand as I absentmindedly watered two huge pots of white impatiens.

"Pat, you need to get dressed! Everyone's going to be here in no time." Doug's voice startled me. As always, he was acting as my alarm clock. Often this was warranted, however this morning I was keeping track of the time.

"I know. As soon as I finish with these plants I'm going to go upstairs and get ready."

I had been enjoying a few moments of solitude outside, away from the hustle and bustle in the house. It was the morning of Bob and Becky's wedding, and it had turned out to be a glorious day. The September sky was pure blue, a gentle breeze lifted the birch leaves which were just beginning to hint at their golden fall color, and even Lake Superior had decided to cooperate with nary a whitecap in sight. We would be able to have the wedding on the deck as we had hoped.

* * * * *

Some months earlier, Bob and Becky came over for Sunday dinner. We were sitting around the dining room table, finishing our dessert and coffee when Bob made the announcement. "Becky and I are planning to get married."

I was not surprised, but I *was* ecstatic. The two of them met when they were working on the student newspaper at Cornell College in Iowa. They started dating and had been together ever since. We loved Becky. She already seemed like a member of the family.

After hugs and congratulations all around, we settled back into our chairs. "There's just one problem," Bob said. "We don't know *where* to get married."

They knew they didn't want a big wedding. They didn't want a lot of formality. And they didn't want to elope.

"You could get married on the deck at Madeline," I offered hopefully, not really sure they would like that idea.

Bob and Becky looked at each other and then both spoke at once.

"That's a great . . . "

"I'd really like . . ."

After a few minutes of discussion, it was settled. They would marry in September on the deck at Birkenloch.

"But what about our brothers?" Becky asked. "I don't know if they'll be able to come."

She had good reason to wonder. Bob and Becky each have only one sibling, and it was impossible to know if either of them would be able to attend the wedding. Steve joined the Peace Corps three months after graduating from college and was working in a tiny village in the Altiplano region of Bolivia. Becky's brother, Tim, had recently entered the Marine Corps and was in the midst of basic training in California.

They decided to hope for the best and go ahead with the September wedding plans.

* * * * *

All morning we had been busy getting everything ready. Bob and Becky had tied white balloons on the Birkenloch sign out by the road. Doug had dressed Bearnard, our wooden welcome bear, in a top hat and bow tie, outfitting him with a sign: "Best Wishes, Becky and Bob!" Stored in the refrigerator were the bridal bouquet, the corsages, and the boutonnieres that Gail, Becky's mom, had created from her garden at home in Wausau. Tacked to the wall of the main room was a large piece of butcher paper containing an illustrated story about Bart the Baboon jointly written by Bob and Becky when they first started dating.

We had hauled our birch and barnboard buffet table out of the porch and placed it in the center front of the deck to create an altar of sorts. Three tall, white pillar candles surrounded by glass hurricanes stood in the center of the table. Becky's parents had placed twenty-five shiny white folding chairs in a semi-circle around the table. Attached to the back of each chair was a brightly colored tissue-paper flower Becky had made. On either side of the altar were tall palm plants and the pots of white impatiens I brought from Minneapolis.

Penny and Keith, both Lutheran ministers, were going to perform the ceremony, and they had led Bob and Becky through a rehearsal. Now all that was left was to eat a quick lunch and get dressed. But I was dallying on the front deck, savoring this moment. Here we were in this beautiful place, surrounded by family, about to celebrate the marriage of our oldest son.

Just four days before, things had been so different. That morning too I had been wearing my robe, but that day I sat stunned in front of the television in our family room in Minneapolis. It was September 11, 2001, and, like millions of people all over the globe, I was trying to absorb the reality that terrorists had attacked the United States on our own soil. For the next few days images of planes crashing into the World Trade Center, the Pentagon, and a field in Pennsylvania covered the newspapers, filled the airwaves and were replayed over and over again on TV, burning themselves into our shared consciousness. As we drove north through Wisconsin to Madeline, we heard more and more of the horrific details on the car radio.

We felt so fortunate that our family was together. Just one day before the terrorists attacked, Steve arrived home from Bolivia. For the previous twelve months I had worried about his safety in a developing country where there had been repeated outbreaks of civil unrest. Ironically it seemed that he may have been safer there than in his own country. We were grateful he arrived home on September 10, since all air travel was halted for days after the attack. In fact, my niece Mary went to the airport in Seattle for three days in a row trying to fly to Minneapolis, but she was never able to get on a plane.

In addition to Mary, Becky's brother, Tim, was not able to attend the wedding. Still in basic training with the Marines, he couldn't get leave. However, twenty-five members of the two families were able to come, and they arrived on the ferry that Saturday. At 3:00 p.m. we heard the crunch of tires on the gravel driveway, and we gathered on the entry porch to greet our guests. Introductions were exchanged all around as we met Becky's extended family for the first time. Then we all adjourned to the deck to wait for the ceremony to begin.

My nephew, Martin, played background music on his guitar as people found their chairs. Doug and I lit one of the pillar candles on the altar to represent the Spaulding family, then Becky's parents lit the Klay candle.

After we returned to our seats, the bride and groom walked through the French doors and onto the deck. Wearing a feathered headband, a simple, long, white cotton dress embellished with embroidery and a beaded necklace she had made herself, Becky looked as though she had stepped out of the Roaring '20s. An abstract-patterned tie that Becky had made for him set off Bob's dark green suit.

As birds twittered and darted among the surrounding trees, the couple said their vows, and then, using flames from each family candle, they lit the unity candle. Both sets of parents gave a blessing to the new couple. As her dad spoke, I glanced over at Becky. Tears rolled down her cheeks. "No, no, don't do that to me," Terry protested. We all laughed, though I too had tear-stained cheeks.

Doug had planned the final moments of the ceremony.

Several months before, when he was prowling around an antique shop in Tomahawk, Wisconsin, Doug had discovered a cast iron school bell complete with an arm to ring it. He decided it was the perfect addition to our deck, particularly in light of the upcoming wedding. On a hot August afternoon, he carefully mounted the old black bell on top of one of the deck posts. He gave strict instructions that no one was to touch it until the wedding. The first ring was to be reserved for the newlyweds.

Now the moment had arrived. Bob and Becky walked to the end of the deck, swung the ringer arm, and the old, black bell clanged loudly, sending its mellow tones down the shore and out across the lake. The guests stood and applauded, and then everyone took a turn ringing the bell as they gathered round the newlyweds with hugs of congratulations.

"Oh, look! Up there!"

One of the guests, gazing skyward, pointed. High overhead soared a pair of magnificent bald eagles. For an instant the sun shone directly on them, igniting their glossy black feathers and white heads. Native Americans believe the eagle is a sign of good fortune. The arrival of this pair certainly seemed an auspicious way to begin a new marriage.

After toasts and champagne, we all drove to Bell Street where Chef Chris had prepared a buffet dinner that was served in the private, second-story room. The evening ended as the younger guests competed to see who would be able to break the blue, star-shaped piñata that Bob and Becky had hung from the ceiling that morning.

There are many photos of that day, but my favorite is the one of Bob and Becky framed between a pair of birch trees as they stand facing the camera with bracken ferns at their feet and vivid blue Lake Superior in the background.

* * * * *

That night, after everyone else had gone to bed, I lingered in the kitchen. As I washed a few odds and ends, I thought about the day. Finally, when I couldn't find anything else to clean, I hung up the dishcloth and walked to the French doors. I pushed open the screen door and went out onto the front deck. The deep blue night sky was studded with stars, and the bright path of the Milky Way stretched out across the lake toward Raspberry Island. The white chairs had been folded and stacked neatly beside the house; the barnboard buffet had been moved back into the porch. The white impatiens, still in place, gleamed in the moonlight. I turned to look back into the house. The stained glass lamps beside the couch cast circles of warm golden light on the floor. The pine log walls glowed.

I thought about our house and why we built it. We wanted a family gathering place, a place to enjoy being together, a place to celebrate special events. Few events could be as special as this one. I knew we built our house for days just such as this.

I glanced into the porch and saw the faded red immigrant trunk with the rope handles that had been passed down from generation to generation in my mother's family. I thought about my parents and Doug's parents, how much I missed them and wished they had been here to share this special day with us. I thought about how frugally they had lived their own lives and how their generosity to us made all of this possible. As tears welled up in my eyes, I whispered softly, "Thank you."

As I looked up into the vast sky, I had the strong sense of our parents looking down at us this day and smiling—smiling to see the circle of family widen and a new member added, smiling to see our family adding and subtracting, growing, and diminishing, yet moving steadily forward across time. I smiled in return.

I thought of families who had lost one of their members on September 11. How could we celebrate while others mourned? But I knew that our celebration was important, perhaps even a necessity. A necessity because this day was an affirmation that life and love go forward, not just for our family but for all families, despite the hatred and destruction of the previous week. This day affirmed that the very ties that bind us together in love make a mockery of the hatred in the world.

I turned back toward the lake and looked down the moonlit channel. There, in the distance, as always, was the beam from Raspberry Island lighthouse, a symbol of security in a world that in the last few days seemed anything but safe and secure.

The light blinked. Then the darkness. I counted the seconds. One, two, three . . . ten . . . twenty . . . thirty. Then, once again the golden light eleven miles away blinked at me.

Solid, dependable lighthouse, punctuating the darkness with the steady rhythm of its beams of light. There was the light . . . now the darkness . . . now the light . . .

Light and dark. Joy and sorrow. Life and death. Co-mingled.

Because of the darkness that follows, I savor the golden light.

ACKNOWLEDGMENTS

This book took longer to complete than our house on Madeline Island. In comparison, Gene, you moved at lightening speed.

I am indebted to many people who assisted in the long labor and birthing of this book. My instructors at the Loft Literary Center offered inspiration and guidance. Among them are Nancy Raeburn, who taught the first memoir classes I took and believed in my book before I did; Elizabeth Jarrett Andrew, who helped me discover and express the deeper themes in my manuscript; and Mary Carroll Moore, Suzanne Nielsen, and Cheri Register whose thoughtful critiques helped shape this book. Paulette Bates Alden offered invaluable suggestions and encouragement on the early chapters.

Members of my writers' groups, Cynthia Entzel, Ann Kempke, Jo Ann Manthey, Helen West, Judy Krauss, Mary Westra, Astrid Slungaard, Anne Crooks, Jerry Fleischaker, and Eugene Kline were willing to read and reread chapter after chapter and offered helpful feedback and insights.

I also want to thank Lindsy O'Brien at Red Step Press whose interest in my book helped give me the confidence to proceed with publication.

Karen Walhof at Quill House Publishers shepherded me through the publishing process, providing the book with excellent copy editing, layout, and cover design.

On car trips to and from Madeline Island, my husband, Doug, never tired of hearing me read aloud every chapter I wrote and rewrote, and he offered encouragement each time my spirits flagged. In forty-three years of marriage we have shared two children, two grandchildren, and many adventures. The one recorded here is surely among the best.

And finally, I offer my heartfelt gratitude to Gene Nelson, without whom there would have been no house and no book. You transformed a pile of logs and lumber into the house of our dreams, and you truly were and are my best tutor in island living.

This is a work of nonfiction, based on my memories. I have tried to be as accurate as possible, but others may remember some of these events differently. There are as many versions of the same story as there are tellers. All of them are different, all of them true.

I have often changed names and details to protect the privacy of the individuals mentioned.

Learn more about my life, this book (including the lost chapter), and Madeline Island at www.patriciaspaulding.com.